DATE DUE

PRINTED IN U.S.A.

D1616858

11/5/21 - BM

Poverty and Place

Poverty and Place

Cancer Prevention among Low-Income Women of Color

Anjanette Wells,
Vetta L. Sanders Thompson,
Will Ross,
Carol Camp Yeakey,
and Sheri Notaro

Foreword by Holden Thorp

LEXINGTON BOOKS
Lanham • Boulder • New York • London

Published by Lexington Books
An imprint of The Rowman & Littlefield Publishing Group, Inc.
4501 Forbes Boulevard, Suite 200, Lanham, Maryland 20706
www.rowman.com

6 Tinworth Street, London SE11 5AL

British Library Cataloguing in Publication Information Available

Library of Congress Cataloging-in-Publication Data

Names: Wells, Anjanette, author. | Thompson, Vetta L. Sanders, author.
Title: Poverty and place : cancer prevention among low-income women of color
    / Anjanette Wells, Vetta L. Sanders Thompson, Will Ross, Carol Camp
    Yeakey, and Sheri Notaro ; foreword by Holden Thorp.
Description: Lanham : Lexington Books, [2019] | Includes bibliographical
    references and index.
Identifiers: LCCN 2018050121 (print) | LCCN 2018051943 (ebook) | ISBN
    9781498522007 (Electronic) | ISBN 9781498521994 (cloth : alk. paper)
Subjects: LCSH: Cancer—Epidemiology—United States. | Poverty—Health
    aspects—United States. | Equality—Health aspects—United States. |
    Health and race—United States. | Social status—Health aspects—United
    States.
Classification: LCC RA645.C3 (ebook) | LCC RA645.C3 W44 2019 (print) | DDC
    614.5/9990973—dc23
LC record available at https://lccn.loc.gov/2018050121

Printed in the United States of America

This book is dedicated to low-income women of color in St. Louis, Missouri, and her sister river city, East St. Louis, Illinois, and to marginalized women across the globe, engaged in the struggle for social justice and healthcare commensurate with their need.

Contents

Foreword

The great universities of America's cities have an enormous responsibility. Like all universities, we are called to produce great scholarship and inspire the next generation of minds with the curiosity that leads to engaged citizenship and a more equitable future. But we are also called to be aware of our location. Our university's full name is not Wash U, Washington U, or even Washington University—it is Washington University *in St. Louis*. We are unapologetically committed to our magnificent, but also troubled, city. And like most institutions, we don't always do a perfect job of meeting those obligations, but we struggle on, knowing that our calling is a worthy one.

For all these reasons, I was ecstatic when Carol Camp Yeakey and Vetta Sanders Thompson came to me with the idea of a working group on "In/Equality in Theory and Practice." These colleagues pulled together scholars from across the university to work on a variety of issues, many focused on health disparities in St. Louis and elsewhere. Long-recognized scholarship on the subject has shown that life expectancy and other outcomes vary enormously over differences of only a few miles within our region due to wide variations in resources across the city and county.

One of the products of their work is this volume, *Poverty and Place: Cancer Prevention among Low-Income Women of Color*. It is a work of outstanding scholarship, but it also one of deep compassion and empathy, as shown by its dedication to low-income women of color and other marginalized groups. It is also a work that holds an institution's feet to the fire in making sure that our rhetoric and actions are in resonance.

We accept the challenge and are immensely proud of our colleagues' vision and scholarship.

Holden Thorp, Provost and
Rita Levi-Montalcini, Distinguished University Professor,
Washington University in St. Louis

Introduction

Cancer in the Face of Race, Poverty, and Place: An Introduction

For as long as there is residential segregation, there will be de facto segregation in every area of life.

—Dr. Martin Luther King, Jr.

Where you live . . . has a powerful impact on your health. Residents of zip codes separated by only a few miles have up to an 18-year difference in life expectancy.

—For the Sake of All

Class and race are potent forces in health and longevity rates in the United States (Scott, 2005). Through original research, *Poverty and Place: Cancer Prevention among Low-Income Women of Color* examines how and why racial and class disparities persist in the most advanced society of the world and what prevention measures might be taken to address such disparities. *Poverty and Place* attempts to fill a void in the research literature. Specifically, in this volume, we look at the many factors that can facilitate or pose a barrier to cancer treatment and adherence, including race and sociocultural barriers, lower socioeconomic standing (which culminates in inadequate social and built environments), information and knowledge, risk-promoting lifestyles, attitudes and behaviors, and exposure to carcinogens as well as diminished access to health care (Freeman 1991; Centers for Disease Control and Prevention [CDC], 2017). We develop a theoretical framework that takes account of these many barriers to support the creation of effective interventions.

Since the 1970s, the scientific community has focused on the documented racial disparities in cancer incidence, mortality, and survival, with data from the Surveillance, Epidemiology and End Results (SEER) Program of the

National Cancer Institute showing that African Americans have experienced higher cancer incidence rates and lower survival rates than white Americans (Henschke, Leffall, & Mason et al., 1973). While few questioned the accuracy of these findings, cancer and health researchers wondered whether race, in and of itself, was the fundamental cause of the disparities in cancer incidence and outcome (Freeman, 1991). This question contributed to more nuanced questions that have pushed our understanding of health disparities and inequity forward.

Over time, research has also suggested a significant link between socioeconomic status and the development of health problems (Adler et al., 1994; Haan, Kaplan, & Syme, 1989; Marmot, Kogevinas, & Elston, 1987). In fact, research from the data set of the ten-year longitudinal study *Atherosclerosis Risk in Communities* suggested that people with lower incomes have a 50% higher risk of heart disease (Franks, 2011). Authors of more recent studies suggest that there is a shortage of studies on the association between socioeconomic status and cancer, due in part to the fact that public health data systems have rarely collected such information (Boscoe et al., 2014).

Socioeconomic status continues to be the strongest predictor of cancer burden across and within racial/ethnic groups. Although no one claims that race or poverty are absolute predictors of cancer incidence and survival rates among the poor, in general, or poor women of color, in particular, each factor serves as a surrogate of human conditions and life circumstances (Freeman, 1991). Why? The reason might have to do with the ecology of race and poverty, seen through the prism of marginalized populations, and the fact that both poverty and race can diminish or accentuate lifestyle issues that impact one's lifestyle issues and opportunities or the lack thereof.

Specifically, this authored volume is the culmination of original research conducted on cancer prevention among low-income women of color in the St. Louis, Missouri, metropolitan region, which is inclusive of the river city of East St. Louis, Illinois. This region represents one of the communities of color that is burdened with cancer disparities; that is, highly segregated urban and older suburban communities of color in decay. Beyond looking at health data relative to screening, diagnostic testing, and a host of lifestyle issues (diet, exercise, smoking, sexual health, mental health, and other predictors of wellness), this volume examines the effects of the local neighborhood and the community impact on lifestyle decisions. In doing so, the data discussed and the stories told provide a telling portrait of the impact of place on cancer prevention in actual communities of low-income women of color. The text touches on issues such as homelessness; residential segregation and housing quality; dis/investment in neighborhoods and communities; access to and provision of adequate and appropriate healthcare; civic engagement or the lack thereof; types of schools and under/achievement; employment and un/ employment; environmental hazards; mortality, morbidity, and longevity rates; curtailment of social welfare programs; and under resourced public services, among others. These aspects of life in the St. Louis metropolitan region will provide a telling portrait of cancer prevention among low-income women of color in actual communities. Photos of the neighborhoods in which our study participants live will show the impact of poor living conditions on health status. Actual vignettes of women impacted by cancer provide human portraits and relate the toll that cancer has had upon low-income women of color and their families.

Cancer is a leading cause of death worldwide (Torre et al., 2015) and in many cases is preventable. This study provides a unique lens to discuss strategies to decrease health inequity. It focuses on four of the most common cancers for low-income women of color: lung cancer, breast cancer, colorec-tal cancer, and cervical cancer (which includes virtually all cases of cervical cancer due to human papillomavirus (HPV) 16 and 18, strains that account for 70% of cervical cancer cases). Consider the following:

- Research has demonstrated that 32 of 39 cancer types are associated with poverty (Boscoe, et al., 2014). Despite overall improvements in care across all races, African Americans still suffer the greatest burden for the most common types of cancer (CDC, 2014). Worse still, the five-year relative survival is lower for African Americans than whites for most cancers at each stage of diagnosis (DeSantis, Naishadham, & Jemal, 2013).
- Breast cancer is the second most common cause of cancer death among African American women, surpassed only by lung cancer (American Cancer Society [ACS], 2015). Overall African American women have an incidence rate similar to that of American White women, yet are 42% more likely to die of breast cancer than White women (CDC, 2017). And, although breast cancer mortality rates have declined among White women nationally, rates have increased among African American women (CDC, 2017).
- The human papillomavirus (HPV) causes 27,000 cancers each year, with cervical cancer being the most prevalent HPV-related cancer (CDC, 2014). Latina women have the highest cervical cancer incidence rate, followed by African American women, and White women. Yet the highest death rate from cervical cancer is among African American women (CDC, 2014; NCI, 2015).
- Colorectal cancer (CRC) is the third most common cancer in women and is also the third most common cause of cancer death among African Ameri-can women in the U.S. (NCI, 2016; CDC, 2014) CRC incidence among

African American men and women is approximately 20% higher and mortality rates about 45% higher than those among whites.

Again, the purpose of *Poverty and Place: Cancer Prevention among Low-Income Women of Color* is to examine how and why such racial and class disparities have become potent forces in health and longevity rates in the United States (Scott, 2005). With over 35 years of experience in addressing minority health and the health of the underserved, as Professor Emeritus at the University of Texas, M.D. Anderson Cancer Center and as Prairie View A&M University's Associate Dean for Research, Lovell Jones sums up the issue by saying:

> In care, treatment and research efforts, differences among ethnic minorities have simply not been noted and treated with the same zeal as "mainstream" medicine and prevention. The same has been true with regard to gender, with women getting the short end of the proverbial stick until very recent times. And in the fight against cancer, the consequences have been particularly tragic (2014).

As one epidemiologist pointed out, "We're creating disparities. It's almost as if it's transforming health . . . into a commodity. Like the distribution of BMWs or goat cheese" (Scott, 2005).

Poverty and Place attempts to fill the aforementioned void in the research literature. Given the growing cost of healthcare and the increasing diversity in our society, there is a strong need to understand the combination of factors that facilitate or pose a barrier to cancer treatment and adherence, for marginalized low-income women of color in society.

DEMOGRAPHIC PROFILE OF THE ST. LOUIS METROPOLITAN AREA: THE IMPORTANCE OF PLACE

The sample population for this original research study is drawn from North City St. Louis, Missouri, and the river city of East St. Louis, Illinois. Both areas comprise the St. Louis Metropolitan Area. Demographic data analysis has identified the incidence rates for invasive and *in situ* cancer for the neighborhoods and zip codes with the highest counts. In reviewing the following data, it is important to note that the U.S. government set the official poverty threshold in 2017 at $24,600 (Mass Law Reform Institute, 2018). Preliminary community mapping data in North St. Louis for zip codes with the highest cancer counts show the following: median household income below the state average ranging from $24,404 to $25,856; unemployed percentage above the state average; African American population percentage *significantly* above the state average; renting percentage above the state average, age of housing stock *significantly* above the state average; and the percentage of population with a bachelor's degree or higher *significantly* below the state average. (City-Data, 2017a). For the zip codes in East St. Louis, Illinois, with the highest cancer counts among low-income women of color, preliminary neighborhood mapping data show the following: median household income *significantly* below the state average, ranging from $18,923 to $26,578; median house value *significantly* below the state average; unemployed percentage above the state average; African American population percentage *significantly* above the state average; and the percentage of population with a bachelor's degree or higher *significantly* below the state average (City-Data, 2017b). What the aforementioned data demonstrate are urban/suburban segments of the St. Louis metropolitan region that are densely segregated by race and class, with stark cancer disparities. The foregoing factors become additive and synergistic and create the perfect storm, which results in cancer health disparities, indeed health inequities, for African Americans in general, but for lower status African American women of color, in particular. As Harold Freeman, MD, queried in the *New York Times* (March 13, 2014), "What does it mean to be black and poor and at the same time to have cancer? . . . This is more than a medical and scientific issue. This is a moral issue."

RESEARCH METHODOLOGY

We executed a mixed-methods study using quantitative data from the 2011 Behavioral Risk Factor surveillance System (BRFSS), a state-based health survey that annually collects information on health conditions, behaviors, preventive practices, and access to healthcare, and the 2011 Missouri Information for Community Assessment (MICA), which provides cancer incidence data for Missouri residents, to examine relationships between lifestyle (e.g., diet, fruit/vegetable consumption, and physical (in)activity), preventive practices (e.g., mammography, Pap smear, HPV vaccination, colorectal cancer screening), and health risk behaviors (e.g., smoking, alcohol use) on health care utilization. Data also include a local survey (337 completed surveys of African Americans ages 50 to 75 recruited in the St. Louis Metropolitan Area, including East St. Louis), as well as quotes from cognitive response interviews used to assist in development of the surveys (Sanders Thompson, Lewis, & Williams, 2013). The survey assessed subjective norms, self-efficacy, family history, physician-perceived risks, attitudes, and beliefs related to colorectal cancer screening (CRCS) and CRC. A similar survey of 200 African American parents, with 30 individual interviews, addressed attitudes and beliefs influencing willingness to obtain HPV vaccination for age-eligible youth. (Sanders Thompson, Arnold, & Notaro, 2012). Similar data sets for East St. Louis, Illinois, will be derived from the Illinois Behavioral Risk Factor Surveillance System (Illinois Department of Public Health, IDPH, 2013).

A qualitative case study is embedded within the aforementioned analyses and includes narratives of the social stressors expressed by low-income women in these areas who are in need of a preventive breast and cervical cancer screening (i.e., mammogram and/Pap testing). Using a template analysis approach (King & Ross, 2003), we will categorize women's stressors into *a priori* sensitizing concepts from Turner and Avison's (2003) stress exposure list (i.e., life events, chronic stressors, lifetime major events, and discrimination stress), which highlights the overwhelming layers of stress that may affect preventive cancer screening and overall health care utilization for these women. Finally, Geographical Information Systems (GIS) is used to capture contextual geographical data within zip codes with the highest cancer mortality rates in the St. Louis Metropolitan region (including East St. Louis, Illinois). Descriptive analyses (means, frequencies, and percentages) will be used to characterize the study sample. Our sample size will include approximately 500 residents.

STRUCTURE OF THE VOLUME

The book is organized into five chapters. The first chapter explores the history, the social determinants of health, using GIS, and pictures of the St. Louis metropolitan area to better illustrate the disparities and prevalence from a ground-level perspective. Research questions that guide the study's development are articulated. The second chapter explores the disparities and prevalence, including incidence and mortality rates of those inhabiting certain zip codes in the St. Louis area. Going beyond mapping and illustrations, the third chapter uses theory to help examine the barriers to preventive health behaviors and screening, using a socioecological model (SEM) perspective and then hones in at an individual micro-level. The fourth chapter uses theory to provide an analysis of our study's findings and introduces a new conceptual model to address some of the gaps and strategies that could be developed to address the barriers. The fifth chapter answers the research questions formulated in chapter 1, provides conclusions to this research study, and provides an analysis of the erosion of the social safety net that bodes ill for society, as a whole. Finally, *Poverty and Place* summarizes the psychological, epidemiological, sociological, and medical literatures to offer effective programmatic considerations for bringing programs to scale with the intention of encouraging future research and action.

ACKNOWLEDGMENTS

No volume is written alone. First, we wish to thank the first author, Professor Anjanette A. Wells, whose original work on cancer prevention provided the intellectual impetus for this project. Second, the authors wish to thank Provost Holden Thorp, the Rita Levi-Montalcini Professor of Medicine and Chemistry at Washington University in St. Louis for bringing our interdisciplinary team together. His BYOI (Bring Your Own Idea) initiative, at Washington University in St. Louis, was designed to break down academic disciplinary boundaries and foster cross disciplinary dialogue. *Poverty and Place: Cancer Prevention among Low-Income Women of Color* is a tangible result of our collaborations. Without such an institutional prompt, as BYOI, this volume might never have been written and written with as much interdisciplinary academic exchange. Special thanks to Matthew Kreuter, Ted Scheel, and Yoo Ran Moon for the opportunity to work on the 2-1-1 patient navigation project and Hanlin Zhou for the careful attention in generating GIS maps of cancer mortality rates in the St. Louis metropolitan region. To current and/or former residents of the St. Louis metropolitan region, specifically Nikisha Bridges, Rodney Holmes, Andrew Hubbard, Ayanna Jones, W. Donnell Jones, and Keith St. John, we are greatly appreciative of your insights in helping us to capture the richness of the region. Similarly, we thank our students, in particular, Chelsea Hoffmaster and Angela Bird, for their assistance assembling data, editing, and compiling references. To Sharese Willis, our editorial assistant, and other reviewers, we sincerely appreciate your thoughtful comments on our draft chapters. Further, we owe a tremendous debt of gratitude to the marginalized African American women in our study who allowed us to intrude upon their lives at a most vulnerable and challenging time. We applaud you for your courage and strength. It is to you that this volume is dedicated. Last but not least, we wish to thank our close friends and infinitely patient families who have endured our need to spend time away from gatherings, on revising drafts, and setting up conference calls in an attempt to capture the right words to further serious discussion on such timely and sensitive subject matter. Of course, the final product is our own creation and one in which we accept full responsibility for its contents. We trust we have rendered the challenging subject matter with honesty, sensitivity, and the rich complexity deserved for the study of cancer prevention among low-income women of color.

A Row of Houses in St. Louis City
photo by Keith St. John

Chapter One

Social Determinants of Health and Their Influence on Health Disparities in the St. Louis Metropolitan Area

> Your zip code should not determine how long you live (or how well), but it does.
>
> —The California Endowment

The growing cost of health care and the increasing diversity in our society underscore the need to understand the combination of factors that facilitate or pose a barrier to cancer prevention, early detection, treatment, and screening adherence among disadvantaged populations. These factors may include race and sociocultural barriers, lower socioeconomic standing—which culminates in inadequate social and built environments—inadequate information and knowledge, risk-promoting lifestyles, attitudes and behaviors, exposure to carcinogens, and diminished access to health care (CDC, 2015; Freeman, 1991). These are all social determinants of health, and, in recent years, public health researchers and practitioners have focused more attention on the role of social determinants of health when discussing health disparities (World Health Organization Commission on Social Determinants of Health & World Health Organization 2008).

Poverty and Place: Cancer Prevention among Low-Income Women of Color, through a case study and original research, explores how cancer health disparities exist due to racial, class inequities, and other social determinants of health that persist in the most advanced society of the world. In this volume, we attempt to answer the following questions:

- How does the cancer incidence for breast, lung, cervical, and colorectal cancer data for St. Louis, Missouri, and East St. Louis, Illinois, residents in the prototype communities compare to state and national averages?

- What are the cancer screening resources and options in St. Louis, Missouri, and in East St. Louis, Illinois?
- What types of patient navigation outreach programs are available in St. Louis, Missouri, and in East St. Louis, Illinois?
- How can existing resources and knowledge of community circumstances and cancer rates be used to address disparities?
- In this chapter we will provide an overview of how the conditions in which people live are inextricably linked to health and the ways in which health is created by the conditions of our society and environment.

SOCIAL DETERMINANTS OF HEALTH

It is important to distinguish the marginalized populations most likely to experience lack of access to favorable social determinants of health. Marginalized populations and communities may include racial and ethnic minorities, low-income and impoverished individuals, individuals with mental and physical disabilities, those marginalized due to sexual orientation, etc. The social determinants of health are defined by the World Health Organization as the conditions in which people "are born, grow, live, work, and age" (WHO Commission on Social Determinants of Health, & World Health Organization, 2008). Health is thus affected by discrimination, adverse early life events, poor education, unemployment, underemployment and job insecurity, economic inequality, poverty, neighborhood deprivation, food insecurity, poor-quality housing, housing instability, inadequate built environment, and poor access to health care. These factors adversely impact the synergistic forces associated with health and disproportionately affect African Americans.

Marmot, Friel, Bell, Houweling, and Taylor (2008) note that social determinants of health are structural in nature and include factors such as socioeconomic status (SES), education, the physical environment, employment, and social support networks, as well as access to health care. By driving healthcare inequality, poverty contributes to the social gradient seen in all countries and in cities around the globe (Marmot et al., 2008). For example, higher rates of cancer incidence and mortality are seen in individuals or population subgroups that do not have access to adequate resources like clean water, fresh air, healthy food options, opportunities for physical activity, and access to affordable healthcare (Marmot et al., 2008).

The social gradient of healthcare inequality is frequently documented at the intersection of one's race/ethnicity and SES. Poorer health outcomes are observed in the United States for individuals with lower incomes, education, occupational status, wealth, as well as those belonging to certain ethnic and racial minority groups (LaVeist, 2005; Williams, 2003). In the United States, poor and low-income neighborhoods are more likely to be unsafe, have exposed garbage or litter, and have poor or dilapidated housing and vandalism. They also are less likely to have sidewalks, parks or playgrounds, recreation centers, or a library (Singh, Siahpush, & Kogan, 2010). Poor members of racial and ethnic minority communities are more likely to live in neighborhoods with concentrated poverty than their White counterparts (Jargowsky, 2015). Individuals respond strongly to social cues within their environment, and as Bronfenbrenner posits in his ecological theory, the environmental influences on an individual's development extends across multiple levels and multiple life periods (Bronfenbrenner, 1995). Evidence is growing that the stress associated with living in poor neighborhoods negatively impacts health across the lifespan (Felitti et al., 1998; Pickett & Pearl, 2001).

Race and income are closely connected in the United States. U.S. Census Bureau data indicate that African Americans are more than twice as likely as Whites to fall below the poverty level. Estimates from 2013 show that 27.2% of all African Americans live below the poverty level, compared to 9.6% of non-Hispanic Whites (DeNavas & Proctor, 2014).

The stress of living with limited resources can contribute to a variety of health problems. Research shows that Americans living in extreme poverty have "more chronic illness, more frequent and severe disease complications, and make greater demands on the health care system" (Kreuter et al., 2012). Research on recently unemployed workers who lost their jobs through no fault of their own shows that they are more likely than continuously employed persons to develop new negative health outcomes such as high blood pressure, diabetes, or heart disease in the ensuing year and a half (Wells, Gulbas, Sanders-Thompson, Shon, & Kreuter, 2013).

The health status of ethnic minorities within the United States has received increased attention as the demographic composition of the country has shifted and national reports have highlighted the persistence of disparities in health (Health Policy Brief, 2011). A demographic shift refers to the transition from both high birth and death rates to lower rates as a region develops into an industrialized system. Overall, minorities have higher rates of diabetes, stroke, and other preventable diseases compared to White Americans (Health Policy Brief, 2011). For example, data from 2010 indicated that African American, American Indian, and Puerto Rican infants continued to have higher mortality rates than those reported for White infants (Mathews & MacDorman, 2013). In addition, African Americans were 30% more likely to die of heart disease and twice as likely to have a stroke (Office of Minority Health [OMH], 2015). In 2013, African Americans were twice as likely to die of diabetic related complications (OMH, 2015). Differences in cancer incidence and mortality have been noted as well and may be useful in highlighting strategies for addressing the issues that produce health inequity (Freeman, 1991).

SOCIAL DETERMINANTS OF HEALTH IN ST. LOUIS

In the case of the greater St. Louis community, the social determinants that negatively affect health outcomes have deep historical roots in the poverty and degraded socioenvironmental setting of the area. Although St. Louis might be Midwestern, its history and traditions are Southern, and it remains one of the most segregated metropolitan areas in the United States (Sauter, 2017). Communities like St. Louis became "intentionally" racially segregated in part because of policies that supported the movement of White families from urban centers into suburban areas, coupled with housing discrimination against African Americans (Gordon, 2009; Phillips, 2016). These policies helped determine how and where the St. Louis populations became stratified by race and by income (Gordon, 2009). Similar policies led to the development of predominantly lower SES and African American communities like Ferguson, Missouri, and have played an integral role in the racial tension behind the police shootings of African American males, such as the unarmed teenager Michael Brown, and the riots that followed (Coy, 2014). The legacy of segregation continues in such St. Louis neighborhoods to this day, resulting in high concentrations of poverty (Coy, 2014).

African American migration patterns between 1915 and 1970 resulted in a White backlash of restrictive housing covenants, zoning laws, and redlining that spawned and codified racial segregation (Wilkerson, 2010). African Americans moved from rural areas in the U.S. South to urban areas in St. Louis and across the nation, lured by factory jobs while filling a labor shortage created by World War I. During this time reasonably representative data for the African American population became more available for official surveillance (Haines, 2001). Many African American who migrated would land in the St. Louis region, particularly East St. Louis, which was a major factory site during that time period. As St. Louis's African American population increased from 6.4% in 1880 to 9.0% in 1920, the United Welfare Association formed to promote segregation as a bulwark against African American incursions into White neighborhoods.

Restrictive covenants were approved by the voters in 1916, essentially constraining African American residents to the northern side of St. Louis City. St. Louis subsequently became the first city in the nation to pass a segregation ordinance by referendum, although the next year such statutes were declared to be unconstitutional by the United States Supreme Court. The segregation practice still carried on through individual property covenants, which were not outlawed until the landmark 1948 Supreme Court ruling in the case of *Shelley v. Kraemer* holding that no one could move to a block on which more than 75% of the residents were of another race (Gordon, 2009; Rothstein, 2014).

As a result of this legacy, St. Louis is now one of the most racially segregated cities in the United States. Its African American population—which in 1999 surpassed the White population as the city's majority group (53.1%)—resides almost exclusively in the northern half of the city (U. S. Census Bureau, 2000). St. Louis, thus, has by far the highest percentage of African American population for any county in the state. During the 1990s, the city's African American population began migrating in two general directions: north into St. Louis County, and south into the city's central corridor. In St. Louis County, the African American population grew by 39% from 1990 to 2000, and for the first time surpassed St. Louis City in total number of African American residents (Rivas, 2011). Twelve municipalities saw a doubling of their African American population during this time period, including five communities whose African American population increased as much as 220 to 750% (U. S. Census Bureau, 2000). Most of this growth occurred in municipalities in an area known as "North County." More than one in five (23%) residents of St. Louis County is African American (233,048 African American residents).

Poverty permeates the region and disproportionately affects the African American population. A persistent gap in the rate of poverty in the past 30 years means that poverty affects close to 1 in 3 African Americans but less than 1 in 10 Whites in St. Louis County and St. Louis City (Tate, 2013). The impact of poverty on children is especially troubling since starting life in poverty has negative consequences for health well into adulthood. Almost half (46%) of African American children under 18 live in poverty in St. Louis County and St. Louis City, (Tate, 2013), which places African American children in St. Louis at greater risk for adverse health outcomes. The 2015 unemployment rate for African Americans in St. Louis was 17.2%, 2.8 times the White rate of 6.1% (Where We Stand, 2015). The unemployment rate increased for both race groups between 2006 and 2015. The White rate was 5.2% in 2006, while the African American rate was 14.7%. These trends mirror national patterns (Tate, 2013).

Education, also a strong and consistent predictor of health, eludes the low-income, African American population in greater St. Louis. One in 10 African Americans in grades 9 through 12 dropped out of school in 2012, and poor performance in key subjects at critical points in their education place many others at risk (Tate, 2013).

SOCIAL DETERMINANTS OF HEALTH IN EAST ST. LOUIS

East St. Louis, St. Louis's sister city and neighbor across the river in Illinois, followed a different historical trajectory. The city is in the Metro-East region of St. Clair County, Southern Illinois and, like St. Louis, reflects the intersection between place and health. Socioeconomically, it is even more depressed than St. Louis; it has high concentrations of poverty and is predominately populated by African Americans (McLaughlin, 2002). At the turn of the twentieth century, East St. Louis was a thriving industrial town built by the "icons of industry," including Andrew Carnegie and J. P. Morgan (Theising, 2003). That all changed when US factories began to employ large numbers of African American workers during World War I. On October 19, 1916, an article in the *East St. Louis Daily Journal* published that, "Fifteen hundred Negroes arrived in East St. Louis on special trains from Tuscaloosa, Alabama, and other southern parts, who were too late to register at the various polling places, are looking for work." (Moore, 1937). They were responding to public notices from local industries that enticed them with competitive job offers and stable income. The eager new workers unwittingly fell into the trap set by industry management, who consequently reduced the wages of all their employees as the labor market swelled with new employees. White employees were seething as they received smaller paychecks and were quick to lay the blame on Black immigrants rather than unscrupulous factory owners.

White workers, also fearing the loss of their jobs, created racially tinged labor unions as a bulwark against further African American incursions (Rudwick, 1964). They began picketing the Aluminum Ore company, which responded by hiring more African American workers. In July of 1917, one of the worst race riots in American history occurred when, in a mob attack or "massacre" (McLaughlin, 2002) scores of African Americans were killed and entire African American neighborhoods were burned down (McLaughlin, 2002). A memorial petition to the U.S. Congress, sent by a citizen committee from East St. Louis, described it as "a very orgy of inhuman butchery during which more than fifty colored men, women and children were beaten with bludgeons, stoned, shot, drowned, hanged or burned to death—all without any effective interference on the part of the police, sheriff or military authorities" In the aftermath, it was estimated that between 50 and 100 African Americans were killed, while thousands were permanently displaced from their homes (McLaughlin, 2002).

During the second half of the twentieth century, Whites simply moved far away from the area (McLaughlin, 2002). This White flight, coupled with the fact that East St. Louis suffered from the mid-century deindustrialization and restructuring of the railroad industry, affected the social and economic status of East St. Louis. A number of prosperous local steel, chemical, meat packing, and other large manufacturing industries and plants began to close, jobs began to move to the South, and these areas were abandoned. In 1960, the East St. Louis Municipal League, in a move to stem the inexorable loss of industry, somehow convinced *Look Magazine* to have it voted "All American City" (Kircherr, 2003). Behind the scenes, however, was a community that looked as if it had been pillaged, bearing the scars of unrelenting racial resentment. Decades of abandonment had generated a textbook illustration of urban decay—environmental waste dumps, vast swaths of vacant lots, half-demolished houses with thick undergrowth, and boarded-up businesses. A depopulation ensued; in 1950, East St. Louis had a population of 82,000, but by

2010 that number had fallen to 27,000 (U. S. Census, 2014). Between 1960 and 1970 alone, the city lost nearly 70% of its businesses (Theising, 2003), further exacerbating its loss of social, economic, and political capital. These changes brought about rapid economic reversals, resulting in communities with high concentrations of families with multiple generations of poverty and associated inner city problems. Ironically, segregation was never the law in Illinois, but its caustic legacy endured, starting in Brooklyn, the oldest all-Black town in Illinois, and continuing with contiguous East St. Louis, which is now 99% Black.

Today, East St. Louis and surrounding communities east of the Mississippi are still struggling to overcome the poverty and associated challenges that have developed in the region. Together, with the African American communities of North St. Louis City and many North St. Louis County communities, the East St. Louis communities stand in contrast to the prosperity displayed in predominantly White regions of Missouri west of the Mississippi. The region has been designated as a *Health Professional Shortage Area*, meaning that there is a region wide lack of healthcare professionals and facilities.

Although health-related data specific to the various East St. Louis communities is somewhat delayed and fragmented (Smith, 2015), the deteriorating social, political, and economic structure account for health statistics that are among the worst in the country. Poverty and poor educational attainment limit access to preventive health and affordable healthcare, especially for children. According to the nonprofit organization Voices for Illinois Children, three-fourths of students in the East St. Louis School District come from low-income families (below 200% of poverty level). In the 2008–2009 school year, the district had a student mobility rate of 37%, compared to 3.7% statewide (Voices for Illinois Children, 2009). The 2017 *County Health Rankings and Roadmaps* reported that out of 102 counties in the state of Illinois, St. Clair County ranks 95th when both mortality and morbidity are analyzed together (poorer health outcomes associated with higher county ratings). For mortality (premature death or the years of potential life lost prior to age 75), the county is 90th out of 102 counties in Illinois, and for morbidity (self-reported fair or poor health, poor physical health days, poor mental days, and low birth weight), the county is 96 out of 102 counties in Illinois. For negative health behaviors (e.g., smoking, diet, exercise, alcohol use, high-risk sexual behavior), the county is 95th out of 102 counties in Illinois (County Health Rankings, 2017).

Geographical Prototypes: St. Louis and East St. Louis

The Greater St. Louis community provides an opportunity to explore cancer needs and how a small region responds to those needs. This information can illuminate health disparities and cancer disparities in general. Because of

considerable residential segregation in St. Louis neighborhoods, many areas
with high African American populations are also areas with concentrated
poverty and poor health (Saint Louis Regional Health Commission, 2012).
These neighborhoods often lack resources like healthy foods, safe green
spaces for recreation, and convenient access to medical care. Residents of zip
codes separated by only few miles have up to an 18 year difference in life
expectancy (Purnell et al., 2016).

For the zip codes in East St. Louis, Illinois, with the highest cancer counts
among low-income women of color, 2015 preliminary neighborhood mapping
data showed the following: median household incomes of $19,697, far below
the state average of $59,588; median house values well below the state average;
an unemployment rate of 11.1% compared with the state average of 5.1%; an
African American population of 95.4%, which is more than 6.5 times greater
than the African American state population (14.1%); and only 5.2% of the population attaining a bachelor's degree or higher, which is also noticeably lower
than the state average of 20.3% (City-Data, 2016). These disparities map onto
the zip codes 62201, 62204, 62205, and 62207 in East St. Louis with the highest poverty rates (figure 1.1). This information depicts the extent to which the
urban/suburban segments of the St. Louis metropolitan region not only suffer
from stark cancer disparities, but are also densely segregated by race and class.

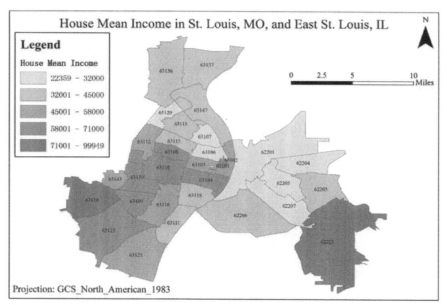

Figure 1.1.   Map of Saint Louis City and East Saint Louis
American Community Survey, 2015

The structural factors become additive and synergistic and create the perfect storm that results in cancer health inequity, for African Americans in general, but especially for lower status African American women of color.

Health Care in the St. Louis Region in the Context of Social Determinants

Despite the reduction in breast cancer death rates (figure 1.2) and the cancer rate mortality decline in St. Louis City and County between 2000 and 2010 (Saint Louis Regional Health Commission, 2012), stubborn racial and ethnic disparity gaps persist. Within St. Louis City, with a population of 320,000, it has been well documented that cancer deaths are concentrated in a small number of zip codes in the City's Northside (figure 1.3). This is most notable for breast cancer (figure 1.4) and cervical cancer (figure 1.5). Although White women are more frequently diagnosed with breast cancer, African American women are 35% more likely to die of the disease. However according to the Missouri Department of Health and Senior Services (MDHSS), the percent of African American women more likely to die of breast cancer in the city of St. Louis is closer to about 60% (MDHSS, 2011). The zip codes with the highest cancer deaths also map onto areas designated as "areas of concern" by the St. Louis City Department of Health (figure 1.6). The critical zip codes in North St. Louis have populations that are 95% African American and, compared with Whites in the metropolitan area, are characterized by lower SES, higher maternal child and sexual risks, poorer life expectancy, and reduced health care access (Purnell et al., 2016; Ross, 2008).

In 2003, the Saint Louis Regional Health Commission (RHC), a regional body charged with developing and implementing a long-range plan to improve healthcare access and delivery to the area's medically underserved population, constructed a series of geocoded maps to highlight the region's adverse health indicators. Data sources included vital record databases from the Missouri Department of Health and Senior Services, the *2000 Census Bureau Report*, and data from the St. Louis City and County Department of Health. The maps presented a striking picture of racial disparities in socioeconomic and health status of area residents. The least favorable outcomes are rooted in the north of St. Louis City and the northern portions of Saint Louis County (Saint Louis Regional Health Commission, 2003).

Among the health indicators that were selected in the RHC study, prostate cancer was two-fold higher in among African American patients compared to Whites, while breast cancer and lung cancer were 30% higher among African Americans compared to Whites (Saint Louis Regional Health Commission, 2003) None of the adverse health indicators identified

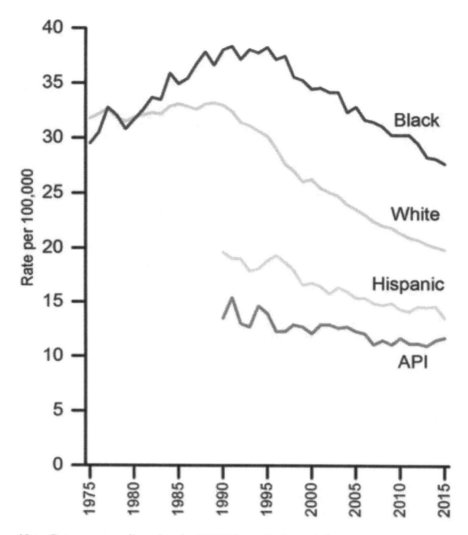

Note: Rates are age adjusted to the 2000 US standard population.

Figure 1.2. Trends in Female Breast Cancer Mortality Rates by Race/Ethnicity, United States

National Center for Health Statistics, Centers for Disease Control and Prevention, 2017. Rates for Hispanics exclude deaths from Louisiana, New Hampshire, and Oklahoma. Data for AI/AN not shown due to small counts and unstable rates. American Cancer Society, Inc., Surveillance Research, 2017. Reprinted with permission, John Wiley and Sons.

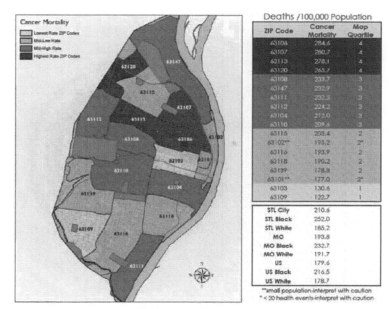

Deaths /100,000 Population

ZIP Code	Cancer Mortality	Map Quartile
63106	284.6	4
63107	260.7	4
63113	278.1	4
63120	265.7	4
63108	233.7	3
63147	232.9	3
63111	232.5	3
63112	224.2	3
63104	212.0	3
63110	209.6	3
63115	203.4	2
63102**	195.2	2*
63116	193.9	2
63118	190.2	2
63139	178.8	2
63101**	177.0	2*
63103	130.6	1
63109	122.7	1

STL City	210.6
STL Black	252.0
STL White	185.2
MO	193.8
MO Black	232.7
MO White	191.7
US	179.6
US Black	216.5
US White	178.7

**small population-interpret with caution
* < 20 health events-interpret with caution

Figure 1.3. Cancer Mortality in St. Louis City
Understanding our Needs. St. Louis City Department of Health Report, 2011.

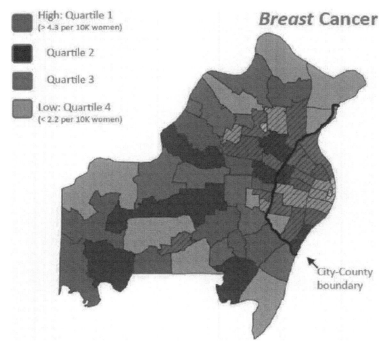

Figure 1.4. Rate of Breast Cancer in the St. Louis Region
Saint Louis Regional Health Commission. (2012). Decade review of health status for St. Louis City and County, 2000–2010: An update to Building a Healthier St. Louis.

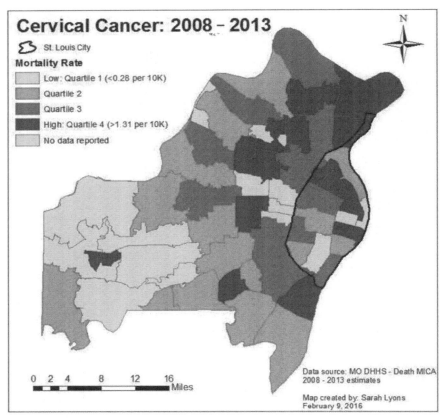

Figure 1.5.   Cervical Cancer Rates St. Louis City and County, 2008–2013
Missouri Department of Health and Senior Services. MICA, 2016.

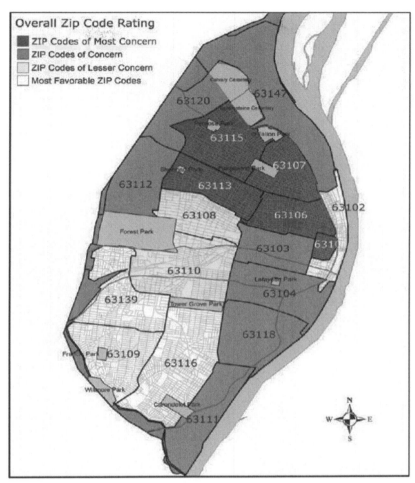

Figure 1.6. Areas of Concern, North St. Louis
Understanding our Needs, St. Louis City Department of Health, 2007.

in the study can be disentangled from the socioeconomic indicators that so glaringly depict the quality of life for African Americans living in the areas of concern (figure 1.7). A follow-up report to the 2003 RHC study cited at least transient reductions in mortality rates for breast, lung, colorectal and prostate cancer (11–24%) in the St. Louis region between 2000–2010 (Saint Lewis Regional Health Commission, 2012).

Conceptual frameworks that explain the persistence of health inequalities traditionally identify barriers in healthcare access (Freeman & Chu, 2005), health behaviors, social factors, physical environmental factors, and macro-policy. The series of graphs included in this chapter highlight the factors that predispose people to poor health in disadvantaged "areas of need" such as North St. Louis. Dr. Heidi Miller, a primary care physician at a community health center in St. Louis City, noted a variety of barriers her patients face, including "lack of transportation, jobs with no health insurance, inability to take time off work, and a lack of awareness about programs that can help" (Munz, 2013). Low health literacy, which contributes to perpetuating health inequities, is concentrated as well in the North St. Louis City and north St. Louis County neighborhoods (Lurie et al., 2008, 2009).

The health disparities and resulting negative outcomes have prompted a variety of responses over the decades to address such barriers. These efforts are evident in the region's promotion of and provision of healthcare through the region's health departments and public hospitals. However, a deteriorating healthcare safety net and the lack of a dedicated tax stream in the city

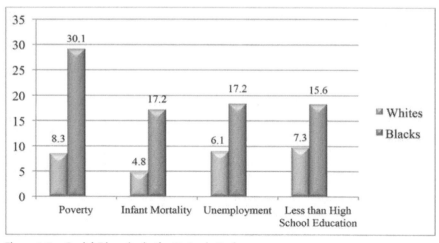

Figure 1.7. Racial Disparity in the St. Louis Region
Where We Stand: The Strategic Assessment of the St. Louis Region. East-West Gateway Council, 2015.
http://www.ewgateway.org/pdffiles/library/presentations/2015-July-WWS.pdf.

of St. Louis to support public health functions (Saint Louis Regional Health Commission, 2015) have hampered these efforts. Toward the latter part of the twentieth century, city profits in St. Louis began to dwindle as a result of a declining population. The city responded to this and changes in overhead legislation by reducing its funding for public health (Berg, 2003) and shifting the allocation of its funds from disease control to reducing healthcare costs and improved healthcare planning. Beginning with the Hill-Burton Act in 1946 (Hoge,1958) through the 1974 National Health Planning Resources Development Act (NHPRDA), the St. Louis community struggled to improve access to healthcare by documenting community need and establishing systems to control overbedding, duplication of services, and increases in healthcare costs.

The increasing paucity of available care, particularly for African Americans, is reflected in the fate of hospitals in the city. In 1906, St. Louis City Hospital opened; it was known as both City No.1 and Max C. Starkloff Hospital. Despite the city's desire to open a public hospital that would provide care to residents irrespective of race (Berg, 2003), the hospital functioned as a segregated facility, with African American patients relegated to the rear part of the second and third floors (Berg, 2003). African American physicians were not extended privileges to practice at City No.1. Only under duress, after 1955, did City No.1 admit and treat all patients irrespective of race, creed, or color. Homer G. Phillips Hospital opened its doors in the city's Northside as a "non-segregated" facility in 1937; however, in practice, it remained deeply segregated throughout its history. The Homer G. Phillips Hospital became the premier training ground for African American medical professionals, many of whom remained to deliver high-quality health care in the St. Louis area and who later assumed prestigious positions throughout the nation. Located in the Ville Neighborhood in North St. Louis, Homer G. Phillips Hospital was a source of immense pride for its patients and the members of the surrounding community, many of whom were employed by the facility. However, although the hospital was constructed as a state-of-the-art medical facility, it was consistently underfunded and understaffed. After the City of St. Louis recognized that it could no longer afford to run two hospitals at a combined deficit of $40 million per year, Homer G. Phillips Hospital was closed on August 17, 1979, under massive citywide protest from the African American community. Its closure was followed by City Hospital No. 1 in 1985, St. Louis County Hospital in 1987, and St. Louis Regional Hospital (a public-private partnership) in 1997.

The closing of St. Louis Regional Hospital prompted a series of community health reports to address the challenges to providing comprehensive, community-based health care. In December 1997, the City of St. Louis Department of Health and Hospitals conducted the *Community Health Needs Assessment* (Cunningham & Tu, 1997). The researchers conducted focus groups with 98 people from various sectors within the community. The research participants identified four major challenges that impacted health status: deteriorating infrastructure in the city, racial polarization, poverty and the consequences of living in poverty, and poor health communications and healthcare access, with many organizations taking a "silo" approach to community health needs. The recommendations included creating a framework for more neighborhood-specific problem solving and action, through more coordination and collaboration of resources.

In the ensuing years, nonprofit health groups and grassroots community organizations advocated for expanded and improved health services in North St. Louis. After the closure of St. Louis Regional Hospital in 1997, the Indigent Care Task Force was created to address the immediate funding crisis for the healthcare safety net. The task force recommended the formation of the Regional Health Commission, a consortium of government representatives, providers of care, and members of the community charged with developing and implementing a long-range plan to improve healthcare access and delivery to the uninsured and underinsured (RHC, 2015).

In 2003, the RHC issued a comprehensive report, *Building a Healthier St. Louis*, detailing striking health disparities based on race, with geocoded maps demonstrating the overlap of poor health indicators, poverty, unemployment, and other social factors, predominantly in North St. Louis. A survey conducted by the RHC in 2005 of more than 800 community health and social agencies echoed those concerns, noting insufficient focus on prevention in high-need populations and limited coordination of health and social agencies.

In its October 2003 report, *Recommendations for Improving the Delivery of Safety Net Primary and Specialty Care Services*, the RHC recommended that current safety net providers form a permanent regional network to coordinate and integrate care to the medically underserved (RHC, 2015). With valuable input from a community and provider advisory committee, regional health leaders moved to develop a safety net provider network, the Integrated Health Network. This network offered the only set of ambulatory care primary and preventive health services in North St. Louis.

In 2007, a broad-based task force, which included representatives from the regional health care safety net and local lawmakers, convened to examine the issue of access to healthcare in North St. Louis. The resulting *North St. Louis Health Care Access Study* (2008) represented the collective thinking of task force members on how to address the documented disparities in healthcare status and access for residents of North St. Louis. The assessment consisted of a triangulation of qualitative data collection and analyses methods that included documentary evidence (reports), secondary data analyses (data from the St. Louis City Health Department and from the North St. Louis health centers and free clinic), focus groups, and structured interviews. The 106 focus group participants were passionate and bitter about what they considered inadequate resources and services in North St. Louis. The report noted the following:

> They (Northside residents) have become disillusioned and skeptical of medical services offered in North St. Louis. They report that their access is severely hindered by their lack of insurance and money. They have no personal wealth and see themselves in communities that have very few assets to help or serve their economic, social or health needs. The residents believe that the services they receive are not equal to the services received by persons with insurance, persons with both Medicaid and Medicare, and by persons who have money to access private physicians. Most of the residents also perceive that the services and facilities in North St. Louis are not equal to the services and facilities in other areas of the region, particularly the Suburbs.

The conclusions of the *North St. Louis Health Care Access Study*, based on extensive focus groups of community residents, highlighted the need for comprehensive healthcare planning that included the creation of partnerships with social support services. To improve historic disparities in healthcare access, reduce health disparities, and improve health outcomes of the medically indigent, leaders of various health safety net institutions entered a period of unparalleled regional collaboration.

The decade of 2000–2010 witnessed an era of unprecedented collaboration among hospitals, community health organizations, and public health agencies, with substantial improvements in chronic disease indicators, as outlined in the 2012 Regional Health Commission report, *Decade Review of Health Status for St. Louis City and County 2000–2010*. In accordance with the report, over the last 10 years, mortality rates for breast, lung, colorectal, and prostate cancer fell 11 to 24%. Nonetheless, despite the overall improvement in health status in the St. Louis region over the past decade, race- and gender-based health disparities continue to be concentrated in economically distressed neighborhoods, particularly in North St. Louis. These disparities will remain intractable until a coordinated approach is undertaken to address the social determinants of health status among African Americans and other racial and ethnic populations.

The residents of North St. Louis well understand the need to address more than the availability of health care. In *A Crisis of Care*, a report on community concerns about health in North St. Louis, Darcell Scharff and Richard Kurz (Kurz, 2003) noted that many of the residents with poor health were more concerned about the communities' social ills that predisposed and enabled poor health. The researchers (Kurz & Scharff, 2003) conducted a total of 13 focus groups in the City of St. Louis between March and April of 2001. These focus groups allowed residents to formulate their main concerns, which included their views on the healthcare system, but explained it in terms of larger structural factors that determine health overall. They frequently reported their profound lack of trust in the healthcare system. An interesting note to point out is that in addition to documenting the attempts to make the healthcare landscape accessible, focus group members also spoke about the economic landscape. The decline in small businesses in the north City area was most concerning, as those businesses provided the bulk of employment in the neighborhood. They also provided basic needs like food and medication from markets and drugstores. The focus group participants identified poverty as the most consistent factor that explained their poor health.

In a similar vein, the recently released *Better Together Public Health Study* (Ross, 2014) lays the fault for the stark health disparities in St. Louis squarely on entrenched poverty and fragmented government. In an accompanying editorial (Ross, 2015), the report's author called for region-wide, comprehensive development to create sustainable, livable, and affordable communities for all; investment in high-quality public education that encompasses early childhood education; an embrace of quality, affordable healthcare for all; and training of a diverse healthcare and public health workforce.

The reports discussed previously in this chapter reflect a growing consensus that the persistence of health disparities in the St. Louis region requires a more robust, regional approach that incorporates the social determinants of health, along with macro-economic policies that mitigate disparities. What has been remarkably consistent over the past several decades are the unrelenting, gripping reports on how poverty and racism continue to bedevil the St. Louis region and impede progress in achieving health equity. There has been notable success in the delivery of coordinated care for the medically underserved, such as the creation of the Integrated Health Network; however, those successes have been sporadic and not widely celebrated or replicated.

Fortunately, some community-based efforts that address social determinants of health in cancer incidence have yielded positive results. The St. Louis region is gaining national attention on a positive breakthrough in health and disparities. On June 9, 2013, the front page article of the *St. Louis Post-Dispatch* celebrated: "Efforts to reduce racial disparities in breast cancer deaths in St. Louis makes headway." (Muntz, 2013) The article focused on progress that the St. Louis region has made in the last 10 years, citing the *Decade Review of Health Status* released in December of 2012, which showed that breast cancer mortality rates for African American women dropped 30% from 2000 to 2010 in the St. Louis City. Nonetheless, there remains an expansive and troubling gap between research and practice in many areas of public health and healthcare.

This chapter has outlined examples of evidence-based, efficacious interventions to reduce cancer disparities in St. Louis. We provided a detailed, ground-level exploration of the history, prevalence, and the influences of the social determinants of health, utilizing GIS (geographic information systems) and illustrations of the neighborhoods in North St. Louis City, Missouri, and East St. Louis, Illinois. GIS and these illustrations depict a host of lifestyle issues that advance or retard cancer treatment and prevention among low-income women of color. We conclude that more attention must be paid to discrepancies between evidence-based interventions to reduce cancer disparities and what occurs in the larger community. In chapter 2 we will discuss in detail cancer disparities by site. In so doing, we report on the global, national, state, and local prevalence of cancer and the significance to the socioeconomic and cultural disparities to cancer outcomes.

An Occupied Home in East St. Louis
photo by Keith St. John

Chapter Two

Cancer Disparities by Site

Today African Americans have the highest mortality rate of any racial and ethnic group for cancer generally and for most major cancers individually.

—Sylvia Matthews Burwell, Secretary, Health & Human Services

In chapter 1, we provided an overview of how poverty and other social determinants of health among African Americans and other racial/ethnic minorities in this St. Louis region can influence cancer morbidity and mortality. In this chapter, we dial back deeper into cancer disparities, by first providing a definition of cancer and a brief description of this group of diseases. We then move to a discussion of cancer inequity, briefly commenting on the significance of the term and a review of global and US data on cancer inequity. The chapter ends with a discussion of the inequities related to cancer that have been observed in Missouri and Illinois, the region used to illustrate the context, life circumstances, economic burden, and options for intervention. Cancer data are provided generally and by cancer sites of interest.

CANCER DEFINITION

A diagnosis of cancer will be given to more than 1 in 3 women and nearly 1 in 2 men in their lifetime (Missouri Department of Health & Senior Services [MDHSS], 2011). Yet among the lay public, there is a limited understanding of the diversity of the diseases grouped together under the cancer label. The complexity of these diseases, limited understanding of them, and their emotional effect (fear, anxiety) impact response to the disease among those diagnosed, as well as their family and friends. This complexity particularly affects responses by lower income individuals and those with limited literacy (Sanders Thompson & Wells, 2014). In many communities, cancer creates significant fears and worries about death, although deaths due to cancer have steadily decreased (National Cancer Institute [NCI], 2015a). Beliefs about the causes of cancer, including concerns over contagion, the role of exposure to the air during surgery, and concerns about radiation exposure during screening, must all be addressed to assist diverse patients to cope with the diagnosis, treatment, and recovery from the disease (NCI, 2015a).

Cancer is not just one disease that begins in different parts of the body, but a group of diseases that cause cells in the body to change abnormally and grow out of control. Usually, the abnormal growth occurs as a lump or mass of cells called a tumor, but some cancers, such as leukemia and most types of lymphoma, do not form tumors. Some tumors may grow slowly, posing little threat to overall health and requiring little or no treatment other than watchful waiting, whereas others grow aggressively and spread throughout the body in a process called metastasis. Types of cancer are generally named after the part of the body in which they start (NCI, 2015a).

The term *cancer* refers to a group of more than 100 diseases, where gene changes in one or several cells in the body lead the cells to divide without stopping (ACS, 2016; NCI, 2015a). The risk of having cancer increases with age because of the time it takes for cancer cells to develop and spread (ACS, 2016). There are many factors that influence who will have cancer within their lifetime. The genetic changes that cause cancer can be inherited or can occur over a person's lifetime because of errors during normal cell division. In addition, these cell changes can occur because of damage due to environmental exposures. Tobacco smoke is a frequent cancer-causing environmental exposure, but other exposures include chemicals, radiation, and sun, among others, as well as viral exposures (NCI, 2015a). In addition, diet and nutrition, physical activity, and weight maintenance are commonly discussed as factors related to cancer risk.

Cancers can vary, but they all cause the rapid overgrowth of cells. As cancer cells grow, abnormal cells often crowd out normal cells, which can impair functioning in the affected part of the body (ACS, 2016a). Cancers are sometimes grouped based on where the cells with abnormal changes are located (NCI, 2015a). The most common terms describing cancer groupings are the following: carcinoma, indicating growth beginning in the skin or tissues that line internal organs; sarcoma, indicating cancers that begin in tissues such as bone, cartilage, fat, muscle, or blood vessels; leukemia, or those cancers that start in tissues that form blood; lymphoma and myeloma, which begin in immune system cells; and cancers that begin in the central nervous system (NCI, 2015a).

Cancerous tumors are termed *malignant*, which means that they can spread into, or invade, nearby tissues through the process previously mentioned called metastasis. Age, family history (genetics), and lifestyle factors (diet, exercise, alcohol or tobacco use) are usually more important risk factors for cancer than environmental contamination (MDHSS, 2016). Cancers may also respond to treatment in different ways, with some responding better to surgery; others responding better to radiation therapy, drug, or chemotherapy; and still others requiring a treatment regimen that combines these options (ACS, 2016). Treatment decisions may also incorporate information about the individual's family history, age, and the presence of other health conditions.

Cancer Inequity

Health disparity refers to differences in incidence, morbidity, and mortality for disease, rates of health and preventive behaviors, as well as quality of life that are likely the result of injustice and inequity in society (Budrys, 2010). The term *health equity* is often used to express health goals and aspirations, defined in *Healthy People 2020* as the "attainment of the highest level of health for all people" (U.S. Department of Health and Human Services, Office of Minority Health, 2010). Researchers and advocates argue for its use because it highlights the issues of social justice that are subtexts of many discussions about disparity (Carter-Pokras & Baquet, 2002), including inequities in cancer incidence and mortality. The use of the term *health inequity* is probably more appropriate and has been widely used in Europe for decades.

Despite the increasing knowledge about cancer risk factors, preventive strategies, and treatment options, cancer does not affect all groups or regions equally, and these differences may be related to complexities in the distribution of resources related to the production of health. The National Cancer Institute defines *cancer health disparities* as "adverse differences in cancer incidence (new cases), cancer prevalence (all existing cases), cancer death (mortality), cancer survivorship, and burden of cancer or related health conditions that exist among specific population groups in the United States" (NCI, 2016a). Many factors are considered when disparities and inequity are discussed, including disability, education, race/ethnicity, gender, geographic location, and income. People who have limited income and limited access to effective healthcare or lack health insurance often bear a greater burden of disease than the general population (NCI, 2016a).

Global Cancer Inequity

The estimated worldwide burden of cancer is expected to increase to an estimated 8 million new cases per year within the next two decades (Stewart &

Wild, 2014). Cancer deaths are expected to rise from an estimated 8.2 million a year to 13 million deaths each year (Stewart & Wild, 2014). The most common cancers diagnosed are lung, breast, and colon, with cancer deaths most often due to lung, liver, and stomach cancers (Stewart & Wild, 2014). Africa, Asia, and Central and South America account for approximately 60% of the world's total cancer cases and about 70% of the world's cancer deaths, which is probably related to lack of early detection and access to treatment (Stewart & Wild, 2014).

Inequities in cancer are observable globally, with cancer decreasing in higher income nations and rising in lower income nations (Torre et al., 2015). For example, in 2012, 14.1 million new cancer cases were diagnosed and 57% of these global cancers were diagnosed in less developed countries (Torre et al., 2015). In addition, many developing countries are disproportionately affected by both a high rate of infection-related cancers (cervix, liver, and stomach) as well as a rising incidence of cancers associated with industrialized lifestyles (obesity, lack of physical activity, etc.) (Stewart & Wild, 2014).

Because of the role that income and education play in health outcomes worldwide, women require special attention as they often have fewer educational opportunities and/or less attainment and make up a larger percentage of those living in poverty (Camp Yeakey, Sanders Thompson, & Wells, 2014). A woman born in a high-income country can expect to live 24 years longer than a woman born in a low-income country (Torre et al., 2015). With respect to cancer, the most common sites of disease and causes of cancer death among women worldwide are breast, colorectal, lung, cervical, and stomach (Centers for Disease Control [CDC], 2015).

Globally in 2008, breast cancer accounted for 23% (1.38 million) of the total new cancer cases and 14% (458,400) of the total cancer deaths (Jemal et al., 2011). Worldwide, there were 521,000 deaths due to breast cancer in 2012 (Stewart & Wild, 2014). Cervical cancer is the fourth most common cancer among women and accounts for 12% of all female cancers (WHO, 2015). Cervical cancer resulted in an estimated 266,000 deaths worldwide in 2012, 7.5% of all female cancer deaths, with 87% of cervical cancer deaths occurring in the less developed nations (WHO, 2015). Colorectal cancer is the third most common cancer in the world. Close to 1.4 million new cases were diagnosed in 2012, with over 54% of colorectal cancers diagnosed in developed countries (Ferlay et al., 2014) and significant variation in rates across the world (WHO, 2015). The strong presence of colorectal cancer in developed countries is not surprising given the lifestyle and nutrition factors that affect rates of colorectal cancer. Finally, internationally, lung cancer accounted for 13% (1.6 million) of the total cancer cases in 2008 (Jemal et al., 2011). Lung cancer accounted for 1.59 million deaths in 2014 (Stewart & Wild, 2014).

Cancer Inequity in the United States

Continued advances in cancer research, detection, and treatment have resulted in a decline in both incidence and mortality rates for all cancers in the United States (DeSantis et al., 2016). For example, in the United States, of those who have a cancer diagnosis, approximately 66% will be alive in 5 years (NCI, 2016c); yet, cancer remains a leading cause of death in the United States, second only to heart disease. Disparities in cancer are well documented (NCI, 2016a) and persist despite the progress made in reducing the burden of cancer (ACS, 2016). African Americans have the highest cancer death rate, which is 25% higher than the death rate for Whites, and the lowest rates of survival of any racial and ethnic group in the United States for most cancers (NCI, 2016a).

Although African Americans continue to have higher cancer death rates than Whites, the disparity has narrowed for all cancers combined in men and women and for lung and prostate cancers in men. However, the racial gap in death rates has widened for breast cancer in women (DeSantis et al., 2016). In addition, the death rates for colorectal cancers have remained the same for colorectal cancer in men (ACS, 2016). It is important to note that these are cancers that are most affected by access to screening and treatment (ACS, 2013). Overall five-year cancer survival for African Americans continues to be lower than that observed among Whites (60% vs. 69%) at every stage for most cancer sites (ACS, 2013).

Other notable race-based health disparities exist among Asian Americans and Pacific Islanders as well. Both of these populations are more frequently diagnosed with stomach or liver cancer than Caucasian Americans, and about two times more likely to die as a result of those cancers. (NCI, 2016a). Although high quality, representative data are difficult to obtain, American Indians and Alaska Natives appear to have higher incidence and death rates for kidney cancer than other racial/ethnic groups (NCI, 2016a).

In addition to race-related cancer health disparities, cancer disparities are noted between men and women and among racial groups of women. Notably, while declines in overall cancer incidence were noted for African American men and White men, incidence slightly decreased among White women, and rates for African American women remained stable from 2000 to 2009 (ACS, 2013). Also, whereas the rate of new cancer cases is highest among White women, followed by African American, Hispanic, Asian/Pacific Islander, and American Indian/Alaska Native women, the same is not true for mortality rates (CDC, 2017a). Mortality rates are highest among African American women, followed by White, American Indian/Alaska Native, Hispanic, and Asian/Pacific Islander women (CDC, 2017a). In particular, African American women have a higher mortality rate for breast and lung cancer compared with White women despite lower incidence rates (ACS, 2013). Furthermore, overall cancer death rates increased significantly for American Indian and Alaska Native women from 1990 to 2009, while overall cancer death rates declined significantly for White women from 1993 to 1998 and 2001 to 2009 (White et al., 2014).

Although Latinas have the highest cervical cancer incidence rate, African American women are more likely to be diagnosed with cervical cancer than are White women and experience the highest overall death rate from cervical cancer (NCI, 2016a). African American women, along with African American men, have the highest incidence and death rates for both colorectal and lung cancers, whereas Hispanics/Latinos have the lowest rates (NCI, 2016a).

Breast Cancer

Breast cancer is the second most common cause of death in U.S. women, second to cardiovascular disease, and is the leading cause of premature mortality. The incidence rate for female breast cancer is 125 per 100,000 (NCI, 2016b). In its projections for 2016, the NCI (2016b) estimated that 246,660 new cases would be diagnosed in the United States in 2016, 14.6% of all new cancer cases. Breast cancer is expected to account for 29% of all new cancer cases among women (Siegel, Ma, Zou, & Jemal, 2014). Based on the data from 2010 to 2012, estimates are that about 12.3% of women will be diagnosed with breast cancer at some point during their lifetime (NCI, 2016b). In 2013, approximately 3,053,450 women were diagnosed with breast cancer in the United States (NCI, 2016b). Most women diagnosed with breast cancer are between the age of 55 and 64 years, and the median age of diagnosis is 62 years (NCI, 2016b). The rates for new female breast cancer cases have been stable from 2004 to 2013, and mortality rates fell on average 1.9% each year over the same period of time (NCI, 2016b).

Breast cancer mortality has decreased by 34% because of improvements in early detection and treatment (Siegal et al., 2014). In accordance with data from 2009 to 2013, breast cancer mortality was 21.5 per 100,000 women per year (NCI, 2016b). The NCI (2016b) anticipated that 40,450 women would die of breast cancer in 2016, 6.8% of all cancer deaths. The percent of breast cancer deaths is highest among women aged 55 to 64 years, with a median age of 68 years (NCI, 2016b). The earlier that breast cancer is diagnosed, the better chance a person has of surviving five years after diagnosis. Approximately 61.4% of women diagnosed with breast cancer are diagnosed at the local stage, the early stage at which the cancer is still confined to the organ of origin (NCI, 2016b). The five-year survival for localized female breast cancer is 98.8%. Based on data from 2006 to 2012, the overall five-year survival rate for female breast cancer is 89.7% (NCI, 2016b).

African American women face an unequal breast cancer burden (ACS, 2013). Overall, African American women have an incidence rate nearly 20% lower than that of American White women, yet are 40% more likely to die of breast cancer than White women (CDC, 2015). From 2002 to 2011 in the United States, the breast cancer incidence rates increased by 0.7% per year among African American women, but remained the same among White women; breast cancer mortality decreased significantly by 1.5% per year among African American women and by 2.0% per year among White women (CDC, 2015). Based on data from the Surveillance, Epidemiology, and End Results Program (NCI, 2016b), breast cancer incidence and mortality rates by race per 100,000 women are noted in table 2.1.

Cervical Cancer

At one time, cervical cancer was the leading cause of cancer death for women in the United States. However, the number of women diagnosed with cervical cancer and the number of deaths from cervical cancer have decreased significantly (CDC, 2014). From 2002 to 2011, the incidence of cervical cancer in the United States decreased significantly by 1.2% per year among White women and by 2.7% per year among African American women. The death rate for cervical cancer also decreased, by 0.8% per year among White women and by 2.3% per year among African American women (CDC, 2015).

Cervical cancer is the third most common gynecological cancer, with 11,967 new cases of cervical cancer diagnosed in the United States each year and 4,100 deaths in 2015 (NCI, 2015b). The incidence for cervical cancer is 25% higher and mortality 95% higher for African Americans compared with Whites (NCI, 2015b). Similarly, disparities are noted among Latinas,

Table 2.1. Cervical Cancer Incidence and Mortality by Race/Ethnicity

	Incidence	Mortality
White	128.0	21.0
Black	125.2	29.6
Asian/Pacific Islander	97.3	11.2
American Indian/Alaska Native	81.2	14.7
Hispanic	92.4	14.5

with incidence 53% higher and mortality 41% higher compared with White women (NCI, 2015b).

The primary cause of cervical cancer is a human papillomavirus (HPV), and approximately 79 million Americans are infected with HPV (CDC, 2014; NCI, 2015b). HPVs are a group of more than 100 virus types (Dunne et al., 2007), more than 30 of which can be transmitted through sexual contact (NCI, 2015a). Although most infections are asymptomatic and resolve on their own, persistent genital HPV infection causes a number of anogenital cancers, most notably cervical cancer (NCI, 2015b). HPV types 16 and 18 are responsible for approximately 70% of cervical cancers worldwide (Bosch & de Sanjose, 2003), and high-risk strains are responsible for approximately 33,200 cancers, including nearly 20,600 among women in the United States each year (CDC, 2014).

Colorectal Cancer

Colorectal Cancer (CRC) is the third most common cancer in both men and women and is also the second most common cause of cancer death among African American men and third among African American Women (ACS, 2015) in the United States. Colorectal cancer includes cancers that begin in the colon (colon cancer) and cancers that begin in the rectum (rectal cancer). In 2013, there were an estimated 1,177,556 people living with colorectal cancer in the United States (NCI, 2016b). In accordance with data from 2010 to 2012, about 4.5% of men and women will be diagnosed with colorectal cancer at some point during their lifetime (NCI, 2016b). The number of new cases of colon and rectal cancer was 41.0 per 100,000 men and women per year, or an estimated 8% (age-adjusted and based on 2009–2013 cases and deaths) of all new cancers in 2016 (NCI, 2016b). The number of deaths was 15.1 per 100,000 men and women per year or an estimated 8.3% (age-adjusted and based on 2009–2013 cases and deaths) of all cancer deaths in 2016 (NCI, 2016b). The five-year survival rate for colorectal cancer was 65.1% from 2006 to 2012 (NCI, 2016a). Colorectal cancer is more common in men than women and among those of African American descent and is most frequently diagnosed among people aged 65 to 74, with a median age of diagnosis at 68 years (NCI, 2016b). However, the median age of diagnosis varies for colon cancer and by sex. The median age of diagnosis for colon cancer among men is 69 years and 73 years for women, with a median age of 63 years for men and 65 years for women for rectal cancer (ACS, 2015).

Among women, Hispanic and Asian/Pacific Islanders have the lowest incidence of colorectal cancer (29.4 and 29.8 per 100,000, respectively). African American women have the highest colorectal cancer incidence among women (44.8 per 100,000), followed by American Indian/Alaska Natives and White women (36.8 and 35.2 per 100,000, respectively) (NCI, 2016b). CRC incidence among African American men and women is approximately 20% higher and mortality rates about 45% higher than those among Whites (ACS, 2014). Deaths due to CRC among African American women and White women follow a similar pattern. Asian/Pacific Islanders and Hispanic women have the lowest mortality from CRC (9.0 and 9.4 per 100,000, respectively; U.S. 2009–2013, age-adjusted) (NCI, 2016b). African American women have the highest colorectal cancer incidence (17.1 per 100,000), followed by American Indian/Alaska Natives and White women (15.1 and 12.3 per 100,000, respectively) (NCI, 2016b).

Lung Cancer

Lung and bronchus cancer constitute the leading cause of cancer death in the United States, accounting for an estimated 158,040 deaths in 2015 alone, which is approximately 27% of all cancer deaths in the United States (Ell et al., 2011). Lung and bronchus cancer are the second leading causes of cancer death among U.S. women (CDC, 2017a). With the exception of skin cancer, lung cancer is the most common cancer diagnosis in both men and women. It is estimated that there were 224,210 new cases in 2014, about 13% of all cancer diagnoses (Siegal et al., 2014), and an estimated 222,200 new cases (14% of all new diagnoses) predicted in 2015 (Ell et al., 2011).

Among women, lung cancer rates have been slow to decline (Siegal et al., 2014). The incidence rate has been declining since the mid-1980s in men, but only since the mid-2000s among women. From 2006 to 2010, lung cancer incidence rates decreased by 1.9% per year in men and by 1.2% per year in women (SEER Cancer Statistics, 1975–2014). Although the incidence rate for lung cancer decreased substantially significantly (0.6% per year) among African American women in the United States from 2002 to 2011 (Kohler et al., 2015), the lifetime probability of developing or dying from invasive lung cancer between 2007 and 2009 in the United States was 5.4%. African Americans have a lower five-year relative survival rate for lung cancer compared with Whites (14% and 18%, respectively; Howlander, et al., 2015 [SEER Cancer Statistics, 1975–2014]). When lung cancer is detected at a localized stage, the five-year survival rate among African Americans is 44%, but only 12% of lung cancer cases are detected at this early stage (DeSantis, et al., 2013). Studies of early-stage lung cancer treatment decisions suggest that perceptions of poor communication of diagnostic certainty between patients and their physicians were associated with a lower likelihood of surgery among both African American and White patients with lung cancer. A lack of regular source of care and the presence of comorbid illness were associated with lower surgical rates for only African American patients (DeSantis et al., 2013).

Cancer Data and Trends in Missouri and Illinois

Cancer health disparities exist on the state level, and many of the trends noted in national data exist on the state level as well. For the purposes of this case study, cancer disparity data are explored for Missouri and Illinois.

Missouri

The 2016 census estimates indicate that Missouri's population is 6,093,000 persons (U.S. Census Bureau, 2016), which is 50.9% female and 49.1% male, with a median age of 38.4 years (Data USA, 2017). The overall state increase in population was 7.0% from 2000 through 2010, somewhat below the national average of 9.7% (Mackun, Wilson, Fischetti, & Goworowska, 2011), with an estimated 1.7% increase in population from 2010 to 2016. African Americans are the largest racial/ethnic group in Missouri. Of the 6,093,000 persons living in the state, African Americans make up 11.8% (695, 213). Missouri's proportion of African Americans is like that of the United States, where African Americans make up 12.6% of the just over 300 million residents (McKinnon, 2001). In Missouri, the African American population increased by almost 85,000 from 2000 to 2012, a change of 13.1% (Missouri Foundation for Health [MFH], 2013). In contrast, the White population increased 5.3% over the same period (MFH, 2013). Of those who reported ethnicity, 4.1% of the population reported Hispanic or Latino ethnicity, 2.2% of individuals indicated that they are Asian American, and 2.2% of individuals indicated two or more races (U.S. Census Bureau, 2016).

The African American population is not distributed evenly throughout the state. One of the largest concentrations of African Americans can be found in the metropolitan area of St. Louis City. Approximately 47.9% of St. Louis City's population is African American (U.S. Census Bureau, 2017). The four counties above the 20% threshold (Pemiscot, Jackson, Mississippi, and St. Louis County) have an African American population ranging from 24 to 27% of the county residents (Index Mundi, 2017).

Although there was a 3.88% increase in household income compared to 2015, the median Missouri household income of $50,238 in 2014 is less than the U.S. median household income of $55,775 (Data USA, 2017). Furthermore, between 2014 and 2015 the poverty rate in Missouri, like in other parts of the country, declined to about 14.8% (Data USA, 2017). This is essentially the same as the U.S. national average (Data USA, 2017). Importantly, income from wages is not equally distributed in the state. In 2015, the Missouri salary wage inequality index was 0.473 (GINI calculation of the wage distribution), which is an increase over 2014 from. However, wages in Missouri are more evenly distributed than national wages (US 2015 GINI index, 4.86). In 2015, approximately 33% of individuals had a bachelor's degree or higher, and 88% of the population had completed high school (Ryan & Bauman, 2016).

In accordance with data from 2010 to 2014 for all cancer sites, an annual average of 31,677 Missourians were diagnosed with cancer, at a rate of 450.5 (448.3, 452.8) cases per 100,000 residents (NCI, 2017). African Americans were diagnosed at a rate of 486.3 (478.5, 494.3) cases per 100,000, which is notably higher than both the state rate and the rate for White Missourians alone—450.8 (448.4, 453.2) cases per 100,000 (National Cancer Institute, 2018). The rates of breast, cervical, colorectal, and lung cancer in Missouri are slightly higher than the rates observed nationally, with a lower rate of diagnosis of breast cancer *in situ* (in its original position, which is at the early stage; NCI, 2016d).

Data indicate that a significant number of Missourians have modifiable risk factors for cancer. Behavioral Risk Factor Surveillance Data for Missouri (MDHSS, 2014) indicated that only 72.5% (69.7–75.2%) and 73.6% (71.1–76.0%) of women reported receiving mammography or Pap testing within recommended guidelines, and only 61.8% (59.4–64.0%) of eligible adults reported any type of CRC screening (fecal occult blood test [FOBT], sigmoidoscopy, or colonoscopy. The CRC screening rate for women in Missouri was slightly better at 67.4% in 2016 (CDC, 2017). The prevalence of cigarette smoking in Missouri was 22.3% in 2015 (Truth Initiative, 2017). A significantly larger proportion of those with less than a high school education compared with those with education beyond high school reported a previous diagnosis of cancer (11.0% versus 6.3%) (MDHSS, 2011). Individuals with household incomes below $15,000 (14.4%) were significantly more likely to report a cancer diagnosis as compared to those with incomes of $25,000 or greater (MDHSS, 2011).

Cancer is second only to heart disease as the leading cause of death among Missourians, and the Missouri cancer mortality rate exceeds the national average (NCI, 2016d). According to Missouri Vital Statistics, in 2010 cancer accounted for nearly one-fourth (22.8%) of all deaths in Missouri. For African Americans, the data for 2011 to 2015 indicate that the death rate was 214.6 per 100,000, which was higher than that of every other racial ethnic group and higher than the US rate of 189.8 (NCI, 2018b). The cancer mortality rate for Asian/Pacific Islanders was the third highest rate (100.3 per 100,000) in Missouri (NCI, 2016d). Missouri African Americans were diagnosed with cancer at a rate of 483.7 per 100,000, which is considerably higher than the state rate for White (including Hispanic) Missourians (447.5) (NCI, 2018c). Because many types of cancer can be treated more successfully if diagnosed early, these late-stage diagnoses partly account for the higher death rates among African Americans. The higher rates of cancer incidence and mortality among African Americans are also often attributed to lower incomes, higher rates of poverty, and less insurance coverage. These factors impact health status by making it more difficult to access timely, high-quality healthcare.

Illinois

Illinois has a population of approximately 13 million, which is 51% female and 49% male, with a median age of 34.7 years. From 2000 to 2010, the population of Illinois grew 3.3% (U.S. Census Bureau, 2016). Hispanics of all races accounted for 16.5% of the population in 2013—a large increase from 2000 when Hispanic residents accounted for 12.3% of the population (IDPH, 2016). In 2013, African Americans made up 14.7% of Illinois' population, which was higher than that of the United States, where African Americans made up 12.6% of the population (IDPH, 2016). The Asian population is smaller than other racial/ethnic groups but is the fastest growing racial/ethnic group in Illinois. Chicago's African American population dropped by 17.2%, falling from 1.05 million in 2000 to 0.87 million in 2010, but remains the largest racial/ethnic group in the city (32.4% of the total population; Hall, 2011). The five Illinois counties that lost the most population between 2000 and 2010 are located in rural areas (MacKun, Wilson, Fischetti, & Goworowska, 2011). In addition, the Illinois foreign-born population grew to 13.5% in 2009 (Lubotsky & Hall, 2011). The median household income for the state is $57,166, with 14.4% of the population living below the poverty level (Mackun, Wilson, Fischetti, & Goworowska, 2011).

Throughout the process of attempting to understand cancer in the region, we have encountered difficulties developing a statistical picture for the portion of the metropolitan area in Illinois (East St. Louis) and indeed for the state itself. We report the limited data available here. A portion of the difficulty encountered probably relates to the realities of Illinois politics and budget issues, a story in itself. Budget delays have had implications for health and human services, as the protracted budget stalemate has eroded an already underfunded public health surveillance infrastructure.

The stalemate also has affected state funding that assisted with healthcare access. Suffice to say, attention is needed to understand the impact of these issues on those who experience poverty and resultant difficulties accessing healthcare. In 2014, each day there were 179 people in Illinois diagnosed with cancer: 26 women were diagnosed with breast cancer, 25 people were diagnosed with lung cancer, and 17 with CRC (Illinois Department of Public Health

[IDPH], 2016a). From 1990 to 2013, there were 1,431,606 Illinois citizens with an invasive cancer reported to the Illinois State Cancer Registry (IDPH, 2016a). Regardless of race, breast cancer was the most commonly diagnosed cancer among Illinois females (29.7% of 796,602 invasive cancers) from 1986 to 2013 (IDPH, 2016a). The cancer incidence rates among Illinois women in 2013 were the following: breast, 129.7 per 100,000; lung/bronchus, 56.9 per 100,000; colorectal, 39.7 per 100,000; and cervical, 28.8 per 100,000 (IDPH, 2016a).

Cancer is also the second most common cause of death in Illinois and the leading cause of death for Illinois citizens aged 45 to 64 years (IDH, 2016b,). Cancer kills more Illinois citizens annually than AIDS, injuries, and homicides combined (IDH, 2016). From 1990 to 2012, 565,115 Illinois residents died from cancer (IDPH, 2015). Lung cancer is the leading cause of cancer death in Illinois for all groups, except Hispanic women. Breast cancer is the second leading cause of cancer death for Illinois women, with the exception of Hispanic women, for whom it is the leading cause of cancer death (IDPH, 2015). CRC is the third leading cause of cancer death among Illinois residents (IDPH, 2015). Among women in Illinois, lung and bronchus cancers were responsible for 23% of cancer deaths from 1990 to 2012, with breast cancer accounting for 16.7% and CRC, 11.4% (IDPH, 2015).

Illinois data also indicate race/ethnicity differences consistent with international and national inequities. Of the cancers diagnosed in 2013, 81.8% were among non-Hispanic Whites, 14.3% among non-Hispanic Blacks, with 6.5% among Hispanics of any race (IDPH, 2016b). African American males had the highest cancer incidence rate. Asian American males and females, as well as other racial/ethnic groups, generally have lower cancer incidence rates than their White or African American counterparts (IDPH, 2016b). While African American males had Illinois's highest cancer mortality rate in 2013, African American females had a cancer mortality rate that was 28% higher than that of White females in Illinois and three times higher than the rate noted for Asian women or women of other racial/ethnic groups (IDPH, 2015). Of the cancer deaths reported from 1990 to 2012, 83.5% were among non-Hispanic Whites, 15.2% among non-Hispanic Blacks, with 2.5% among Hispanics of any race (IDPH, 2015).

Missouri and Illinois Cancer by Site

In this section, we provide limited data comparing incidence and mortality in Illinois and Missouri by cancer site.

I know for me, my sister was diagnosed with breast cancer when she was like 27 years old, and I know when I reached the age of 30, being her sister, I was told, you're going to need to stay up on your mammograms and all of that. So, beginning at the age of 30, I had a mammogram every year. I'm from the Pennsylvania area, so when we transitioned and moved here, I kept up with that but, for a little thing like getting busy with your job occurred, and it just . . . I rescheduled, rescheduled, and what happened was . . . two years went by and I went in for a hysterectomy, and it was when I was recuperating from that I had detected a mass, and then I had my mammogram, and then I had a diagnostic mammogram, and then I was diagnosed. So unfortunately, I so-called did what I was supposed to do for the entirety, but that short little window . . . do you know what I mean? So . . . (Focus Group Participant)

The breast cancer prevalence in Missouri is 1.60%, which is slightly lower than the national prevalence (CDC, 2015). In Missouri, the breast cancer incidence rate is 122.6 per 100,000. The mortality rate is 23.8 per 100,000, which is slightly higher than the national rate, but the breast cancer mortality rate in Missouri decreased between 2007 and 2011 (CDC, 2015). The breast cancer prevalence in Illinois is 1.65%, which is slightly lower than the national prevalence (CDC, 2016). The Illinois incidence rate is 127.4 per 100,000 with a mortality rate of 23.4 per 100,000, which is also higher than the national rate (CDC, 2016). Illinois data indicate that although African American women have a lower incidence rate than White women (including Hispanics), they have a mortality rate that is close to 1.5 times higher than White women (CDC, 2016).

Illinois and Missouri cervical cancer rates range from 7.6 to 8.7 per 100,000 (age-adjusted to the 2000 U.S. standard population) (CDC, 2017b). In Missouri, the cervical cancer incidence rate is 8.1 per 100,000, and the mortality rate is 2.5 per 100,000, which is slightly higher than the national rates. The Illinois incidence rate is similar at 8.4 per 100,000, and the mortality rate is 2.6 per 100,000—also higher than the national rates (CDC, 2017).

Mine is fear. When I started going to my lady doctor I was telling you about, when she ran my family history the first thing she did was write me out a referral to get a colonoscopy. I carried that slip around for a year. Then, I decided to go on and have it done. I had three polyps. Had I not went . . . (Focus Group Participant)

The National Immunization Survey released in the fall of 2015 provides the most recent HPV vaccination rates. Currently the national rate for females with at least one dose of HPV vaccine is 62.8%. Illinois has a rate very close to the national average, 62% (Reagan–Steiner et al., 2015). Missouri's rate of HPV vaccination, 59.3%, is lower than the national rate and Illinois one dose vaccination percentage. The vaccination rate among Missouri girls with at least three doses of the HPV vaccine is now 31.5% compared to the national rate of 41.9%. Again, Illinois has a rate that is closer to the national average, 40.2 (Reagan–Steiner et al., 2015). The national percentage for males receiving one dose of HPV vaccine is 49.8% for one dose and 28.1% for three doses of vaccine, as compared with Illinois' rate of 44.3 and 26.8% and Missouri's rate of 44.7 and 25.1% (Reagan–Steiner et al., 2015). Illinois and Missouri HPV vaccination rates for males are more similar and are both below the national average.

In 2014, the most recent year for which data are available, CRC incidence in Missouri was in the third highest quartile at 40.3 (38.1–42.2) per 100,000 (NCI & CDC, 2011–2015). The Illinois incidence was in the highest quartile and slightly higher than that observed in Missouri. Illinois colorectal cancer incidence was 42.3 (42.3–49.4) (NCI & CDC, 2011–2015). Mortality rates in both states were in the third highest quartile, with Missouri's CRC mortality at 14.5 (14.5–15.6) per 100,000 and Illinois mortality at 15 (14.5–15.6) (NCI & CDC, 2011–2015).

Missouri has a stable rate of lung cancer incidence (63.7%), although higher than the national rate of (CDC, 2015). Regarding Missouri women, nine counties had incidence rates considerably higher than the state rates, with five counties having lower incidence rates than the state rates (MDHSS, 2011). Additionally, although mortality rates are decreasing, Missouri still has higher lung cancer mortality rates than national rates (45.5%) (MDHSS, 2011).

Now that we have a better picture of the extent of the problem for this region, in chapter 3 we will shift our focus to cancer screening guidelines, in addition to the socioeconomic and cultural barriers to health that impact cancer outcomes. We discuss in detail cancer prevention behaviors and lifestyle choices. The chapter examined cancer screening guidelines, noting how the complexities based on age, family history and personal history of screening and disease led to difficulties in comprehension, decision-making and adherence among those with less education, concentrated among the poor. Quotes from providers, navigators and patients in the St. Louis region noted the barriers that low-income women, living in segregated communities faced as they attempted to coordinate work schedules, transportation needs, appointments for other health conditions, while coping with fears and worries related to costs, lack of insurance and the toll that a potential diagnosis might take on the them and their families.

A Vacant Home in St. Louis City
photo by W. Donnell Jones

Chapter Three

Health Behaviors, Lifestyles, and Prevention

> I just feel like white people have always been able to get the best of care. Blacks die more from breast cancer because we're not prevalent to getting the care or the money to go to the doctors.
>
> —Focus Group Participant

Chapter 1 detailed the aspects of life in the St. Louis metropolitan region that set the stage for persistent cancer disparities in the region. The history of racial discrimination, violence and segregation described persists in various forms, resulting in persistent and concentrated poverty in geographical regions occupied by people of color. The chapter highlights the links between a destructive racial history and the current socioeconomic and health status of people of color, particularly women. The adverse confluence of social determinants creates barriers to cancer prevention and results in cancer disparities in incidence, late stage disease and mortality among low-income women of color. Chapter 2 continues the discussion of the cancer disparities, noting the similarity in the social patterning of disease incidence and outcomes at the global, national and state levels. As noted in *A Crisis of Care,* within the St. Louis Region the social and environmental context described (homelessness, housing quality, dis/investment in neighborhoods and communities; access to and provision of adequate and appropriate healthcare; types of schools and under/achievement; employment and un/employment; and under resourced public services) increases stress and distracts residents from the preventive health behaviors and screenings that might reduce disparities in incidence and mortality. This chapter explores the socioeconomic and cultural factors influencing cancer prevention.

The levels of poverty and racial segregation in addition to areas of limited food and healthcare access found in the St. Louis region are the social determinants (Marmot, 2005; Zenk et al., 2005) detailed in chapter 1. These social determinants are often associated with the inability to engage in cancer prevention behaviors. If we want to eliminate health disparities related to cancer, the best place to begin is likely prevention. Preventive behaviors can reduce the risk of developing many cancers, including those that affect women at high rates—breast, cervical, colorectal, and lung. New cancer cases and cancer deaths could be prevented if individuals adopted healthier lifestyles, such as avoiding tobacco products, maintaining a healthy body weight, and being physically active. However, we know—because of national and local data and the voices of women themselves—that there are significant variations in adherence to healthy lifestyle recommendations. Cancer screening is one such recommendation. However, although cancer screening rates have steadily increased overall, substantial variation exists by race and ethnicity, and this variation affects cancer risks and mortality.

This chapter provides an overview of the social and cultural attitudes and the concerns that residential segregation, poverty, and low income sometimes produce or intensify, resulting in low adherence to health recommendations, particularly cancer screening. The chapter includes quotes from cancer health care providers, navigators, and St. Louis women who participated in the focus groups. (Throughout this chapter "providers" will refer to cancer healthcare providers who participated in research; "navigators" will refer to navigator participants; and "focus group participants" will refer to St. Louis women who participated in focus group research.) These quotes illustrate some of the barriers noted in the cancer prevention literature regarding how socioeconomic and cultural barriers to health behaviors and cancer screening affect cancer outcomes, but the quotes also expressly illustrate experiences that are lived and discussed in the St. Louis region. The quotes are drawn from women who participated in focus groups conducted as a part of the community outreach effort of the Siteman Cancer Center's Program for the Elimination of Cancer Disparities (Sanders Thompson et al., 2015), as well as focus groups conducted as a part of formative work to address colorectal and breast cancer in the African American community (Thompson, Kalesan, Wells, Williams, & Caito, 2010; Wells, Shon, McGowan, & James, 2015).

We begin this chapter by supplementing the discussion in Chapter 1 on the socioecological framework and factors that affect health as well as cancer mortality and morbidity. The chapter includes a review of cancer screening guidelines; data on cancer screening by age, race, and ethnicity; and screening rates and the barriers that affect screening. The chapter ends with a consideration of how adherence theory can guide efforts to organize and understand interventions to address health disparities in lifestyle choices and cancer-screening behavior.

SOCIOCULTURAL FACTORS INFLUENCING HEALTH

Although it has not always been the case, culture is now generally accepted as a factor that affects health (Napier, Ancarno, Butler, Calabrese, Chater, Chatterjee, 2014). Culture affects how individuals and populations understand what it means to be healthy or to be sick or ill. It also shapes beliefs about the causes of these states and what can and should be done about them. For this reason, culture affects a range of health behaviors, both those that prevent disease or illness and those that are necessary to treat these states. Culture affects decision-making about what individuals and groups expect and prefer. For instance, in the case of cancer, culture affects how much people may value advice to eat certain foods, maintain a particular weight, engage in physical activity, or seek and repeat cancer screening or treatment. However, our ability to integrate culture into our efforts to address disparities in cancer incidence, mortality, and morbidity depends on our understanding of what culture means.

A number of definitions of culture have been put forward. Culture goes beyond food, dress, music, and art and can be defined as the "shared beliefs, values, traditions, and behavior patterns of a particular group, may focus on the function of beliefs, values and behavior, as well as the process of constructing these (Faulkner, Baldwin, Lindsley, & Hecht, M. L. (2006). Dana (2005) asserts that culture "permeates the person as a source of pride, strength, and vitality as well as a personal rendering of what is involved in being a human being that involves values, beliefs, modes of thought, affects, language, and behaviors" (p. 23). The influence of these cultural beliefs, values, and behaviors may persist in some form across generations, even as support and modeling of the cultural traditions diminish.

Culture is transmitted to community members through socialization in the family, schools, churches, and other social and community organizations in ways that are not obvious to members of the group. Cultural elements are observed by others as shared language, social norms, and traditions. It is important to realize that recognition of cultural differences is not synonymous with an understanding of culture, which is critical to efforts to promote health and treat disease and illness. A sociocultural perspective encourages examination of culture and the way specific features of culture affect health attitudes and behaviors. These influences include issues such as perceptions of health, illness, and disability; attitudes toward healthcare systems and institutions; preferences for type of health information and how it is communicated; help-seeking behaviors; and preferences for the treatments that are considered as acceptable (Helman, 2000).

Ongoing research has demonstrated links between culture and a variety of health concerns, including symptom recognition, ability to communicate symptoms to healthcare providers, expectations for care, medication adherence, and preventive care adherence (Smedley, Stith, & Nelson, 2003). Cultural norms regulate many of these responses to diseases such as cancer. Whether a person is comfortable with a cancer screening procedure is culturally bound. The types of help that will be sought have some cultural component. Examples include prayer, herbs, traditional medicine, and the coping skills that are used to manage fears and anxiety related to signs and symptoms of disease as they first emerge. If there are strong emotional reactions or uncertainties about the best course of action, cultural norms and attitudes are likely to have an even stronger influence on health behavior and decisions. This is largely due to the profound impact of culture in determining how people characterize health and illness, determine the origin of illness, delineate how to sustain health, and plan ways to restore health during illness (Napier, et al., 2014). The strong tie between culture and health behavior is demonstrated in the following quote from one of the St. Louis focus group participants:

> Focus Group Participant: Trying to be our own doctors. Listening to what our parents . . . what they did for an illness. You talk about it and they say, why don't you try.

Many marginalized and underserved groups have a system of attitudes, beliefs, and practices that are composed of a worldview that emerges as a result of interactions within, among, and between group members and the dominant culture. These cultural realities influence people's reactions, which may be gender specific, as gender norms and expectations interact with cultural norms and expectations. Using this socially constructed lens to guide their perceptions and interpretations facilitates the development of a health conception that is used to determine ways to protect or maintain health, restore health, and retain social support when sick (Helman, 2000).

Any proposed connection among culture, health behavior, and health attitudes requires some qualification. First, there is not always a direct link between a person's health beliefs and the health behaviors that they adopt (Mulatu & Berry, 2001), as it is possible to maintain health beliefs that are inconsistent with each another and with behavior. For example, a woman may engage in smoking that is viewed as ceremonial, as she diligently adheres to a physical activity and dietary routine to avoid the breast cancer that her mother was diagnosed with. Most individuals recognize the overlapping and interconnected treatment domains: popular, folk, and professional (Helman, 2000). They may engage in one or more of these domains, sometimes engaging in multiple simultaneously (Mulatu & Berry, 2001). Consider three religious women—one who initially elects herbal remedies to treat colorectal cancer, another who might pray and request the prayers of others, and a third who might immediately elect to receive surgical treatment. The second woman may eventually elect to receive surgery and the first and third women may ask for prayer as they undergo treatment.

Individuals move freely between and among treatment approaches, even with the unique features of the popular, folk, and professional sectors in their explanations and treatments for an illness as well as the role of the provider and patient within the helping relationship. In general, a person's tendency to adopt the health activities of a particular domain depends on trust and perceptions regarding the ability of that system to relieve physical discomfort or emotional distress.

Beliefs, attitudes, and behaviors concerning health and well-being are dynamic and may change with time and circumstances and what women in St. Louis believe about cancer is constantly changing. This changing landscape is based on shared experiences with cancer and the cancer detection and treatment system, as well as the variety of sources of information about the disease increasingly available in the community. For instance, one woman notes:

Focus Group Participant: From the people I know if they catch it in time, they do survive. I have a co-worker and she had cervical cancer or something. And she said that they did the surgery and she's fine. So I believe if you get screened, take the treatments in time, you can survive.

One factor likely to produce changes in cancer disparities is socioeconomic status; however, as noted in chapters 1 and 2, persistent poverty, low-income and un/under-employment are characteristic of North St. Louis, MO and East St. Louis, IL. Another factor capable of producing change is exposure to health-related knowledge and expertise within or outside of the culture. Influences from outside of the culture are more likely if the appropriate context for influence or persuasion exists, hence our growing interest in models of culturally appropriate health communication and intervention as well as culturally sensitive and appropriate patient care and interaction.

A Crisis of Care, described in chapter 1, was one of the first efforts to address issues of the social determinants of health in the St. Louis region (Kurz & Scharff, 2003). Other researchers have made efforts to observe and understand family relationships, rules for emotional expression, communication and affective styles, collectivism, individualism, spirituality and religiosity, myths, and time orientation and how these seem to influence health attitudes and behaviors, as they affect health and as these factors affect attitudes about cancer in the St. Louis region (Sanders Thompson, Arnold, & Notaro, 2011; Sanders Thompson, Lewis, & Williams, 2013; Sanders Thompson, Arnold, & Notaro, 2012; Cogbill, Sanders Thompson, & Deshpande, 2011; Wells, Gulbas, Thompson, Shon, & Kreuter, 2014). The findings inform the efforts of navigators and lay health advisors and the development of tailored and targeted health information designed to address the unique cultural and structural barriers that confront the marginalized communities.

As discussed in chapter 2, cancer care is not equitable across demographic categories. While socioeconomic status is a major variable affecting access to preventive services, several studies have demonstrated a relationship between sociocultural attitudes and self-reported screening, intent to screen, and cancer attitudes among African Americans (Sanders Thompson, Harris, Clark, Purnell, & Deshpande, 2014). Cancer fatalism and mistrust of the medical system have been associated with decreased utilization of colorectal cancer screening (CRCS; Sanders Thompson et al., 2014). Associations have also been found between privacy concerns and attitudes about CRCS barriers (e.g., costs, transportation, time, etc.), which suggest the need to consider tailored education and navigation strategies rather than targeted ones to address the needs of individuals with high privacy concerns (Sanders Thompson et al., 2014), but all of these issues are related to the importance of a provider's recommendation of CRCS (Klabunde et al., 2005; Sanders Thompson, Lander, Xu, & Shyu, 2014).

Women, Culture, and Cancer

In St. Louis, as in other regions, the importance of culture is readily observed in certain features of women's reactions to cancer. For example, certain health topics, diseases, and medical procedures are not discussed among women in the African American community, and cancer is one of these (Sanders Thompson, Harris, Clark, Purnell, & Deshpande, 2014). Some of the silence is related to beliefs about the disease, but the silence is often because of the emphasis on being strong, Black women; being role models for children and in the community; and having the desire to protect loved ones that may be related to the structural violence and discrimination discussed in earlier chapters. A focus group participant noted:

> Navigator: In the African American women's culture, there's this whole secrecy and so the goal is to put on your best face, be strong, keep yourself well dressed, your hair done and that's the façade and you talk about. . . . There's just this culture of secrecy I've heard and had some of my ladies describe to me as being present. And so working to try and penetrate that culture in helping women. . . .

It's the educational piece. . . ."Here's why it's important to know what your family tree looks like." And "here's why it's important for you to talk about breast health and the importance of mammograms."

Another navigator suggests:

Navigator: The taboo and the secrecy is not only in the African American community. It's also very big in the Hispanic community.

Often women do not want others to worry about them or feel burdened by their illness. Some of the most pressing burdens noted are financial—time off from work, co-pays, transportation, and the costs of treatment if needed. A navigator in the St. Louis region observed:

Navigator: In the Latino community, I see a lot that they have fear to lose their job. . . . Like if you call them they say, "Well, I have to work, and I need to call off like 3 weeks in advance. . . ." They are afraid they might get fired, which is a big barrier in the Latino community.

In addition, women have their own concerns. The fears related to cancer that are expressed by women in racial/ethnic communities affect reactions to the diagnosis and treatment decisions, but are not solely cultural. In Chapter 2 we note the role of economic factors and concerns on cancer incidence and mortality. Similar concerns may also affect cancer prevention. Minority women may find themselves concerned about the effects of treatments that affect their ability to work, care for children, or meet other obligations. Other issues emerge, which may be unique. Will radiation therapy darken or alter the skin and affect appearance? Does surgery really make cancer worse? Will having surgery make the cancer spread? These were all concerns expressed by the women who participated in our study:

Navigator: One of the main barriers that I've noticed with men and women, male and female, is the caregiving. They always put families and children before themselves. And so what I've noticed is that I have to tell them, "Well, if you're responsible for that person and you're not here to take care of that person, then who are they going to have?" And I have to put it in a sense to where it's reality, and they have to think, "Yeah, okay, I am this person's provider."

Focus Group Participant: And, um, the chemo, it took her hair, but she was fine. It was fine. They gave her radiation that turned her skin black. I mean *black*, and my sister was light skinned. And, um, after that, I noticed her, her looks, a thing about her looks, which she wasn't hung up on but, that took it. It just took it like . . . it took her someplace else.

There are a number of issues that women may suddenly and unexpectedly face after receiving cancer treatment, such as menopausal symptoms (i.e., "hot flashes"), changes in sexual desire and response, concerns about infertility and pregnancy, as well as the need to understand and discuss genetic and family breast cancer risk.

> Focus Group Participant: Because every time it's something new in life. Going through the change. Going through the change and coming out of this cancer, and then fighting other problems in your life, and children. . . . Don't you all get me started! I'm trying to be cool.

Seeing themselves as strong and long-suffering, many African American and Latina women will not readily seek the support of others to cope with concerns. Women, particularly ethnic minority women, are used to providing support. How do they cope with the fears, the changes that they experience? Who answers their questions?

Religion and Spirituality

Religion and spirituality have been noted in the cancer literature as a strong cultural influence and source of support. Our research indicates that religiosity and the role that religion and religious institutions play in St. Louis is strong (Thompson et al., 2010; Sanders Thompson, Harris, Clark, Purnell, & Deshpande, 2014). Religiosity and spirituality can provide the strength to have a mammogram or colonoscopy so that cancers can be detected early. Religious beliefs may also affect whether a parent will consider use of the human papillomavirus (HPV) vaccination to prevent infection and reduce risk of cervical cancer (Sanders Thompson et al., 2012). Religion and spirituality can provide a sense of hope that God will take care of the individual's needs in the event cancer is discovered. Women may use their faith to assist in making critical decisions about care, acknowledging that God has given physicians the knowledge necessary to provide appropriate care. A focus group participant attests to this notion:

> Focus Group Participant: When they said I had cancer, I didn't believe it. I just couldn't believe it! But then once I figured that it was, then I was satisfied, okay. So, then I said, "I have my husband. I have my children. I have church members to help me. Most of all I have Jesus." I said, "That's what helped me. His word, given that word." And so she [peer coach] said, "Well that's good. But don't you need to talk it over with somebody?" I said, "Not really, because I accept it." And I said, "I had the surgery so I don't have it no more." And so she would come, and we would talk, we had good talks.

Although many women in racial and ethnic communities use religiosity and spirituality in health decision-making, their approach varies, as shown in the responses of two of the participants:

> Focus Group Participant: I always trust God first. I always pray for guidance and protection. And if it's something he put on this earth to help his people, then, yes, you know, I want that to be given to my daughter. I'm led by the Holy Spirit. It led me to make the right decision that this would help her, you know, then yeah.

> Focus Group Participant: God gave us five senses, and we know when we need to take care of business. My spiritual sense wouldn't affect my health decision at all, you know, because I mean I would use—that can be separated, you know. This is real life right here. I mean and this is spiritual over here, you know. So, no, it wouldn't affect it.

Churches provide a range of support mechanisms regarding health, from cancer prevention to support after diagnosis. Some host mammography vans, provide breast cancer education through health ministries and fairs, and are places to disseminate cancer education materials.

> Navigator: I think a lot of times too [about] the churches where we put the flyers up and . . . when there's a coordinator, having people sign up for the mammography van.

Prayer is one tool of religion that some women in the study used as a coping strategy to deal with negative thoughts, fears, and stressors that came with receiving a cancer diagnosis and cancer treatment. In addition, the church can organize to provide women with the emotional support that they may need.

> Focus Group Participant: I was in the cancer ministry at our church, so it did help because I was with women who had gone through this. My best friend was there, and she had been through this right before me. Right before my best friend, my cousin had went through it, but she had passed on. So, I had a lot of help as I'm taking treatments.

Other Culturally Appropriate Support

Although women are strong, have learned to cope with adversity, and have a strong faith, a cancer diagnosis may render these standard coping resources insufficient. Navigators and women participating in focus groups note the importance of women feeling free to discuss their decisions, feelings, and concerns with their loved ones. They also note the importance of women feeling comfortable requesting and expecting the support they need, despite a sense of responsibility towards family members and friends. When family and friends are not enough, women in ethnic minority communities should have access to other culturally appropriate sources of support. Navigators often fit the definition of culturally appropriate support when they are members of the community who understand the social, economic, and cultural issues faced by women who are being screened for or diagnosed with cancer.

> Navigator: I talk to them just like I'm talking to my friend when I call them. When I ask for them, I am very professional . . . a lot of times they think I'm a bill collector . . . once I tell them who I am, they're like, "Oh, it's a friend," and that right there allows to me gain their trust.

The importance of sociocultural issues extends beyond efforts to cope with a disease that can frighten women. Culture affects how we approach the lifestyle issues that affect cancer risk and our ability to reduce disparities. When and what we eat are influenced by cultural and social norms that may alter willingness to listen to dietary recommendations. Similarly, cultural and social expectations related to appearance may affect willingness to implement changes to achieve recommended levels of physical activity. Next, we explore how sociocultural, as well as economic and other social determinants affect lifestyle choices that affect women's cancer risk.

Disparities in Health Behaviors and Lifestyles

The data presented in chapter 1 illustrates why increased awareness of the social determinants of health has led health and public health practitioners and researchers to examine the health, safety, and well-being of diverse segments of our population. Even when we consider that behavior plays an important part in explaining the higher incidence of chronic diseases like cancer, heart disease, and diabetes, the behaviors of interest happen within a context. Data indicate that there are associations among neighborhood characteristics, social class, and race/ethnicity (Diez Roux & Mair, 2010). The existence of these associations suggests that poor individuals and racial/ethnic minorities have less access to the resources that support a healthy lifestyle (Diez Roux & Mair, 2010). Successful intervention with chronic diseases, such as cancer, requires recognition that social and environmental contexts matter for overall health, as illustrated in chapters 1 and 2. Quotes from members of the community allude to the roles that income, education, health literacy, health insurance, and transportation can play in smoking, physical activity, diet, cancer screening behavior, and even votes on policy decisions that affect health behaviors such as smoking. We also consider how the socioeconomic concerns that operate and are sometimes intensified in segregated environments inform health behaviors regarding cancer.

> Navigator: Even people who are identified with breast cancer, the first question out of their mouth a lot of times isn't, oh my God, I have this cancer. It's how am I going to pay for it? Which just makes me always so sad that that's their first thought.

> Navigator: If you're having a hard time coming up with $15, $20 just to see the doctor, then thinking about breast cancer treatment, you're talking about possible surgery, maybe chemo, maybe radiation, maybe all three; medication, follow-up appointments. Now you're talking about something that's as a full-time working person, I'm like, I probably would have that question as well. We have to, everyone has to live until you die. So even as a person who is sick, you don't want to be faced with starvation or homelessness. You don't want to get to a certain point and you're getting treatment. I mean, to me, the worst thing would be initiating treatment and then having to stop. Because some of them have to pick and choose over attending their appointments or putting food on the table or paying a bill or something like that. I hear that too sometimes. It's either or. Do I go here because I really need to? Or I need food on the table too so it's like, I have to make a choice.

Chapter 2, using cancer statistics, illustrates how health is diminished in nations, states and communities that do not have equity, particularly in the social determinants that shape health outcomes (Budrys, 2010; LaVeist, 2005; Williams, Neighbors, & Jackson, 2003). As noted, data indicate that a significant number of individuals in Missouri and Illinois have modifiable risk factors for cancer and we take this opportunity to illustrate the role of culture and social determinants in adherence to recommended health behaviors. Using examples provided by women in the St. Louis region, we explore how social determinants affect efforts to engage in lifestyles associated with cancer prevention, as well as cancer screening adherence.

> Focus Group Participant: I cannot afford going to the doctor, paying for medicine, and trying to eat and trying to live in or have an apartment. And for me as far as insurance is concerned, I don't have any insurance because (a) I can't afford it, (b) when I did have insurance, it was my check, at least half my check. And for me and my daughter to survive, I can't pay that and eat and have a place to live.

Depending on public transportation can also be a barrier to receiving care:

> Focus Group Participant: You have to get from point A to point B if you don't have a car. You can go one place in one day because you have one transfer per

bus. So, if you go to a clinic, you gotta make sure it is on the bus route and it's on the second one or the first one. And if it's not, you are in trouble.

Finally, educational issues can result in a lack of understanding or limited understanding of prevention measures and later treatment options and decisions:

Navigator: I don't know if the ladies really understand the importance of it; the lack of education. It sounds good in the moment when they're signing up.

Smoking and physical inactivity are two major risk factors for multiple chronic diseases (American Cancer Society [ACS], 2013). Leisure time physical activity is significantly lower among non-Hispanic African Americans than among non-Hispanic Whites, (ACS, 2013), which places African Americans at higher risk for lung cancer and other types of cancers. Socioeconomic factors, environmental context, and cultural factors may all play a role. It is notable that lower education levels are correlated with lower income, increased rates of smoking, and shorter life expectancy (Galea, Tracy, Hoggatt, DiMaggio, & Karpati, 2011). In addition, environment affects willingness to engage in physical activity. For example, how safe is the community for walking and jogging? What are the conditions of parks and recreation centers? Is there adequate programming that meets the work and interests of the communities served? Safety is often a major issue in St. Louis due to the crime statistics reported year after year. In this residentially segregated region, there is the perception that the safe places for physical activity are in other parts of the region:

Focus Group Participant: If you can't go out on your porch or yard because you are too scared of a drive-by shooting. . . . I'm not saying that there's more crime everywhere . . . but let's be real. You know in some areas there's more crime than there is in others. Let's just be real.

Nationally, residential segregation is more prominent among African Americans than other racial ethnic minority groups (O'Keefe, Meltzer, & Bethea, 2015) and St. Louis is no exception as discussed in chapter 1. Although most residential segregation concentrates low-income and racial/ethnic minority residents into poorer quality, low-resource areas, this experience is most acute for African Americans. Hyper-segregated communities generally restrict access to "quality healthcare, fresh produce, recreational facilities, and economic mobility," all of which are required to support health and well-being and may influence risk of cancer mortality (O'Keefe et al., 2015, p. 2). Consistent with Missouri and Illinois lung cancer patterns mapped in chapter 1 and presented in chapter 2, O'Keefe et al., (2015) note that lung cancer mortality among African Americans was observed to be higher than that observed among Whites, but was highest among African Americans living in the most segregated neighborhoods, with a 10% higher lung cancer mortality rate compared with African Americans who reside in the least segregated neighborhoods. This difference persisted after adjusting for socioeconomic status (SES). In addition, racial segregation accounted for approximately 8.9% of differences in breast cancer healthcare (i.e., lower mammography access and late-stage cancer diagnosis) observed in one study (Haas et al., 2008). When physicians and mammography services are not in your community, transportation matters for access. Public transportation may be available, but routes to services may require multiple transfers, leading to costs and time expenditures that can decrease the motivation for prevention and care. A navigator's comments highlight one of the complexities for isolated communities attempting to access the services designed and implemented to improve health outcomes:

> Navigator: I always tell them, "If you cannot make this appointment, that's okay. Just call me and let me know, and I will send transportation for you. . . . [Paying for transportation] is something that Show Me Healthy Women and Komen do. But they only work at specific times. . . . You cannot let that woman go home by herself; if they don't have any transportation . . . you can't just leave it up to chance.

Education is another factor that figures into health disparities. It affects literacy, which affects health literacy, and health literacy affects health outcomes. Compared with those with high health literacy, individuals with low levels of health literacy have more hospitalizations and emergency care, less preventive care, and poorer overall health status, and older adults with low health literacy have higher mortality rates (Berkman, Sheridan, Donahue, Halpern, & Crotty, 2011).

The disparities in education that consistently correlate with cancer disparities in north and East St. Louis (chapter 1) suggest the need to consider health literacy. In a systematic review on health literacy, researchers (Berkman et al., 2011) note that lower health literacy is associated with less knowledge and comprehension of recommendations and information, which can include recommendations on diet, physical activity, and screening. Low health literacy has also been associated with the inability to interpret health messages and the inability to take medications as instructed (Berkman et al., 2011). Willems, De Maesschalck, Deveugele, Derese, and De Maeseneer (2005) suggest that SES and education affect patient-provider communication patterns, such as asking questions. Physicians are noted to communicate less with patients who seem less educated and less communicative, which likely affects patients' experiences and their ability to overcome health literacy obstacles (Willems et al., 2005). Patients who lack health information about cancer are likely to have misconceptions about prevention and screening.

Cancer prevention guidelines can be one site of complexity for those with low health literacy, as explained by participants in our study:

> Navigator: The fact that the guidelines of when you can get your pap or when you can get your mammogram are always changing. . . . "Well you need your pap every 3 years. Oh no, wait. You only need your pap every 5 years." They get confused and don't know their timelines . . . and it's hard to keep a structured setting of when their timelines are because well that changed last year. . . . They don't know who to believe or what's legitimate, and they don't know which avenue to take because they've been told so many separate things, so many different times.

> Provider: I think from a provider perspective, I'm just as confused as the women because those guidelines are changing. It looks like every 6 months there's some change. . . . And they don't inform you.

As the study participants demonstrate, a complex set of social and economic factors accounts for many health outcomes, including health behaviors relevant to cancer. Tobacco use and exposure affect fourteen types of cancer, and we know that individuals with lower incomes and education smoke longer and, although they make attempts to quit, are less successful in doing so (Houston, Scarinci, Person, & Greene, 2005). The complex set of factors driving these realities are important to explore.

Tobacco Use and Exposure

Cigarette smoking is the leading cause of lung cancer (U.S. Department of Health and Human Services [USDHHS], 2014). Compared with nonsmokers, women who smoke are about 25.7 times more likely to have lung cancer (US-DHHS, 2014). Smoking causes 80% of lung cancer in women (USDHHS, 2014) and 90% of lung cancer deaths among women. In addition, adults who are exposed to secondhand smoke at home or at work increase their risk of having lung cancer because the concentrations of many cancer-causing chemicals are higher in secondhand smoke than in the smoke inhaled by smokers. African Americans, American Indians/Alaska Natives, and Native Hawaiians/Other Pacific Islanders experience health disparities regarding the adverse effects of tobacco use and secondhand smoke exposure (National Cancer Institute [NCI], 2017). A participant in one of our St. Louis studies shared her experience:

> Focus Group Participant: I smoked from age 13. Back in the day, you didn't know cigarettes were cancerous. So, I smoked from 13 to 33. And one night,

I went to work, and it was kind of drizzling, and I had to kind of jog to Union Station across the street to the post office. I was out of breath. The cigarettes that I had in that pack, I said that when I get through with these I'm not smoking anymore. I never picked up another cigarette. And I never started back because it had been too hard to quit.

Houston, et al., (2005) note that individuals who are poor and those who are less well educated are more likely to smoke. Smoking rates are close to 40% among individuals with less than a high school education or a general education diploma (GED) compared to 5% among college graduates (Jamal et al., 2016). Moreover, individuals in lower SES groups have substantially longer durations of smoking and lower cessation rates than those in higher SES groups (Singh, Williams, Siahpush, & Mulhollen, 2012). Lower education, ethnic minority status, and poorer health are associated with lower levels of receiving recommendations from health professions, including advice to quit smoking. These differences persist, even as factors such as number of cigarettes, income, presence of other health conditions, health insurance, sex, and age (Houston et al., 2005) are taken into account. It is important to note that there are significant variations in smoking among ethnic minority women. Smoking rates among Latina and Asian women are still below 10%, but much higher smoking rates have been found among Cuban and Puerto Rican women (Jamal et al., 2016). Despite tobacco's role in cancer disparities, not every state has adopted policy options, such as increasing cigarette and tobacco taxes that protect low-income, less well educated and minorities from smoking related cancers. Despite higher lung cancer rates than the national average (chapter 2) and smoking rates higher than the national average (MICA), residents of north St. Louis live in such a state. Missouri legislators and voters have repeatedly defeated initiatives to increase tobacco taxes, although the state has the lowest cigarette tax in the country at 17 cents a pack (Scarboro, 2017).

National data assist us in examining factors that may affect tobacco use among racial/ethnic and low-income women. Several researchers note a relationship between perceived stress and smoking among African American women (Jesse, Graham, & Swanson, 2006; Webb & Carey, 2008; Nguyen, Subramanian, Sorensen, Tsang, & Wright, 2010). In one study, researchers found a positive association between perceived stress and current smoking in a community-based sample of African American women (Webb & Carey, 2008). In addition, researchers found positive associations between perceived stress and smoking when they examined correlates of smoking status among pregnant African American women (Jesse et al., 2006; Nguyen et al., 2010).

Researchers have suggested that racism and discrimination play a role in tobacco smoking and may increase the risk of smoking, decrease the chances of quitting, and ultimately increase health risk. The studies linking racial discrimination and current smoking are primarily cross-sectional and focused on African Americans, and the evidence is less clear for other racial/ethnic groups and those with better financial resources, suggesting a role for income and stress in smoking status (Jesse et al., 2006; Carey & Webb, 2008; Nguyen et al., 2010) The St. Louis region is no stranger to discrimination and racial/ethnic unrest (Banks & Sanders Thompson, 2016). Research on perceived experiences of discrimination in St. Louis suggest that all racial and ethnic minorities report these experiences and that they report some distress in response (Sanders Thompson, 2006).

In addition, evidence exists that tobacco advertising may affect smoking disparities in low-income racial/ethnic communities, as tobacco advertising seems to be disproportionately targeted toward low-income and minority communities (NCI, 2017). These communities typically lack the resources to provide robust tobacco prevention programs, to treat tobacco use, or both. Drives through St. Louis communities make clear the differences in tobacco advertising, whether on buildings or at street level on many corners.

Education and literacy issues further complicate smoking levels in low-income and minority communities. For example, the reason for providing warning messages on cigarette packages is to give individuals information on the hazards of smoking that will deter the behavior or encourage the decision to quit (McQueen et al., 2015). Greater message processing has been associated with greater intentions to quit or to change smoking behaviors (Hammond, Fong, McDonald, Cameron, & Brown, 2003). To be effective, the warning labels must be accepted as believable (increases processing) and must provide those reading them with the information on smoking harm (increases knowledge of harms that deter). However, people with low education, language barriers, or both may misunderstand the written warning labels used in the United States, including some terms (McQueen et al., 2015). The misunderstandings that can occur may limit the extent to which the printed warning labels on cigarette packaging can motivate individuals to avoid, reduce, or quit tobacco use. The information processing barriers described for smoking behavior may have relevant policy implications, such as reactions of Missouri voters to tobacco tax increase initiatives.

As noted in chapter 1, the St. Louis region has a lower percentage of college-educated individuals than the national average, and this is more acute among African Americans and other ethnic minorities, suggesting the need for additional tobacco control resources. Chapter 2 highlights higher lung cancer rates and the disparities within the state. The Precaution Adoption Process Model (Weinstein & Sandman, 2002) suggests that awareness of a health risk is necessary but not sufficient for behavior change. Thus, it is important to evaluate whether comprehension of smoking and secondhand smoke risks reaches levels optimal enough to motivate exploration of resources to quit. Because of the value of decreasing smoking, the Illinois and Missouri Tobacco Quit Lines offer telephone counseling and resource materials to help citizens to stop tobacco use (Missouri Department of Health and Senior Services [MDHSS], 2016a). However, those who are most affected must be aware of the resources and have the ability to access them.

Physical Activity

In recent years, health and public health organizations and practitioners have increased their emphasis on the importance of physical activity. Much of this interest is due to increases in morbidity and mortality associated with chronic diseases (e.g., cardiovascular disease, diabetes). Insufficient physical activity is a common risk factor for most chronic diseases, including cancer (U.S. Department of Health & Human Services [USDHHS] 2009). Participation in regular physical activity has been associated with decreased mortality, decreased morbidity (e.g., risk for having chronic conditions), and health-promoting benefits (e.g., maintenance of a healthy weight; increased health of bones, muscles, and joints; and good mental health) (USDHHS, 2009).

In 2008, the USDHHS developed physical activity guidelines for the nation, in which it adopted the ACSM guidelines but increased the vigorous physical activity recommendation from 60 to 75 minutes per week (USDHHS, 2008). The USDHHS recommends that adults 18 to 64 engage in some physical activity, as some physical activity is better than no physical activity and has health benefits. The guidelines go on to suggest that individuals engage in 150 minutes of moderate activity or 75 minutes of vigorous activity (USDHHS, 2008).

Despite the known health benefits of physical activity, national data indicate that adherence to recommendations is less than ideal. Diez Roux and Mair (2010) note a positive relationship between physical activity and resources within the community. The presence of a safe community, parks, good sidewalks, and biking and walking trails make physical activity more likely, although other factors may still affect levels of activity and consistency. As highlighted in chapter 1, these resource issues are characteristic of the St. Louis region and many other communities with large racial/ethnic and low-income communities.

Several factors have been shown to be associated with physical activity among African Americans and other ethnic minorities, such as marital status, education, income, and health status (Seefeldt, Malina, & Clark, 2002; Ainsworth, Wilcox, Thompson, Richter, & Henderson, 2003; Egede, 2003;

Wilbur, Chandler, Dancy, & Lee, 2003; Fontaine et al., 2005). Studies indicate that physical activity occurs more often among those who are more educated and have higher family incomes, whereas the relationship between marital status and physical activity is less clear (Ainsworth et al., 2003; Wilbur et al., 2003). Some have found that physical activity is more likely among married persons (Ainsworth et al., 2003), whereas others have found the opposite (Wilbur et al., 2003). Women also cite job demands, physical tiredness, physical illnesses, expectations and needs of the family and others in the community, economic constraints (money for gyms and classes), major life changes or traumas, safety issues, weather, and environment as reasons for lack of physical activity. In addition, African American women note the hassle of personal care (e.g., showering, keeping hair looking good) and a lack of facilities and opportunities (Ainsworth et al., 2003).

The Missouri Information for Community Assessment (MICA) system indicated that in 2011, 25.9% of residents of St. Louis indicated that they had engaged in no leisure time physical activity, which is significant differently from rates in the surrounding county, but not statistically different from rates in the state (USDHHS, 2017). African Americans reporting no leisure time physical activity was higher (27.7%). (Hispanic data were not available). In our work in the St. Louis region (excluding East St. Louis), we found that the rate of physical activity was higher than the rates obtained from state sources; most participants in our study reported some participation in physical activity (84.5%). However, only 58.7% were found to be adherent to USDHHS guidelines. Participants who were married or employed were, respectively, 67% and 60% more likely than their counterparts to engage in enough physical activity to meet current USDHHS recommendations (OR=1.67 [95%: 1.04, 2.70], OR=1.60 [95%CI: 1.09, 2.34]) (Cogbill et al., 2011). Those who reported a family income less than $20,000 were 40% less likely to engage in sufficient physical activity recommendations (OR=0.60 [95%CI: 0.38, 0.95]). Consistent with the physical activity literature, those who had a family history of a chronic illness were 2.47 times more likely to be adherent to physical activity recommendations (95%CI: 1.20, 5.07), but those who had a personal history of chronic disease were 74% less likely to meet guidelines for physical activity. Because African American men are typically more active than women, not surprisingly, when physical activity adherence was stratified by gender, 60.1% of men and 57.6% of women were adherent to recommendations. Women who were employed or scored higher on religiosity (OR=1.72 [95%CI: 1.22, 2.42], OR=1.93 [95%CI: 1.03, 3.61]) were more likely to be adherent. Clearly, physical activity is a health behavior that might be improved to decrease cancer risk and mortality.

Dietary Behavior

The types of food an individual consumes influences development and progression of chronic diseases, including various cancers (Mayne, 2003; Keku, Millikan, Martin, Rahkra-Burris, & Sandler, 2003). Fruits and vegetables, which are high in antioxidants and other healthy elements, have been shown to prevent such conditions, but are irregularly consumed by Americans. Lack of health education in communities or from providers may contribute to low-consumption of fruits and vegetables. Fruit and vegetable consumption does not receive significant amounts of attention in the media, the main source of news and education for many individuals (Rolnick et al., 2009). It has also been suggested that physicians, who are generally respected sources of medical information, and other professionals have not done enough to promote fruit and vegetable consumption. However, more importantly, there is recognition that people do not eat based on food groups or nutrients (USDHHS & USDA, 2015). The latest dietary guidelines, in recognition of how people really eat, are focused on patterns of food consumption.

The 2015–2020 dietary guidelines (USDHHS & USDA, 2015) include only suggested numerical values (i.e., numbers and percentages) of nutrients to assist individuals and families in staying within calorie limits. The guidelines suggest that individuals and families consume "less than 10% of calories per day from added sugars" (p. xiii), "less than 10% of calories per day from saturated fats" (p. xiii), and less than 2300 mg of sodium per day (individuals 14 and older). In order to achieve the goal of high-quality nutrients within calorie limits, the guidelines suggest "selection of nutrient-dense foods across and within all food groups in the recommended amounts" (p. xiii). The 2015–2020 guidelines encourage consumption of vegetables from all subgroups, a variety of fruits and grains, particularly whole fruits and grains; low-fat or fat-free dairy, a variety of proteins, and oils. However, it is important to remember that even these guidelines require numerical skills to calculate the percentage of calories coming from restricted sources; they also require knowledge of food nutrients (e.g., saturated versus unsaturated fats, sodium, and whole grains). Literacy and numeracy skills matter. A focus group participant alluded to the role of education in health behaviors:

> Focus Group Participant: With a little more education, maybe higher in the economic, you know branch. . . . They deal with things, they eat differently, they live differently than maybe the lower income. And a lot of it depends on education. It's education and where you are economically.

Low SES is associated with an unhealthy diet and other health behaviors that might contribute to obesity (Kahng, 2010). Studies suggest that, on average, individuals who are poor do not meet federal recommendations for fruit and vegetable consumption (Golan, Stewart, Kuchler & Dong, 2008). In addition, members of poor households consume fewer servings of whole grains and low-fat dairy products than households with higher incomes. A number of factors that could account for disparities in healthy eating associated with income include affordability, availability (i.e., presence of supermarkets, grocery stores, farmers' markets), and information on healthy eating necessary to make good decisions. According to Golan et al. (2008), low-income households receiving maximum benefits from the Supplemental Nutrition Assistance Program (SNAP) should be able to afford a healthy diet. However, low-income families may spend more of their income and time on food when attempting to eat a healthy diet. In addition, affordability of food is an issue for low-income households that do not receive SNAP benefits or that receive less than maximum benefits (Golan et al., 2008).

Research indicates that income is not the sole factor in the health behaviors of the poor and near poor. According to Diez Roux and Mair (2010), systematic reviews indicate that neighborhoods with better access to supermarkets or other stores that provide healthy food options report healthier food intake. When neighborhoods lack these resources, community members are at greater risk of poor nutrition. Interventions attempting to increase fruit and vegetable consumption have too often focused on changing individual health behaviors and improving health communication (Baker et al., 2006). However, today, researchers and practitioners more often recognize that health education is not a panacea.

In addition to individual behavioral factors, social, economic, and environmental factors play a role in health outcomes. As emphasized in chapter 1, these health determinants often help to direct behavioral factors. Shopping for fresh produce and unprocessed foods in large or chain grocery stores is less expensive, but many African American neighborhoods lack such businesses in close proximity (Baker et al., 2006). The financial, transportation, and time limitations render it difficult for individuals living in such communities to obtain healthy foods. Other studies hint at the effects of mental health on health behaviors and have suggested the use of stress management to increase fruit and vegetable consumption (Block et al., 2004). Hence, although changes in health behaviors are the goal of prevention, researchers and practitioners must look at the true underlying causes for individuals' unhealthy choices, which are likely multifaceted and multilayered.

Partnering with ethnic minority institutions is a culture-specific intervention that has demonstrated effectiveness with ethnic minorities (Satia, 2009). These institutions and organizations (churches, sororities/fraternities, HBCUs, community groups, etc.) may also provide venues for program intervention. In addition, reviews of the literature suggest that it is important to consider the cultural values and norms of the racial/ethnic group to be served, adapt the traditional foods of the group and consider "hiring 'ethnically matched' staff or staff that participants can identify with" (Satia, 2009, p. 5). Finally, the ability to include the participant's family and friends into the program in some way has been found to be helpful.

Recommendations for Screening Cancer

Navigator: What I hear from women in their position is, "Okay, so now I've found something wrong. I have no money. I have no resources. How am I going to now care for my kids, care for my aging parents, care for myself; what is that going to look like, how am I going to access this care when I don't have a pot to throw out the window?"

Provider: So, while we're saying we are going to take care of the patient, the hoops that we as clinicians are having to jump through to get the care to the patients precludes us from getting out in the community and bringing you in and saying, let me help. Because I'm spending so much time on the phone or trying to figure out how to help them. . . . Which pot am I going to be able to pull from to get some coverage? . . . in the case of undocumented immigrants, there are no pots.

The cancer objectives for Healthy People 2020 focus on monitoring trends in cancer incidence, mortality, and survival to better assess the progress made toward decreasing the burden of cancer in the United States (Office of Disease Prevention and Health Promotion, 2017). The objectives reflect the importance of promoting evidence-based screening for lung, breast, cervical, and colorectal cancer by measuring the use of screening tests identified in the U.S. Preventive Services Task Force recommendations (USPSTF, 2017).

Breast Cancer Screening

Focus Group Participant: It's [cancer is] scary. . . . But my grandmother, she had breast cancer. She had both of her breasts removed. And it eventually killed her, though. She died. But she had to have both removed. That's why that's a fear of mine, is that breast cancer. Because I saw how she suffered. Because I was with her and she really suffered. And I wouldn't want to suffer like that. And I think I was mad at the doctors because they were keeping her alive.

Clinical breast exams and regular mammogram screening are currently the best ways to detect breast cancer at the earliest possible stage. Mammography is a screening test found to be one of the best ways to detect breast cancer accurately and reduces the likelihood of late-stage breast cancer and subsequent mortality when the cancer is detected early when it is easier to treat (Elmore, Armstrong, Lehman, & Fletcher, 2005). Five-year relative survival rates for common cancers, such as breast cancer, is 90 to 100%, if they are discovered and treated before spreading beyond the organ where the cancer began (MDHSS, 2016b). The USPSTF recommends biennial screening mammography for women aged 50 to 74 years. The decision to start screening mammography in women prior to age 50 years should be an individual one. Women who place a higher value on the potential benefit than the potential harms may choose to begin biennial screening between the ages of 40 and 49 years. For women who are at average risk for breast cancer, the greatest mammography benefits provided by the Affordable Care Act (i.e., "Obamacare") (Patient Protection and Affordable Care Act, 2010) allow for biennial screening for women ages 50 to 74 years. Compared with women in other age groups, women aged 60 to 69 years are most likely to avoid breast cancer death through mammography (USPSTF, 2016).

Several agencies provide mammography screening guidelines. Although there is general agreement among various guidelines on the benefits of breast cancer screening, the age of screening initiation and the frequency of the screening remain controversial. In 2009, the USPSTF recommended against routine breast cancer screening in women younger than 50 years (NCI, 2016a).

Mammography use varies by age, with greater utilization among women 40 to 49 years (NCI, 2016a). In 2013, 72.6% of women aged 50 to 74 years had a mammogram within the previous 2 years (NCI, 2016b). The screening percentage was lower for Hispanic women (66.7%) compared with White women (73.3%) and African American women (72.5%; NCI, 2016b). In addition, screening rates vary by poverty level, such that the screening percentage is 77.7% among women who are at or above 200% of the federal poverty level and 58.8% among those below 200% of the federal poverty level (NCI, 2016b). In addition, mammography use varies by education level, with 59.5% of women with less than a high school education (50 to 74 years) being screened in the last 2 years (NCI, 2016b). Studies indicate that mammography is twice as high among the insured (54.8%) compared with the uninsured (22.3%); however, it is too early to tell whether the Affordable Care Act reduces this disparity in states that have expanded Medicaid (Smith et al., 2015).

A range of factors have been identified to account for disparities in breast cancer mortality. Studies suggest that a lack of medical insurance, lack of a usual source of care, or both play a role in disparities in breast cancer outcomes (NCI, 2016b). Lack of coverage and a usual source of care are barriers to early detection and screening and may contribute to unequal access to improvements in cancer treatment and the observed differences in survival between African American and White women (NCI, 2016b). In addition, research indicates that aggressive breast tumors are more common in younger African American and Latino women living in low SES areas (NCI, 2016b). These more aggressive forms of breast cancer are less responsive to standard breast cancer treatments, which result in poorer survival (NCI, 2016a).

Economic barriers have also been noted, including cost of mammography, lack of access to screening services, appointment barriers, long wait times for screening, and language barriers (Peek, Sayad, & Markwardt, 2008; Sarma, 2015; Stoll et al., 2015). An analysis of the Siteman Cancer Center's Breast Health Outreach Program data illustrates the role that economic factors may play among women in the St. Louis region (Drake, Abadin, Lyons, Chang, Steward, Kraenzle & Goodman, 2015). Women who were aged 50–65, uninsured, or African-American had higher odds of a repeat visit to the mobile mammography van compared with younger women who were insured, or Caucasian. One focus group participant emphasizes the barrier to care posed by the lack of insurance:

> Focus Group Participant: Sometimes they don't even recommend tests for people without insurance. Those tests aren't available to them. . . . And if you don't have any insurance at all . . . people are working out there, but you'd be surprised, a lot of people don't have the insurance. And that's the main factor right there.

Long wait times are also noted as an impediment:

> Focus Group Participant: That's one thing I hate about going to the clinic is when you have to sit all day to be seen.

In addition, women have reported fearing a mammogram, providing as a reason that it may be painful (Peek at al., 2008; Stoll et al., 2015). A focus group participant expressed her fear of having a mammogram, although she did not note pain as the reason:

> Focus Group Participant: Just to let you know . . . I still don't take mammograms. I just feel that all that radiation will give you cancer, so I just don't take it. I mean now we discuss about the radiation . . . I mean about taking the mammogram, but I just told her I just . . . I just don't believe in it. I met women that has . . . took the mammogram and two months later found out that they had breast cancer, and they couldn't . . . they were shocked, because they had taken the mammogram. Even the girl at the church literally takes it regularly, and it didn't pick it up. So, I said, well why do I need to take it?

Other commonly reported barriers to mammography include healthcare system–level barriers such as the lack of a recommendation for a mammogram from a healthcare provider and lack of a usual healthcare provider (Peek et al., 2008; Sarma, 2015). A lack of trust in hospitals and doctors has been cited as barriers to breast cancer screening, particularly among minority women (Sarma, 2015). Several factors have been associated with whether women receive a recommendation for breast cancer screening from a provider. Women who have health insurance, request a mammogram, have an annual income above the federal poverty line, and have at least a high school education are more likely to receive a recommendation than women without health insurance, who have incomes below the poverty level and less than a high school education (Sarma, 2015). Provider attitudes about the screening guidelines may affect the recommendations that women receive. This may result in confusion among less well-educated women and can affect adherence, as suggested in the navigator comment below:

> Navigator: I know we have a real issue in our clinics with the providers being split in half when they get the mammograms because of the taskforce. I've got some providers who believe every year is fine, and then I've got some providers who are encouraging women to come back in 2 years and so we're kind of struggling with that as well. We're trying to get all the doctors on one page.

St. Louis data are similar to those in the national literature. Women reported fears of cost (40%), mammogram-related pain (13%) and bad news (13%) as barriers to breast cancer screening (Fayanju, Kraenzle, Drake, Oka & Goodman, 2014). Women with insurance did not report perceiving cost as a barrier. St. Louis women have also reported distrust of hospitals and medical providers (Thompson et al., 2010; Sanders Thompson, Harris, et al., 2012; Sanders Thompson, 2014).

Screening and Survival Rates

Although racial disparities in the screening rates between U.S. African American and White women have disappeared, inequities in breast cancer outcomes still exist. Breast cancer screening rates ranged from 45.9% in Hispanic women to 52.6% in non-Hispanic African American women. Screening rates were twice as high among the insured (54.8%) compared with the uninsured (22.3%; Smith et al., 2015). In addition, the aggregated screening rates obscure other inequities associated with screening. These factors include low quality of equipment in certain areas, high patient-provider ratio in certain poor resource areas, and uncertainty about where to target interventions locally to increase screening (Schootman et al., 2008). A provider in the navigator study noted, along with other systemic issues, shortages in providers available to treat poor and low-income women:

> Provider: So, I think there's the piece of not having enough providers, but I also think it's the efficiency and streamlining of the system. . . . If I see Cherise and I've worked her up and done what I can for her breast pain and referred her to the next higher level of care but then she just comes back to me . . . there's another cost incurred; there's direct and indirect costs that are being incurred with that approach financially . . . and you've now wasted time for the provider and for the patient . . . and there is the possibility of the patient not coming back.

Navigators discussed the imposition of referral and appointment requirements that increase costs for women:

> Navigator: The state of Missouri is just shifting the cost. It's just a huge barrier, not only for the patients but then for the providers who want to do the right thing at the right time.

> Navigator: They need two referrals in order to pay for it. . . . It's just like they don't want them to come. They don't want to provide any more free services so they are making it difficult for the patients to come.

Moreover, overall improvements might mask disparities in screening practice for much smaller areas (Schootman et al., 2008). Thus, to reduce the incidence of late-stage breast cancer diagnoses, the issue becomes where to target interventions locally (geographic targeting) to increase mammography use. The strategies proposed to address concerns include flexible clinic hours, health education and mobile mammography vans (Drake, et al., 2015; Schootman et al., 2008). Providers offer the following comments.

> Provider: Well, for me, because I work with so many chronically ill patients and this is kind of a subset of probably what you're looking at, they have so many appointments. I mean their life just consists of so many doctors' appointments. And I think as a healthcare system we need to do a better job of finding ways to decrease the number because we know that the more appointments that they have, the more likely they're going to miss. Mammograms are important for our female patients, especially over 40. But when you have someone who is coming in so many times for so many other things and this is kind of like, "You're talking about preventative care versus acute care because I actually have something wrong with me that I know. This is a little bit more flexible. I can keep rescheduling this or I don't have to go or I don't feel like going." So we need to find ways to make sure that the preventative care is somehow wrapped up into a different appointment; really to condense those appointments and that's what

we do with a service that we have called "Diabetic Cluster." We just take it, and we condense it, and you get everything in one room. You get to talk to the doctor, you talk to the healthcare coach, you talk to the dietician and whoever else may be coming that day; the pharmacist. Instead of having six different appointments, really to try to make it a convenient service. And I think that could possibly impact the rates of screening.

And for women, I'm sorry—we have, you know, our annual OB/GYN appointment. I don't see why that's not wrapped into that. That's not tied together while they're already there. And with people in general, it's best to just get them while you already have them there. They're more likely to cooperate. They've already taken the day off. They've already paid their co-pay one time. They have already given the information that they need. Every time that you let them walk out the door you risk them not coming back or, when they come back, not having something that they need. And so you increase the risk of them not being screened.

Cervical Cancer Screening

Focus Group Participant: In my husband's family two of his nieces, one was 19 and she had to have a hysterectomy because she had cancer of the cervix.

Focus Group Participant: Right now, I feel like it's killing my daughter. Because she had to have a partial hysterectomy. And she been complaining about more pain in that area.

Cervical cancer screening is the checking of a woman's cervix for cancer before there are signs or symptoms of the disease, which can be done by means of the Papanicolaou test, best known as the Pap test (or Pap smear). The prevalence of having a Pap test or smear is significantly lower among non-Hispanic African American women than non-Hispanic White women. In recent years, with recognition of the slow progression of the disease, the success of the HPV vaccine, and more sophisticated screening tests, guidelines for cervical cancer assessments have shifted. Cervical cancer incidence and mortality rates have declined since the introduction of the Pap test in the mid-twentieth century, and the rates continue to decline to this day.

The Pap test is used to look for precancerous cells in the cervix that may become cervical cancer if they are not treated appropriately (CDC, 2015) or removed (ACS, 2013). The USPSTF (2016) recommends screening for cervical cancer in women aged 21 to 65 years with cytology (Pap smear) every 3 years. The USPSTF (2016) recommends testing every 5 years for women aged 30 to 65 years who want to lengthen the screening interval, which can be done if their cervical screening is conducted using a combination of cytology and HPV testing. Although the guidelines suggest that screening end at age

65 for women who have had two or three consecutive negative results in the previous decade, experts report the new findings do not necessarily point to the need to revisit. Cervical cancer progresses so slowly, with so many early warning stages, that it is highly unlikely that a 65-year-old woman who had met guideline requirements would subsequently have the disease.

Objectives of Healthy People 2020 for cervical cancer screening are to increase the percentage of women who receive cervical cancer screenings and to increase public education regarding the newest prevention methods that are proven effective at reducing cancer rates (USPTF, 2017). The outcomes have sometimes been measured by assessing the number of girls and boys who receive at least one dose of the HPV vaccine (CDC, 2015). Ways to improve screening include promoting evidence-based interventions for screening and early detection exams. In addition, another non-patient (individual level) strategy is to increase healthcare providers' awareness of current cancer screening guidelines and follow-up recommendations by, in part, educating providers on the newest prevention methods for them to discuss with their patients (NCI, DEA, 2014).

Vaccines to prevent HPV infection make cervical cancer highly preventable (CDC, 2010, 2011, 2014) since cervical cancers are caused by persistent infection with HPV. The HPV vaccination, available since 2006 for females and 2009 for males (CDC, 2010, 2011, 2014; Markowitz et al., 2007), provides protection against HPV-16 and HPV-18 (Markowitz et al., 2007; CDC, 2010), the carcinogenic strains responsible for causing 70% of cervical cancers worldwide (Bosch, Lorincz, Munoz, Meijer, & Shah, 2002). The Advisory Committee on Immunization Practices (ACIP) recommends routine HPV vaccination in girls and boys aged 11 to 12 years (CDC, 2010, 2011; Markowitz et al., 2007). Although "catch-up" vaccination is an option (females 13–26 years and males 13–21 years; CDC, 2010, 2011; Markowitz et al., 2007), this information may confuse parents and young adults (Wisk, Allchin, & Witt, 2014).

Although vaccination rates remain lower than expected, prevalence of the four HPV strains targeted by the vaccines decreased 56% among girls 15 to 19 between 2007 and 2010 (Elam-Evans et al., 2014). It is estimated that "if current vaccination levels increased to 80%, an additional 53,000 future cases of cervical cancer would be prevented among girls who are now 12 years old and younger over the course of their lifetimes" (NCI DEA, 2014, p. 15).

Screening and Survival Rates

Five- and 10-year relative survival rates for cervical cancer patients are 68% and 64%, respectively. Almost half of patients with cervical cancer

(47%) are diagnosed when the cancer is localized, for which the 5 year survival is 91% (ACS, 2013). The racial disparity noted in studies of cervical cancer mortality was thought to have narrowed because cervical cancer death rates for African American women were declining. However, a recent study shows that the gap is far greater than believed. The new rates do not reflect a rise in the number of deaths, which recent estimates put at more than 4,000 a year in the United States. Typically, death rates for cervical cancer are calculated by assessing the number of women who die from a disease against the general population at risk for it. However, the epidemiologists who analyzed health data from 2000 to 2012 excluded from the larger population women who had had hysterectomies. A hysterectomy almost always removes the cervix, thus reducing the possibility that a woman will have cervical cancer. Although studies show that the disease is preventable and, if detected early, treatable, many of these patients never had Pap smears. In a new analysis of existing data from 2000–2017, the mortality rate for African American women was 10.1 per 100,000 (Beavis, Gravitt, & Rositch, 2017). For White women, it was 4.7 per 100,000. In previous studies, those figures were 5.7 and 3.2, respectively (Beavis, et al., 2017).

African American women are the only race/ethnic group to show a progressive trend in screening (having had a Pap test in the previous 3 years) among women aged 18 years and older (CDC, 2014). In addition, the percentages of cervical cancer screening vary by education level, with women with the most education most likely to have had a Pap test in the previous 3 years (CDC, 2014). The percentages of cervical cancer screening also vary by age, with women aged 18 to 44 years most likely to have had a Pap test in the previous 3 years, followed by older women (CDC, 2014).

Between 2005 and 2013, cervical cancer screening declined by 4.4% (Siegal et al., 2014). In 2013, cervical cancer screening rates ranged from 70.6% in Asian women to 82.8% in non-Hispanic White women and were 25% higher among insured women (85.6%) compared with uninsured women (60.6%) (Smith et al., 2015). Hispanic and Asian women were also less likely to have had a Pap smear within the previous 3 years than were White, African American, or American Indian/Alaska Native women.

Many barriers exist to the completion of cervical cancer screening. For instance, lower rates of cervical cancer screening have been documented for women with mental illness (Aggarwal, Pandurangi, & Smith, 2013). Additionally, systemic barriers influence cervical cancer screening among Latina women. St. Louis navigators note that despite their reassurances to the contrary, fear of deportation due to immigration status serves as an obstacle to screening for some women:

Navigator: They become afraid and that's where we are losing them. When they start out, they are undocumented, and we start asking a lot of questions. "Do you have social security? How long have you been in the United States? Do you have paperwork? Do you have this, do you have that?" Then, they say immigration is going to report me. And even if you tell them everything here is confidential, you are not going to be reported, we still lose a lot of them because they don't want to come back and take a chance.

Navigator: They are fearful that they are going to be reported to immigration, yes. But we assure them, no, no, no and most of the times we are successful. . . . They trust us, yeah, but it takes a while in that situation to gain the trust. It's very difficult because of that overriding fear of deportation.

Navigators also note that there are financial issues that are prevalent among the racial and ethnic minority women they encounter.

Navigator: Most of them are illegal immigrants. So, once they're diagnosed, they stop. There's not money. It's like they're diagnosed. . . . Okay, the county pays for the diagnostic mammogram, the ultrasound, the biopsy, and that's it. . . . And so no treatment.

Some women may not know that cervical cancer is a preventable disease, or they may know about the prevention but do not have access to healthcare facilities where they can be examined (Szaboova, Svihrova, & Hudeckova, 2014). Among those who participate in screening regularly, groups of working women with higher education and income were found to have higher levels of information about the prevention of the disease (Szaboova, Svihrova, & Hudeckova, 2014). Several researchers have found a link between low SES and a lack of knowledge about cervical cancer screening services and low participation in screening programs (Szaboova et al., 2014), an issue that women participating in focus groups noted:

Focus Group Participant: In order to get better, you do have to catch it in time before it spreads. Where can I go if I don't have health insurance?

Psychological barriers were found to be based on the lack of knowledge about screening, fear of the examinations, fear of a positive test result, fear that the examination would be uncomfortable and painful, feelings of shame in front of the doctor, and a preference for women to perform the examination (Marlow, Waller, & Wardle, 2015; Szaboova et al., 2014).

Navigator: A lot of people are just scared to go and hear them say you got it. I think the fear comes from people who don't have any money and not having healthcare, or good healthcare, and not being able to go and be hospitalized and get treatments they need if they have it.

Distrust of healthcare professionals because of previous negative experiences also has been found but has been found to be related primarily to lower education and lower SES (Szaboova et al., 2014). Women in the focus group discussed their concerns about a history of medical mistreatment of women of color:

Focus Group Participant: I know there's a big issue. They say half of the hysterectomies they did on Black women were not necessary. So that's a big issue.

Behavioral and cultural barriers to cervical cancer screening include feelings that they would be neglecting family responsibilities and child care at the time of visiting the doctor in addition to feelings related to the fear of the examination (Marlow et al., 2015; Szaboova et al., 2014). Navigators discussed how they try to assist clients in putting their social and cultural expectations in perspective as they attempt to manage the demands of cancer preventive behavior.

Navigator: Caregivers have other barriers, but caregiving seems to be the main part as far as not showing up. . . . "I can't come because I have my grandchildren to take care of or my children."

Geographical barriers to cervical cancer screening include a lack of access to healthcare facilities, centers, and health services that perform the screenings, along with long distances and expensive transport (Marlow et al., 2015; Szaboova et al., 2014). Access issues may also include the wait times and the lack of scheduling flexibility, as noted below:

Focus Group Participant: A lot of times you go and sit hour, hour-and-a-half, before they see you, but if you be late five minutes and they want to charge you.

Human Papillomavirus Vaccination

Just as there are significant racial disparities in cervical cancer prevalence, incidence, and mortality, there are disparities in HPV infection rates. The President's Cancer Panel has called underutilization of HPV vaccine "a serious but correctable threat to our progress against cancer" (NCI Division of Extramural Activities [DEA] President's Cancer Panel, 2014, p. 1). In an effort to increase HPV vaccination, the panel has called for the development of communication and intervention tools that promote in-depth discussion between adolescents' parents or caregivers and healthcare providers" (NCI DEA President's Cancer Panel, 2014, p. 2). Any emergence of differential HPV vaccination rates has the potential to impact cervical cancer disparities.

According to National Health and Nutrition Examination Survey data from 2003 and 2004, the prevalence of any HPV infection was significantly higher among non-Hispanic African American women (Dunne et al., 2007). The overall prevalence of HPV-16 among African American women (sero-prevalence estimates based on surveys and serum collected) is estimated to be 19.1% compared with 12.5% among White women (Stone et al., 2002). However, now, several vaccines target the HPV subtypes that are responsible for most cervical cancers. A quadrivalent vaccine is recommended for females and males 11 to 12 years of age (HPV-16, -18, -6, and -11), but it may be given as young as 9 and as old as 26 years (CDC, 2010; Markowitz et al., 2007). A bivalent vaccine is recommended for girls aged 11 to 12 years (HPV-16 and -18) (CDC, 2010), but it may be given as young as 10 and as old as 25 years (Markowitz et al., 2007). A recently approved vaccine covers nine strains of the HPV virus (Robinson, ACIP, & ACIP Child/Adolescent Immunization Work Group, 2016). Although vaccination may further decrease incidents of cervical cancer, any disparities in the adoption of vaccination may exacerbate cervical cancer disparities.

HPV vaccination plays a strong role in cervical cancer prevention. Although HPV vaccination has been available for 8 years and is recommended by the CDC and the Advisory Council on Immunization Practices (CDC, 2010, 2011), uptake in U.S. males and females remains low (Reagan-Steiner et al., 2015). Researchers found in the National Immunization Survey–Teen (NIS–Teen) 2014 that only about 60% of U.S. girls aged 13 to 17 years received at least one dose of the HPV vaccine, with approximately 36.8% having received the full three-shot regimen (Reagan–Steiner et al., 2015). See table 3.1. Of note, statistically significant higher proportions of Hispanic, African American, and American Indian/Alaska Native adolescent females compared to White females reportedly received at least one dose of the HPV vaccine, with Hispanic and African American females also more likely than White females to report receipt of two doses of the HPV vaccine (Reagan–Steiner et al., 2015). Only Hispanic adolescent females reported statistically significant higher receipt of three doses of HPV vaccine than White females (Reagan-Steiner et al., 2015). Male HPV vaccination followed a similar pattern. Interestingly, those living below the poverty level reported higher proportions of 1-, 2-, and 3-dose HPV vaccination compared with those living at or above the poverty level (Reagan-Steiner et al., 2015). However, a study of healthcare provider practice as it relates to HPV vaccination recommendation indicated that only about one third of healthcare providers serving low-income, ethnic minority, and immigrant patients provided recommendations for HPV vaccinations (Bruno, Wilson, Gany, & Aragones, 2014).

Table 3.1. NIS-Teen 2014: Estimated HPV Vaccination Coverage for U.S. Adolescents Aged 13–17 years (n = 20,827)

Category	Female[a]			Male[a]		
	≥ 1 dose	≥ 2 doses	≥ 3 doses	≥ 1 dose	≥ 2 doses	≥ 3 doses
Total	56.7 (±1.9)	46.9 (±1.9)	36.8 (±1.9)	33.6 (±1.8)	22.6 (±1.6)	13.4 (±1.3)
Race/ethnicity						
White	56.1 (±2.2)	47.1 (±2.2)	37.5 (±2.1)	36.4 (±2.0)	27.4 (±1.9)	18.8 (±1.7)
Black	66.4 (±4.8)[b]	53.0 (±5.1)[b]	39.0 (±5.0)	42.1 (±4.9)[b]	32.0 (±4.8)	20.4 (±4.0)
Hispanic	66.3 (±5.1)[b]	57.4 (±5.1)[b]	46.9 (±5.2)[b]	54.2 (±4.9)[b]	39.4 (±4.9)[b]	27.8 (±4.7)[b]
Income						
Below poverty level	67.2 (±4.2)[c]	58.0 (±4.3)[c]	44.7 (±4.3)[c]	51.6 (±4.0)[c]	39.4 (±4.1)[c]	27.2 (±3.9)[c]
At or above poverty level	57.7 (±2.1)	47.9 (±2.2)	37.9 (±2.1)	39.5 (±2.1)	29.5 (±2.0)	20.2 (±1.8)

[a]Reported as % (95% CI). [b]p <0.05; White serves as referent group; [c]p <0.05; at or above poverty serves as referent group.

Physician recommendation (Daley et al., 2010; Rambout et al., 2013; Sanders Thompson et al., 2011) and safety concerns (Sanders Thompson et al., 2011) have been cited as strong influences on parents' and young adults' decisions to obtain HPV vaccination. It is worth noting that, regarding HPV vaccination, religious beliefs, vaccination at free or community clinics versus private physicians, transportation, and perceptions related to community norms and attitudes are not major issues among African American parents (Sanders Thompson et al., 2012). Quotes from interviews conducted with St. Louis region mothers of girls eligible for HPV vaccination are included to illustrate some of the concerns noted in the general literature (Sanders Thompson, Arnold & Notaro, 2012):

> Mother of Girl Eligible for HPV Vaccination: Well, when she went for her physical, her pediatrician said that she wanted to wait for her to get the vaccination, because, I guess, the drug, or something with the vaccination hasn't been FDA approved for at least 5 years. So, she didn't recommend her to get it just yet.

> Mother of Girl Eligible for HPV Vaccination: You know, people scared to get vaccinated and stuff like that. Because even the flu shot, you know, I work at a medical place where we offer a flu shot. And I was telling one of my friends about this flu shot, and she said, "I'm not doing that! You know, they got us set up to kill all these Black people." And I looked at her, and I mean, to me ignorance is just such a bliss. And I'm like, "What?" "Girl, that's the way to wipe us out!" I said, "A flu shot?" I said, "That would've wiped us out years ago. But you do get a little sick behind it sometimes." And I have, but that's just normal! You know?

Some parents are concerned about early initiation of sexual behavior as a result of a false sense of security associated with HPV vaccination (Allen et al., 2010). However, knowledge on HPVs association with the development of cervical and other cancers, genital warts, and its status as the most frequent sexually transmitted disease have been weakly associated or not associated at all with HPV vaccination uptake and completion (Bendik, Mayo, & Parker, 2011; Schmidt & Parsons, 2014).

> Mother of Girls Eligible for HPV Vaccination: That's not true. That's not true. Because I do have a daughter that is sexually active, and I have a daughter that is not sexually active. It has nothing to do with sex. I explained to my children, "It's not about trying to have sex or be grown. It's about your health, what's most important for you. It's about cancer.

To date, unique factors associated with college women's intent to receive HPV vaccination include perceptions of vaccination (Allen et al., 2010) and knowledge of genital warts (Boehner, Howe, Bernstein, & Rosenthal, 2003) as socially normative. White women eligible for catch-up vaccination (18–26) were reportedly more likely to be vaccinated as compared with African American and Asian American women (Boehner et al., 2003).

Colorectal Cancer Screening

> Focus Group Participant: It's called fear. It's called shame. You don't want anyone to know that you got colorectal cancer. The fear is about it is cancer, the word that when you say it means that you are going to die.

> Focus Group Participant: You have to know your retirement plan. My mother retired and she used to have good insurance. She was set for retirement, but Medicare doesn't pay for everything. She cannot afford going to the doctor, paying for tests, and trying to eat, and trying to live or have an apartment. You have to have a supplement.

For most adults, the most important risk factor for colorectal cancer (CRC) is older age. Other factors associated with CRC include family history of colorectal cancer, male sex, and African American ethnicity (USPSTF, 2016). Research shows that screening for CRC as recommended helps prevent cancer through early detection and removal of precancerous polyps. However, the USPSTF report indicates that with increasing age there is increased risk of serious adverse CRCS events, including perforation and bleeding (USPSTF, 2016). Therefore, the decision to screen for CRC in adults aged 76 to 85 years should be made by the physician and patient, considering the individual's health and prior screening history (USPSTF, 2016). Individuals in this age range who have never been screened are more likely to benefit from screening than previously screened individuals in this age group. In addition, it is recommended that factors in decision-making about screening after age 75 years should include whether comorbid conditions are present that might limit life expectancy and the ability to withstand CRC treatment if cancer is detected (USPSTF, 2017).

Although there is no definitive evidence of greater benefit of one test over another, there is some evidence that suggests screening may be increased by offering patients, particularly women, a choice between invasive procedures, such as colonoscopy, and noninvasive test options, such as fecal occult blood testing (FOBT) or fecal immunochemical test (FIT; Joseph, King, Miller, Richardson, & CDC, 2012). Numerous barriers to CRCS are reported, including not wanting to handle stool or keep stool cards in the house when completing FOBT, fear or avoidance of bowel preparation, fear of having a tube inserted through the rectum, and fear of pain or discomfort (Jones et al., 2010.) In addition, other factors associated with CRCS include access to a regular healthcare provider and having health insurance. Physician recommendation to screen, lack of knowledge, fear, embarrassment, lack of symptoms or current health problems, cost, and competing demands also matter, with competing demands potentially important among women (Klabunde et al., 2005; Guessous et al., 2010).

According to the ACS Society (2012), CRC incidence rates have decreased due to increased use of CRCS tests that permit detection and removal of polyps. Rates for new CRC cases have been falling on average 3.2% each year over the last 10 years, and death rates have fallen, on average, 2.7% each year over the period from 2004 to 2013 (NCI, 2016c). The ACS states that from 2004 to 2008, annual declines in CRC incidence among White men were much larger than those noted among African American men (2.9% versus 0.8%, respectively), while among women, declines in CRC incidence among Whites (2.2% per year) and African Americans (1.7% per year) were similar (ACS, 2015). The percentage of individuals who received CRCS increased between 2008 and 2015. The percentage of people aged 50 and older who ever had a blood stool test increased from 39.7% in 2008 to 43% in 2015 (CDC, 2015). The percentage of people who ever had a flexible sigmoidoscopy (FSIG) or colonoscopy (COL) increased from 61.4% in 2008 to 65% in 2015 (CDC, 2015).

A large proportion of CRCs could be prevented by avoiding risk factors such as obesity, physical inactivity, and high consumption of red and processed meat; however, screening is very important to the prevention of CRC. Regular screening with a FOBT, a SIG, or COL may reduce incidence through early detection and removal of precancerous polyps (Levin, Lieberman, McFarland, Smith, Brooks, Andrews, Dash, et al., 2008), may facilitate earlier detection of CRC, and may facilitate lower mortality (ACS, 2015; NCI, 2016c). More than 90% of CRC is diagnosed after age 50 (NCI, 2016c); however, diagnosis at an early, localized stage of CRC is important for long-term survival. When diagnosed at an early stage, the CRC 5-year survival rate is 90%; however, only 39% of CRC patients (based on data from the Surveillance, Epidemiology End Results program 2006 to 2012) are diagnosed at this stage (NCI, 2016c).

Most screening guidelines recommend that for those at average risk, CRCS should begin at age 50. The most recent USPSTF guidelines recommend use of common methods of screening, which must be completed regularly at appropriate intervals. The USPSTF recommends one of five available CRC screening tests (note that the following list also includes an additional combined-methods option): an annual guaiac FOBT (gFOBT), FIT, a FSIG, a combination of annual FIT and FSIG, a COL every 7 to 10 years, as well as computed tomographic colonography (CTC).

Each screening strategy has different advantages and limitations, and, to date, there are no empirical data to demonstrate that any of the strategies provide a greater net benefit than the others because they have not been compared with each other in a scientifically rigorous way (Lin et al., 2016). However, the American College of Gastroenterology continues to recommend that African Americans be screened at age 45 years rather than 50 (Rex et al., 2017). The American College of Gastroenterology also suggests screening at 40 years of age for individuals with one first-degree relative (or two second-degree relatives) diagnosed as having CRC. If a close relative had CRC or a polyp diagnosed before age 60 years, the American College of Gastroenterology recommends CRCS 10 years younger than the relative was when the earliest cancer or polyp was diagnosed (Rex et al., 2017). The screening guidelines of the ACS (Byers et al., 1997), the most widely disseminated, recommend that those aged 50 years and older have one of the following: a FOBT and FSIG (if normal, FOBT should be repeated annually and FSIG every 5 years), colonoscopy (repeated every 10 years if normal), or double-contrast barium enema (DCBE; if normal, repeated every 5 to 10 years).

Screening and Survival Rates for Colorectal Cancer

As noted in chapter 2, women have fewer CRC cases and fewer significant polyps than men; however, screening is equally important in both populations, and the guidelines for screening are the same for both. However, the prevalence of CRCS remains lower than rates for breast and cervical cancer screening, even among those with insurance. A comment by one of the St. Louis focus group participants shows that women might have less awareness about colorectal cancer:

> Focus Group Participant: I thought that it was man's disease. I didn't know that women could get colorectal cancer.

The prevalence of having had CRCS is about 60% among both African Americans and Whites in Missouri, with both groups potentially experiencing an improvement in early detection and appropriate screening for the cancer with the implementation of evidence-based guidelines (MDHHS, 2011).

Disparities in CRCS rates may assist in understanding the CRC disparities discussed in chapter 2. Hispanics and African Americans are reportedly less likely than Whites to have up-to-date CRCS (O'Keefe et al., 2015). Analysis of data from the Behavior Risk Factor Surveillance Survey for 2002 to 2008 indicate that non-Hispanic Whites had the highest overall prevalence of CRCS, followed by African Americans and Asian/Pacific Islanders (Steele et al., 2013). American Indians/Alaska Natives and Hispanics had lower CRCS rates during the same period as compared with African Americans (Steele et al., 2013). In 2010, the national CRCS prevalence was approximately 64.5%, 63.4% for Missouri, and 58.3% for Illinois (Steele et al., 2013). In the same year, CRCS test use was observed to increase with the patient's age, educational level, and household income, with greater disparities noted for COL than for SIG and FOBT use (Steele et al., 2013). CRCS using annual FOBT or SIG/COL within 10 years was related to income and health insurance, which are known to be strong predictors of CRCS (Steele et al., 2013). Additional research is needed to understand the effects of poverty and sociocultural status on screening independent of insurance status (Steele et al., 2013). Medicare has covered CRCS since 2001, which has increased CRCS among older persons (Steele et al., 2013). The implementation of the Affordable Care Act has removed financial barriers to CRCS by mandating coverage of preventive health services without co-pay requirements.

CRC screening rates are low overall and are well below the Healthy People 2020 goal of 70.5% (NCI, 2017). The current rate for women is 63.4% (61.8–65.0%). The low rates of screening for CRC appear to be due to lack of awareness and inadequate provider counseling rather than lack of patient screening acceptance (Wee, McCarthy, & Phillips, 2005). Focus group participants note the use of the Internet to gain information and clarity on CRCS but also note the role of a physician's ability to explain screening:

Focus Group Participant: Some of it is what you don't know. Doing some research. The Internet can tell you anything that you want to know.

Focus Group Participant: My doctor comes down to my level. He's not talking above my head a lot of things I don't understand. And if he does get back up there, I say, "Well I didn't quite get that. Would you run that by me again?" So, I've got to feel . . . I've got to have a comfort zone with him.

Studies have presented issues that primary care providers report among CRCS patients. They note embarrassment and anxiety about testing, test cost, and lack of insurance coverage as factors in patient CRCS adherence (Klabunde et al., 2005). Suggested CRCS improvement strategies include increasing CRCS capacity and increasing healthcare providers' awareness of current cancer screening guidelines and follow-up recommendations.

During our efforts to promote CRC in St. Louis, participants openly discussed how acquiring knowledge about CRC has kept them motivated to remain screening adherent. Although this knowledge is insufficient to assure access to and utilization of screening, patients who are unmotivated are more difficult to assist. In the quotes below, focus group participants talk about their level of CRC awareness.

Focus Group Participant: I don't know nothing about colorectal cancer. Nothing.

Focus Group Participant: Well um, I guess when I first found out that I had to have it. . . and it was because there was a possibility that I might have polyps. I admit, I didn't know what a polyp was, you know, until this came about and then I read. All I knew it was something below the waist. That's the way I looked at it. I looked at it below the waist. But I didn't know there could be polyps inside. Those polyps could be removed and there are some instances where it cannot be removed. But that, I had to learn on my own. A colonoscopy.

Thus, dissemination of culturally sensitive information on the early detection of CRC that also takes into account literacy seems like an important strategy. Comments related to colorectal cancer knowledge, concerns, and experiences provide local examples of some of knowledge and issues (emotional, gender, and economic) that affect screening (Sanders Thompson, Lewis, & Williams, 2013):

Focus Group Participant: I think people in lower income brackets, health concern is not one of the problems. You have to concentrate on where you're going to stay, how you're going to eat.

Focus Group Participant: When you go to better schools. Better housing. You eat differently. You can even cook differently. As you become educated, and maybe in a different income bracket, you know you eat differently—you might eat more vegetables or more fruit.

Lung Cancer Screening

Although a number of steps can be taken to reduce one's chance of having lung cancer, not smoking is the main prevention strategy. For those who smoke, the USPSTF recommends annual screening for lung cancer with low-dose computed tomography (LDCT) in adults aged 55 to 80 years who have a 30 pack-year smoking history and currently smoke or have quit within the previous 15 years; screening should be discontinued once a person has not smoked for 15 years or has a health problem that substantially limits life expectancy or the ability or willingness to have curative lung surgery (USPSTF, 2013). The ACS has similar guidelines, recommending that clinicians with access to high-volume, high-quality lung cancer screening and treatment centers initiate a discussion about lung cancer screening with patients aged 55 to 74 years who have at least a 30 pack-year smoking history, currently smoke, or have quit within the previous 15 years, and who are in relatively good health (ACS, 2017). For current smokers, screening should include smoking cessation efforts (Wender et al., 2013).

Lung Cancer Screening and Survival Rates

Most lung cancer cases are diagnosed at a late stage; however, residents of more deprived areas are significantly more likely to be diagnosed with late-stage lung cancer (Singh et al., 2012). Differences in preferred treatment for lung cancer may also contribute to higher cancer mortality rates (Singh et al., 2012). Whereas LDCT screening can be useful, smoking cessation efforts should accompany lung cancer screening for adults who are current smokers (Wender et al., 2013), and adults should be informed that screening will not detect all lung cancers.

Several factors can affect a patient's willingness to adhere to LDCT screening. The main barrier to CT scanning for lung cancer is likely to be insurance coverage for the test, which would be a burden for those on limited and fixed incomes (Delmerico, Hyland, Celestino, Reid, & Cummings, 2014; Singh et al., 2012). In addition, patients may fear the harms of LDCT screening, which include anxiety due to abnormal testing results and the need for additional imaging tests and biopsy procedures associated with false-positive results (Delmerico et al., 2014). In addition, the response to LDCT screening may vary by smoker status. Among current smokers, the most commonly cited reasons for not being screened were not wanting to find out whether they had cancer and lack of insurance (Delmerico et al., 2014). Among former smokers, the most commonly cited reason for not having the screening was a belief that they did not have lung cancer (Delmerico et al., 2014).

The 5-year overall relative survival rate for lung cancer is lower in African Americans than in Whites: 13% and 16%, respectively (O'Keefe et al., 2015). When lung cancer is detected at a localized stage, the 5-year relative survival rate among African Americans is 44%; however, only 12% of lung cancer cases are detected at this early stage because symptoms generally do not appear until the disease is advanced. (DeSantis, Naishadham, & Jemal, 2013). Studies have shown that when lung cancer is diagnosed early, African Americans are less likely than Whites to undergo surgery—the treatment with the best chance for cure—even after accounting for socioeconomic factors (DeSantis et al., 2013).

African American women (66.7%) have lower incidence rates than White women (68.2%), including Hispanic women (https://ww5.komen.org/Breast-Cancer/DisparitiesInBreastCancerScreening.html). The mortality rate for African American women (49.2%) is also lower than among White women (52.5%) (https://ww5.komen.org/BreastCancer/DisparitiesInBreastCancerScreening.html). At baseline, 50.6 lung cancer deaths per 100,000 population occurred in 2007 (age adjusted to the year 2000 standard population). The target objective is 45.5 deaths, based on a target-setting method of 10% improvement.

SES, particularly in lung cancer mortality as described here and in chapter 2, may be related to differences in tobacco regulation and advertising, availability of cigarettes, public awareness of the harmful effects of smoking, smoking cessation support, cancer screening, and healthcare factors (Singh et al., 2012). For example, gas stations and convenience stores in the low-income community North St. Louis display more cigarette advertising on outside windows, walls and sidewalks than are observed in higher income communities in the region. Research has suggested the need to determine best practices for promoting cessation among smokers and a time highlighted in the literature is when they are seeking lung cancer screening (Wender et al., 2013). Healthcare disparities may also contribute to disparities in stage of diagnosis. Limited access to care due to provider unavailability, lack of transportation, lower rates of cancer screening in more disadvantaged areas may account for the high rates of late-stage cancer diagnoses observed. Participants in our cancer studies are very sensitive to issues of healthcare access.

Focus Group Participant: I wonder if I lose my job today or tomorrow how am I going to be seen. You know that is an issue in the United States. They don't want to pay for the poor people to be seen medically.

Summary

Although better screening and treatment have contributed to the improvement of cancer outcomes and mortality in the nation, as in chapter 2, we see that not all Americans have benefited from these advances. One way to eliminate cancer disparities and to achieve equity is to increase the proportion of adults who are counseled about and adhere to mammogram, cervical (Pap) tests, and CRCS consistent with current guidelines. However, the question remains: Why do low-income and minority, predominantly African American women, get breast, cervical, colorectal, and lung cancers, and why do they die from them? And with such pronounced racial and age divides?

Navigator: And the one reason I'm getting from all of them is, I forgot. . . . I wonder if, [pause] some of what I think is that maybe they just don't see the value. And so because they don't see the value that mammography and early detection warrants, so it just gets slid onto the back burner because they've got so many other things going on in their lives.

According to Healthy People 2020, one major cancer-related goal is to reduce the number of new cancer cases, as well as the illness, disability, and death caused by cancer. However, low-income women and women of color—the population of greatest risk for death due to cancer—are the least likely to have access to and/or utilize secondary prevention procedures such as mammography to detect breast cancer, LDCT to detect lung cancer, Pap testing to detect cervical cancer, and CRCS to detect colorectal cancer.

Under former President Barak Obama, the Affordable Care Act took effect in 2010 and emphasized prevention services, including no-cost screenings for breast, colorectal, and cervical cancers. The evidence shows that essentially no one should die of cancer, as screening for lung, cervical, colorectal, and breast cancers helps to find these diseases at an early, often highly treatable stage. However, any resulting benefits of the Affordable Care Act for cancer mortality would not be evident this early since cancer takes years to develop. It is unknown whether the repeal of "Obamacare" will ever occur and if it does what will take its place. After three failed attempts at repeal in 2017, it remains unclear whether the future holds similar coverage or something altogether different that reflects the desires of current or future administrations.

Cancer Screening Disparities: The Importance of Theory

The earliest theories used to organize interventions to enhance cancer screening focused on individual characteristics and interpersonal relationships and concerns. Later efforts to improve screening for cancer and to promote prevention also included sociocultural concerns and variables as discussed at the beginning of this chapter. The history and use of theory to guide screening and health behavior intervention is more fully developed in chapter 4. However, we end this chapter with a discussion of how theory may begin to take into account the unique needs of low-income racial/ethnic minority women.

In addition to the social determinants discussed in chapter 1 and the cultural issues and concerns integrated here, among the important determinants of health behavior are positive and negative attitudes about behavior and social normative perceptions that each influence intention to engage in healthy behaviors that can include physical activity, healthy eating, smoking cessation or non-initiation, and screening (Kallgren, Reno & Cialdini, 2000; Rimal & Real, 2005;). Social normative perceptions are based on what someone believes people close to them feel about the behavior, and how motivated they are to please those people, or the pressure felt to comply. These perceptions influence individual and group emotional reactions to behavior, as well as beliefs and cognitions related to behavior; in this case, cancer screening is a primary focus.

Focus Group Participant: My aunt went through colon cancer. No problem with radiation. And she's one of those people been clean for 5 years and I think that's some kind of mark or something, if you've been . . . for 5 years. I've had other friends going through breast cancer and they're fine, so it's changing my way of thinking. The more people that's hit close to you.

Dutta (2007) suggests that cultural appropriateness and sensitivity could assist in overcoming educational and literacy barriers to cancer communication
and interventions. Cultural theorizing suggests that identification (ethnic identity) with other people of color or low-income women dictates the importance
of the subjective norms of these groups. In addition, community health and cancer mortality concerns provide further influences that may increase motivation
to change cancer-related behaviors. However, the interaction of these and other
variables that affect response to attitudes and subjective norms are affected by
other group social and cultural constraints—trust of the medical system, norms
around the role of women, privacy, and other issues—and complicate our ability to determine the best course of action when addressing population-level
behaviors. This interaction is shown in the words of one of the St. Louis focus
group participants, words expressed in a discussion about CRC:

> Focus Group Participant: If you go to the doctor for it, all they going to do is
> make it worse. Yeah, once they start cutting on you, you ain't ever going to get
> any better. That's all I've heard. They say once the air hits it, it spreads.

A wide range of factors can be included when social and cultural perspectives are considered. Social factors may include identity, level of ac-
culturation, levels of economic and social resources, along with accessibility
to, attitudes toward, and interaction with major social institutions (Dutta,
2007; Rimal & Real, 2005). Despite efforts to attend to potential social determinants of health, interpersonal theories are focused on the individual and
do not adequately organize what we know about the role of structural factors
in screening behavior. In addition, these individually focused theories do
not offer practical guidance to practitioners, health educators, and lay health
advisors assisting women in low resource situations to access screening and
health behaviors that are most likely to prevent cancer.

Changing Preventive Behaviors and Screening Adherence
Barriers through Theory

Although guidelines for screening adherence can help to reduce cancer mortality among low-income women and women of color, many women do not
receive recommended tests and screenings. When we look at the difference
between minority patients and White patients, the rich and poor, the poorly
educated and well educated, we find similar disparities, with the quality of
assessment and follow-up treatment potentially being different. The question becomes the following: How do we get adequate preventive care to all
people? The complexities of the system require knowledgeable personnel
who are committed to seeing care through, from beginning to end.

Provider: We don't have enough people so it's a lot of work. . . . It's only a staff of six so like I said previously in the navigator meetings, it's really a play by play, role by role type situation . . . if we haven't heard from the patient and we've called, sent letters, looked in the system to see if you followed-up with your doctor and you haven't, then we will make a home visit just to make sure you're okay. . . . We play every role.

Addressing the questions and issues that drive cancer disparities requires the identification of barriers to healthy lifestyles, screening and treatment, as well as a theoretical framework to understand why these obstacles function as barriers. This framework, in turn, will guide the development of intervention strategies. Meichenbaum and Turk (1987), which will be discussed in more detail in chapter 4, have used an adherence theory framework for identifying and categorizing correlates to medical treatment. Their theory is particularly appropriate for studying barriers to screening for this population, since barriers can operate at successively embedded dimensions of influence. Once these barriers or enablers to treatment have been established, this theoretical framework can help us understand and predict why unscreened women do not adhere to recommended guidelines.

In accordance with Meichenbaum and Turk's (1987) adherence dimensions, barriers can be categorized into the following dimensions: (a) characteristics of the patient, (b) characteristics of screening regimens, and (c) the relationship between the healthcare provider and the patient. Table 3.2 adapts Meichenbaum and Turk's adherence theory to illustrate the four dimensions of barriers to screening for lung, breast, and cervical cancer, in addition to CRC. Table 3.2 reflects the dimensions of adherence theory developed and elaborated on in chapter 4. Chapter 4 presents the intervention needs of women living in high poverty, segregated and resource-constrained environments, as illustrated by the St. Louis region. We turn to theories more capable of integrating the implications of these complex issues into intervention and support for low-income and ethnic minority women facing cancer.

Table 3.2. Barriers to Lung, Breast, Cervical, and Colorectal Cancer Screening

Barrier Dimensions	Lung Cancer Screening	Breast Cancer Screening (Mammogram)	Cervical Cancer Screening (Pap)	Colorectal Cancer Screening (Colonoscopy)
Individual Characteristics	• Fear • Health literacy • Insurance coverage	• Fear • Health literacy • Time • Geographic location • Past negative healthcare experiences • Low socioeconomic status • Age • Education level • Social support • Insurance coverage • Childcare • Marital status • Family history • Language	• Fear • Health literacy • Time • Geographic location • Past negative healthcare experiences • Low socioeconomic status • Age • Education level • Social support • Embarrassment/shame	• Fear • Health literacy • Time • Geographic location • Childcare
Characteristics of Screening Regimens		• Inconvenience of screening • Impact on body image	• Inconvenience of screening • Safety concerns • Confusing/extensive protocol for follow-up	• Inconvenience of screening

Category		
Relationship Between Healthcare Provider and Patient	• Negative interactions and distrust of healthcare professionals • Wait times for appointments and test results • Lack of recommendation for screening from healthcare professional • Poor communication and misinformation • Delays in appointments	• Negative interactions and distrust of healthcare professionals • Wait times for appointments and test results • Being uncomfortable with male doctors • Lack of explanation for diagnosis, tests, and results • Lack of recommendation from healthcare professional
Sociocultural	• Community cultural norms to delay care and prioritize acute or deteriorating conditions over preventive healthcare.	• Scarcity of community resources • Cultural values and religious beliefs • Position of women in society and their affiliation with different ethnic and cultural groups • Women's attitudes toward cancer prevention • Feelings of neglecting family responsibilities and child care at the time of visiting the doctor • Fear of the examination and feelings of shame • Women in some cultural groups were discouraged from screening if the doctor was male and they were prejudiced to such examinations • Forgetting the term of screening appointments was also considered to be one of the behavioral barriers

A Row of Vacant Businesses on Dr. M. L. King Drive in St. Louis City
photo by W. Donnell Jones

Chapter Four

From Theories to Practice, into Feasible Solutions

We have just identified the extent to which barriers and stressors limit screening. But this is only part of the solution. It is not enough to just know what gets in the way of screening. We must understand the barriers and stressors within a theoretical context. We need evidence-based approaches that address multiple determinants of cancer disparities. Such approaches are essential to their elimination. This is congruent with a holistic approach and the aim of alleviating suffering to reverse the social conditions that produce suffering. Multilevel approaches are needed that recognize determinants of health, from the biological to the socioecological perspective. This chapter will provide an overview of theory as it relates to the intervention needs of women living in high poverty and in segregated and resource-constrained environments.

In this chapter, we will present five cases of qualitative research studies, which will be used to illustrate these women's perspectives on screening and cancer, and the stressors and barriers that make it challenging to adhere to the screening recommendations discussed in chapter 3. The strength of these qualitative case studies was in the use of three types of triangulation throughout, to enhance the overall rigor and credibility of the findings: (a) data triangulation (the use of a variety of data sources), (b) investigator triangulation (the use of multiple theoretical interviewers), and (c) theory triangulation (the use of multiple theoretical perspectives to interpret a single set of data) (Denzin, 1978; Patton, 2002). Grounded theory (Glaser & Strauss, 1967) was used throughout to explore and generate new theory on cancer screening adherence and delay (Creswell & Maietta, 2002). Several forms of triangulation were used as a primary strategy for enhancing the rigor and trustworthiness for this qualitative research study (Padgett, 1998). The influence of sociocultural, psychosocial, provider, and health system factors on screening behavior adherence were explored using semi-structured, individual, face-to-face interviews and focus groups, template analysis, secondary audio narrative recordings and telephone interviews, and provider focus groups. These inductive methods of data collection elicited patient and provider perspectives on cancer, the utility of cancer screening, barriers to completing cancer screening, reasons for non-adherence and screening delay, and viable provider strategies for improving adherence among these populations of women in certain communities. Such an approach allowed for a systematic and triangulated organization of findings, while reflecting on existing theoretical constructs. Such exploration generated further related discussion about the experience of cancer and cancer screening, help-seeking behaviors, stigma, cancer self-management, family support, and other culturally mediated coping resources such as religion and other multilevel barriers and facilitative factors to cancer screening.

THEORETICAL ADHERENCE FOUNDATIONS

Despite attempts to adapt existing health behavior theories to real-world screening adherence, we still are in need of theoretically meaningful screening adherence models that are relevant to low-income women of color. Although existing studies are extremely important in understanding the prevalence and scope of the factors involved with screening behavior, such studies have been mostly atheoretical in nature. Absent in research is a true guiding theoretical framework essential to understanding and subsequently intervening with screening adherence behavior among low-income women of color. Although related studies have used mostly individual models of health decision-making—e.g., the Health Belief Model (Givens et al., 2006; Reece, 2003; Sher, McGinn, Sirey, & Meyers, 2005)—in explaining adherence problems, these models tend to be somewhat incomplete because of the limited focus on individual thought processes (i.e., perception) in predicting screening behavior (Glantz, Rimer, & Lewis, 2002).

Although an array of theories have been applied in past studies, there seem to be two overarching categories or dimensions of theories that have been used to investigate health behavior and to predict adherence with other population categories. The most commonly investigated theories of health behavior that can help predict adherence and incorporate elements of outcome expectancies, outcome values, self-efficacy expectancies, and intentions include the following: Hochbaum's (1958) Health Belief Model, Fishbein and Ajzen's (1975) Theory of Planned Behavior (TPB), Roger's (1975) Protection Motivation Theory, Bandura's (1977, 1986) Social-Cognitive Theory, and Strecher, DeVellis, Becker, and Rosenstock's

(1986) Self-Efficacy Model (Brawley & Culos-Reed, 2000). In addition, theories that are commonly used to predict adherence to treatment and to address the processes of behavior change include: Bandura's (1977; 1986) Social-Cognitive Theory, Marlatt and Gordon's (1985) Relapse Prevention Model, Prochaska's (1979) Transtheoretical Model (TTM), and Weinstein's (1988) Precaution Adoption Process Model (Brawley & Culos-Reed, 2000). Additionally, a motivational component is central to most theories used to study health behavior for either prediction or behavior change purposes (Brawley & Culos-Reed, 2000). Christensen and Johnson (2002) offer a simple linear model of understanding adherence with medical treatment regimens, which is derived from previous theory and research in personality, social, and clinical psychology concerning the value of an interactionist perspective. Although somewhat limited, the core tenets of this framework suggest that factors that influence adherence can be better understood through the interaction of patients' characteristics, types of adherence intervention, illness characteristics, and medical context. This array of theories includes aspects of social, cognitive, personal agency, and environmental constructs shown to be predictors of adherence.

New ideas for adherence interventions should first be examined within the context of existing theories (e.g., TPB) and established results (Brawley & Culos-Reed, 2000). Foundational adherence theories and previous literature can significantly contribute to the knowledge base for guiding the development of new adherence interventions (Pinto & Floyd, 2008). Specifically, regarding this research, the TPB provides a solid knowledge base within an organized framework from which to begin addressing essential findings and concepts from this literature review about screening adherence among low-income and minority cancer patients. This theory focuses on theoretical constructs that are concerned with individual motivational factors as determinants of the likelihood of performing a specific behavior (Montano & Kasprzyk, 2002). The TPB includes measures of attitude and social normative perceptions (that determine behavioral intention, which in turn affects behavior) and perceived control over performance of the behavior (Montano & Kasprzyk, 2002). The TPB includes the following eleven constructs: behavioral beliefs, evaluations of behavioral outcomes, normative beliefs, motivation to comply, control beliefs, perceived power, attitude toward behavior, subjective norm, perceived behavioral control, behavioral intention, and behavior. This theory assumes that all other factors—including demographics and environment—operate through the model constructs and do not independently contribute to explaining the likelihood of performing a behavior (Montano & Kasprzyk, 2002). This literature shows many key adherence components that can be applied to TPB theoretical constructs.

The TPB is well suited to guide a beginning inquiry of factors involved with screening adherence. The premise of the full TPB model is based on behavioral intention, which is the person's subjective probability that the behavior in question will be performed (Montano & Kasprzyk, 2002), in this case that behavior being *screening*. As such, intention is assumed to be the most powerful predictor of change, and if intention can be changed, behavior can be changed. Intention is thought to be shaped by three primary factors: attitude toward the behavior (made up of behavioral beliefs and evaluations of behavioral outcomes), subjective norm (made up of normative beliefs and the motivation to comply), and perceived behavioral control (made up of control beliefs and perceived power).

The TPB posits that, not only is it important to understand individual perspectives and intentions, but also to consider the influence of multidimensional, environmental, physical, and social factors (Alvidrez & Arean, 2002; Chyun, Amend, Newlin, Langerman, & Melkus, 2003; Cooper, Hill, & Powe, 2002; Glantz et al., 2002; Green, Richard, & Potvin, 1996; Moreno-John et al., 2004; Pierce, Chadiha, Vargas, & Mosley, 2003). These multidimensional elements are embedded in the Subjective Norm construct of the TPB (Fishbein, 1967; Fishbein & Ajzen, 1975). The quality of one's social networks (Van Heeringen & Zivkov, 1996), family time commitments, family obligations, and family conflict can limit or enable adherence behavior (Brown & Topcu, 2003; Fouad et al., 2001). Not only do others in our environment contribute to the decisions we make, but also our beliefs about the resources, opportunities, obstacles, and impediments in our lives that will influence our decision to follow through with treatment, which is an additional important consideration in the Perceived Behavioral Control construct (Fishbein, 1967; Fishbein & Ajzen, 1975).

Despite the frequently blurring constructs, the TPB (Fishbein, 1967; Fishbein & Ajzen, 1975) seems to be the most appropriate existing theoretical model, as it considers the inherent nature of individual cost-benefit analysis whereby the individual must weigh the literal and figurative "cost" of not adhering to screening guidelines with the benefits of screening adherence and maintenance. This theory can be used to inform the intervention and help in identifying the "active" ingredients of those interventions (Pinto & Floyd, 2008). Thus, the TPB is a promising approach to a further exploration and understanding of adherence screening.

Similarly, the Theory of Planned Behavior, a health behavior model that has significant limitations for conceptualizing, also provides a good beginning conceptualization to important influences, with its focus on categories of micro- and meso-level systems. Although these areas are extremely important, we see that for this diverse population, there are weighty ethnic, cultural, and political influences. Appraisals of stressors and coping responses are often rooted in cultural experiences and may vary with minority and socioeconomic status (Montano & Kasprzyk, 2002). Although TPB proved a good starting point, it was limited in its focus on categories of micro- and meso-level systems. Although cultural barriers were somewhat abstract and difficult to articulate at times for this population, the "multiple confounding barriers" and individual variables might also have been influenced by non-predominant environmental, political/ organizational, and cultural factors. These macro-level system influences are critical for consideration with low-income women of color.

A solution to this gap in TPB can be feasibly considered using the Integrated Behavior Model (IBM) (Kasprzyk, Montano, & Fishbein, 1998), an extension to the TPB model which essentially reconfigures and adds to the TPB and has elements from the Health Belief Model, the Social Cognitive Theory, and the Transtheoretical Model. The predictors in the IBM have evolved from the TPB, but with slightly new construct names that predict the intention to perform a behavior: attitudes, perceived norms, and personal agency (Kasprzyk et al., 1998). Four new components are added alongside "intention," as additional proximal predictors of the final behavior: knowledge and skills to perform the behavior, salience of the behavior, environmental constraints, and habit (Kasprzyk et al., 1998). Based on the findings of this study, the IBM knowledge constraints, salience of the behavior, and environmental constraints, capture several components that the TPB did not include. For this population, future constructs to consider would include primary elements of pre-existing motivation and self-efficacy, which could be added to the model to help determine the likelihood to participate and continue treatment. In addition, sociocultural barriers and aspects of influence should be considered relevant for this population. Future research and intervention strategies should focus on actual determinants and facilitators of regular preventive health behavior within a theoretical framework that incorporates environmental elements, as well as cultural, ethnic, and socioeconomic diversity. In terms of a socioecological context, we should point intervention strategies to four avenues toward cultural competence: (a) individual clinical care, (b) healthcare providers, (c) among community stakeholders and businesses, and (d) policy.

In addition to understanding adherence from a theoretical perspective, we must also understand the barriers and stressors within a cultural context. A cultural lens allows us to develop and organize interventions to truly address unique lifestyle choices and screening behavior by developing and customizing theory.

Cultural Influences in Theory

Cancer prevention and the experience of cancer do not escape the influence of cultural factors. This is not always well understood by many people, as it is known to have different meanings that may easily be attached to it (Bailey et al., 2005). Beliefs about the causes of cancer and its symptoms may affect the types of preventive measures and treatment sought, given that culture provides unwritten definitions of how individuals and families respond (Bailey et al., 2005). For this reason, critical limitations persist in our knowledge about generalizing for use among racial/ethnic minorities the interventions that have proved effective when tested primarily with samples of Whites. Much work is needed to design and test interventions tailored to racial/ethnic and lower SES populations. Therefore, theory-based strategies for change require specific data from particular groups.

Especially in studies of racial/ethnic minority groups, it is important to emphasize important elements of cultural relevance since many of the retention barriers that stem from the beliefs and attitudes occurring within a sociocultural context impact one's beliefs and attitudes (Wells & Zebrack, 2008). Individuals from diverse cultural groups have views that differ from Western biomedical models (Schraufnagel, Wagner, Miranda, & Roy–Byrne, 2006), particularly regarding stigma (Garfield, 1963; Reece, 2003). Additionally, the nonsharing of illness representations, treatment, and appraisal rules are common for non-Western patients who access Western and traditional medicine (Leventhal, Diefenbach, & Leventhal, 1992). As such, the Cultural Explanatory Model adds explanatory theoretical power to the TPB model in screening adherence for ethnic minority populations (Kleinmann, Eisenber, & Good, 1978). This sociocultural framework assumes that cultural and social-contextual factors will interactively shape the clinical process and patient outcomes. For example, fatalistic beliefs are generally believed to be more often associated with ethnic/racial minority patients than Caucasian patients, which may similarly affect health services use (Schraufnagel et al., 2006). In general, a patient's past experiences, both cultural and personal, will strongly influence their beliefs, which in turn will shape their attitudes and/or preferences (Schraufnagel et al., 2006). Attitudes or preferences will strongly determine someone's acceptance of treatment as well as the person's motivation (inherent in the Subjective Norm component of the TPB) to screening. This will, in turn, influence the likelihood that a person will seek cancer screening.

Bernal's Ecological Framework (Bernal & Castro,1994) goes a step further in serving as a guide for developing socioculturally sensitive treatments and adapting existing psychosocial treatments to specific ethnic minority groups (Bernal & Castro, 1994). This general theoretical framework consists of eight dimensions of treatment interventions: language, persons, metaphors, content, concepts, goals, methods, and context, which can be used to inform screening adherence adaptations. It is important to produce more clinical findings, which can contribute toward a clearer understanding of how individuals from other cultures need to have their adaptive efforts to cancer understood within the context of their own culture (Spinetta, 1984). Thus, heightened awareness of patients' cultural perspectives and care preferences is important in screening assessment, diagnosis, and treatment (Bailey et al., 2005; Wells & Zebrack, 2008).

Another Cultural Explanatory Model that has been used as a theoretical framework to centralize culture in the study of health behaviors and to integrate culturally relevant factors in the development of interventions is the Positive-Existential-Negative-3 (PEN-3) Model cultural model (Hall, et al., 2015; Iwelunmor, Newsome, & Airhihenbuwa, 2014). This model aims to help explain decision-making influences on health practices and explores not only how cultural context shapes health beliefs and practice, but also how family systems play a critical role in enabling or nurturing positive health behaviors and health outcomes. This model posits that there are positive influences (which consist of nurturers and enablers who influence the community to engage in health practices relevant to cancer prevention and control), existential influences (which have no positive or negative effects on health), and negative influences (which consist of attitudes, beliefs, and behaviors that place individuals at risk for cancer and are influenced by the family and community). This model has credibility in research as a framework for health behavior, with African American populations (Hall, et al., 2015; Iwelunmor, Newsome, & Airhihenbuwa, 2014).

Theoretical Implications

Future interventions should offer a balance between theory and practice. Even those contributions designed to provide an overview of relevant theory should offer suggestions or implications for practice that arise from those theoretical models. Discussions about the application of theory to practice need to provide adequate detail to be useful for intervention development. For theory to help drive interventions, it must focus attention on how to select the important factors that we can influence from among many factors associated with behavior (Montano & Kasprzyk, 2002).

A systematic construction of adherence categorization dimensions were first useful in the development of a conceptual model to think categorically about screening adherence and follow-up, in promoting health prevention and treatment programs (Logan & Freeman, 2000). Findings reveal that the classic work of Meichenbaum and Turk (1987) on their systematic models of medical adherence framework provide a good starting point to thinking about possible ways to organize the ecological characteristics of dropout. However, Meichenbaum and Turk's (1987) barrier dimensions offer a somewhat limited perspective that conceals important family, cultural, and political influences (within the "characteristics of the patient") on the decision to participate and in screening by grouping these within the "characteristics of the patient." For example, low-income, minority women diagnosed with cancer who dropped out of a depression treatment clinical trial described several family-related barriers (e.g., family caregiver issues, moving in with family, or strained relationships), which seemed to indirectly influence patient discontinuation of treatment (Wells, Palinkas, & Ell, 2014). If we were to use Meichenbaum and Turk's (1987) model to categorize the barriers or stressors, we would obscure the importance of family influences, although the research suggests that screening adherence should be investigated in relation to family and cultural beliefs, perspectives, and meanings (Vega et al., 2007). If we were to use Meichenbaum and Turk's (1987) model to categorize the barriers or stressors, we would have to include these family-related barriers within the "characteristics of the patient," which blur the importance of family influences. Andersen and Newman's (2005) model of health use offers a more useful heuristic for categorizing the dropout and adherence factors, distinguishing the family, and other societal, health services system, and individual factors.

Rather than to test these theories, the intent was first to build theory through the generation of a heuristic model of patient decision-making with respect to screening adherence. Sensitizing concepts (Blumer, 1954), based on Turner and Avison (2003) and Meichenbaum and Turk's (1987) adherence variable categorizations provided a starting point to explore these barriers and factors. The first case study example uses Turner and Avison's (2003) theory categorization to describe the stressors and barriers involved in non-adherence for low-income women in the St. Louis region.

Case Example #1: Stressors/Barriers[1]

A variety of individual stressors have been identified as obstacles for low-income women in using mammography and Pap testing (Allen, Shelton, Harden, & Goldman, 2008; Eggleston, 2007; Frelix, 2000; Gabram, 2008; Mendez, 2009; Moy, 2006; Percac-Lima, 2010; Sadler, 2007; Peek, 2004; Peipins, 2011; Reiter, 2012). These include low knowledge, financial and insurance barriers, logistical barriers (for example, scheduling difficulties, appointments interfering with work and/or childcare, and transportation-related issues), cultural norms, psychological or emotional states, and low social or practical support. Provider communication barriers (e.g., lack of adequate explanation about the procedure, diagnosis, or results; inadequate appointment/results notification; and language barriers) also affect rates of breast and cervical cancer screening (Pecac-Lima, 2010). Awareness of and sensitivity to these complex stressors and barriers are likely to improve low-income women's participation in breast and cervical cancer screening.

Study Objective

The objectives of this project are to identify the types of stressors/ barriers experienced by a sample of low-income, female United Way 2-1-1 Missouri callers (ages 40 or older) in need of a mammogram and/or Pap test.

Analytic Sample

Data for the present study were derived from recorded interactions between navigators and women 2-1-1 callers who needed a mammogram and/or Pap test based on current guidelines from NCI and USPSTF. Inclusion eligibility included all United Way 2-1-1 callers who were low-income, aged 40+ years and unscreened for mammography within the past year, and/or aged 18+ years and untested for Pap smear within the past 3 years (based on current guidelines from NCI and the USPSTF). Exclusion criteria included women who did not speak English.

Methods

Descriptive analyses (means, frequencies, and percentages) were used to characterize the study sample. A template analysis approach (a structured technique for analyzing qualitative data, with the key advantage being the researchers' ability to create a more structured analysis for their data [Brooks, et al., 2015; Cassall, 2008]) was used to identify general issues related to stressors expressed by 2-1-1 callers, based on *a priori* sensitizing concepts from the literature, which include *recent life events, chronic stressors, lifetime major events,* and *discrimination stress.*

Stressors Experienced by Women

Table 4.1 describes the full range of stressors and barriers reported by 2-1-1 callers that might interfere with behaviors like getting a mammogram or Pap test. Such barriers can be categorized into Turner and Avison's (2003) stress exposure list, which includes *recent life events, chronic stressors, lifetime major events,* and *discrimination stress,* and has been tested with minority and low-income groups. Illustrative quote numbers 2, 10, and 19 in Table 4.1 represent examples of structural barriers.

Table 4.1. Stressors and Barriers

Turner & Avison's (2003) Stressor Categories	Stressor Definitions	Types of Stressors/ Stressor Subtypes	Illustrative Quotes
Life Events	Things that happened to women or person close to them in the past 12 months	Financial/ insurance – Utilities disconnected/ inability to pay – Facing foreclosure – Denied Medicare – Recently uninsured Job-related stress – Recent unemployment Housing situations – Severe weather damage to home – Relocation to new home in new city – Recent homelessness – Poor living conditions – General housing stress Physical/ mental health issues – Recent hospitalization – Recent injury/surgery – Diagnosis of disease – General physical health issues – Substance addiction Legal issues Under house arrest Carjacking/Robbery Caregiving demands Illness of relative	1. *"My gas is being turned off tomorrow, and I've gotten no help whatsoever. I've been on the phone for 4 days."* (48-year-old White, divorced female, no children, unable to work [unknown reason], with 4+ years of college, receiving between $15,000 and $19,999/ year; in need of a mammography screening) (Financial, Utilities Disconnected/Inability to Pay) 2. *"I had a doctor, but now that I have no insurance, he won't see me."* (51-year-old, divorced White female without any children, out of work for less than 1 year, receiving less than $5,000/ year income, with highest level of education between 9-11 grade; in need of a Pap testing) (Financial/Insurance, Recently Uninsured)

3. *"My life is just too stressful. My lease expires the 31st of August. I don't know what their intentions are . . . the problem is the world doesn't care. Nobody gives a crap what you feel like. Right now, I'm doing the best I can."* (58-year-old White female, who has never been married and has no children, unable to work and receiving less than $5,000 income/ year, and with 4+ years of college; in need of a mammography screening) (Housing Situation, General Housing Stress)

4. *"The attorney said 'Why don't you just move?' and I told him that it was easier said than done . . . I haven't even unpacked from the move over a year ago . . . I wish that we could resolve issues here and get on an amicable agreement. I know this is not the ideal place for me, but I need to be here until I'm in a better position financially and physically."* (59-year-old who describes self as American Indian/Native Alaskan (with more than 1 race ethnicity), divorced with no children, student with 1–3 years of college, and receiving between $5,000 and $9,999/year; in need of a mammography screening) (Legal issues, Poor living conditions)

(continued)

Table 4.1. *(Continued)*

Turner & Avison's (2003) Stressor Categories	*Stressor Definitions*	*Types of Stressors/ Stressor Subtypes*	*Illustrative Quotes*
			5. *"I'm homeless. I'm temporarily with my mom because I'm injured, but she doesn't let me stay with her. My mom's tired of me because I'm an alcoholic . . . my (common law) husband is in jail in Colorado, and he has 3 more months, so I have to figure out what to do [until he gets out]. It depends on my mom's husband [if I get to stay or not]."* (30-year-old African American, never married with children, out of work for less than 1 year, and 12th grade or higher education, and receiving between $5,000 and $9,999/year; in need of a Pap testing) (Housing Problems, Homelessness, Substance Addiction)
			6. *"I found out he ([my son] has a congenital birth defect in his hands and feet so now we have to take him to a pediatric plastic surgeon, so my health isn't the most important thing right now. I've been spending most of my time running around trying to take care of him that I haven't had time to work on me."* (37-year-old, African American female who is separated, unable to work, 8th grade education, and receiving between $5,000 and $9,999/year; in need of a Pap testing) (Caregiver Issues, Illness of relative)

Chronic Strain	Situations that sometimes come up in people's lives	Financial strain from basic necessities/insurance	- Inability to obtain assistance with food/utilities - Rent/mortgage payment assistance - Insufficient money for emergencies - Bankruptcy - Infant needs - Clothing needs - Uninsured - Prescription payment assistance needed	7. "I just get to the point where I am getting tired of everyone being like 'no we can't help you, we can't do this because of that,' it's frustrating" (56-year-old, African American female who has never been married and never had any children, been out of work for more than 1 year, receiving less than $5,000 income/year, and with 1-3 years of college; in need of mammography screening) (Financial/Unemployment, Problem Accessing Healthcare Systems, Trouble navigating health/social service system)
		Unemployment/ Employment commitment	- Unemployed - Working multiple jobs	
		Housing problems	- Landlord issues - Unsafe/unsanitary living conditions - Homelessness - Moving in with family or friends/strained relationships	
		Problems accessing healthcare systems	- Difficulty finding time for appointment - Long wait times to see doctor - Lack of transportation or car - Rural area without nearby health providers - Trouble navigating health/ social service system	8. "My life is really bad right now. I mean it's good and I'm upbeat, but there's lots of things I need to do." (45-year-old, divorced White female, with children, unable to work (unknown reason) receiving between $15,000 and $19,999/ year and having 4+ years of college; in need of a mammography screening) (Financial strain, Stress)

(continued)

Table 4.1. *(Continued)*

Turner & Avison's (2003) Stressor Categories	Stressor Definitions	Types of Stressors/ Stressor Subtypes	Illustrative Quotes
		Physical health – Dental/vision problems – Trying to quit smoking – Inability to work due to disability – General fear of doctors – Chronic pain from illness/ accident	9. *"I'm in one of those situations where I have to use the services that I used to refer other people to."* (56-year-old divorced African American female with children, who has 4+ years of college, and employed for wages; in need of mammography screening) (Emotional Issues, Stress)
		Mental/emotional/ addiction issues – Depression – Stress – Undetermined mental illness – Fear of doctors/ – Mammogram/mammogram results – Addiction recovery – Drugs/alcohol – Trying to quit smoking	10. *"Most people want you to pay $25 to get seen. I don't even have 25 cents. I don't have money."* (40-year-old, African American female with children, who has never been married, who has been out of work for less than 1 year and receiving between $15,000 and $19,999/year income, and having either a 12th grade high school diploma or GED; in need of a mammography screening) (Financial strain from basic necessities, Unemployment, Uninsured)
		Legal issues Caregiver issues Need legal assistance Taking care of ill/elderly relatives	

11. "I have a lot of other things going on, and I haven't had time to call. That's [a Pap] like the least of my worries . . . those resources that they give me don't work out and there's so many people out here hurting (financially). I just have to keep trying. I don't know how much longer I will be in this situation. Nothing has changed, and it seems to have taken a turn for the worse . . ." (40-year-old, African American female with children, who has never been married, who has been out of work for less than 1 year and receiving between $15,000 and $19,999/year income, and having high school education; in need of a Pap testing) (Financial strain from basic necessities, Unemployment)

12. "I've just been so sidetracked with trying to find a job and honestly that's the only thing that matters to me right now until I can feel 'grounded' or get on stable ground . . . trying to find a job is hard, and that's the only thing I can see myself doing right now." (43-year-old White female who has never been married and has children, been out of work for more than 1 year, did not complete high school, and receiving between $15,000 and $19,999/year; in need of a Pap testing) (Unemployment)

(continued)

Table 4.1. (Continued)

Turner & Avison's (2003) Stressor Categories	Stressor Definitions	Types of Stressors/ Stressor Subtypes	Illustrative Quotes
			13. *"Because I catch the bus from a noon appointment, I didn't get home until 3:00"* (48-year-old White, divorced female, no children, unable to work [unknown reason], with 4+ years of college, earning between $15,000 and $19,999/year; in need of a mammography screening) (Problems accessing healthcare systems, Unable to work)
			14. *"I've been so angry and so aggressive . . . in the evening, it's like I'm falling into a bottomless pit of depression . . . I'm sorry for going on so much, but I really have nobody to talk to. I have no family and suicide runs in my family."* (48-year-old divorced White female who is head of household, with children, has been out of work for less than 1 year and receiving between $5,000 and $9,000/year, with a 12th grade high school diploma or GED; in need of a Pap testing) (Mental/ Emotional Issues, Stress)

Life Trauma	More serious events that could have happened at any time	Illness/disability	– Disease diagnosis – Poor disability prognosis – Accident resulting in permanent disability	15. *"I was a former drug user and I may have Hep C . . . I don't know . . . I didn't normally share needles, but last time I shot up, I did. I was a heroin user."* (45-year-old, divorced White female, with children, unable to work [unknown reason] earning between $15,000 and $19,999/year and having 4+ years of college; in need of a mammography screening) (Addiction issues)
		Family member's death/loss	– Miscarriage – Cancer death in family – Sudden death of relative	
		Other traumatic psychosocial issues	– Domestic violence – Molestation – Shame related to rape Negative healthcare experience	16. *"I feel a lot of shame [about being raped], and I pretend that it's okay, but it's not."* (34-year-old, unknown race/ethnicity, member of an unmarried couple, out of work for more than 1 year and receiving between $15,000 and $19,999/year, and only completing between grades 1–8; in need of a Pap testing) (Traumatic Psychosocial issues, Shame related to rape)

(continued)

Table 4.1. *(Continued)*

Turner & Avison's (2003) Stressor Categories	Stressor Definitions	Types of Stressors/ Stressor Subtypes	Illustrative Quotes
			17. "I came home, and I cried (after being diagnosed with a bone disease). I'm very panicked right now [about affording healthcare] because it took 6 1/2 weeks to even get contacted (by the unemployment office). . . . I prefer [de-identified hospital] because I received a bad surgery from another hospital and I don't want to go to that hospital, even though it is close to my house. I don't want to go there" (51-year-old White divorced female, who has been out of work for less than 1 year and earning under $5,000/year, and only attended kindergarten; in need of a Pap testing) (Unemployment, Illness, Mistreatment from healthcare providers, Disease diagnosis)
Discrimination	Biased/unfair treatment experienced from other people	Mistreatment from healthcare providers – Not treated fairly at medical facility Previous bad experience with clinic staff	18. "I went and the lady was so rude. I was telling her about the free program, and she had went off on me and I told her I was never coming to that clinic ever again. She was like 'Do you know why you came in here? Just wait over here.' She was yelling at me like I was five (years

old), and I said that maybe I could come back and she said 'We may still be busy, and you still might get me.' She was just rude! I was really embarrassed because there were so many people there." (55-year-old, married [unknown race/ethnicity] homemaker with children, family income between $35,000 and $49,999/year, with a 12th grade high school diploma or a GED; in need of Pap testing) (Mistreatment from healthcare providers, Previous bad experience with clinic staff)

19. "You call (the clinics) and you never get through and the people you do contact are so nasty . . . I don't feel like going through that." (40-year-old, African American female with children, who has never been married, who has been out of work for less than 1 year and earning between $15,000 and $19,999/year income, and having either a 12th grade high school diploma or GED; in need of a Pap testing) (Mistreatment from healthcare providers, Not treated fairly at medical facility)

Solutions Point to the Socioecological Model Levels

For prevention and intervention strategies to decrease the experience of disparities at the population level, multilevel socioecological factors must be accounted for and addressed. Addressing these causes and contributors to women's health disparities is a complex process that requires intervention from a socioecological framework. Addressing barriers to women's disparities is a complex process that requires intervention at multiple levels of influence. This adapted model (Figure 4.1) coalesces the psychological, epidemiological, sociological, and medical literatures to offer possible approaches and considerations for bringing programs to scale with the intention of encouraging future research and intervention in screening adherence.

Figure 4.1. The concentric segments indicate the relationships between SEM levels of influence. The individual woman's screening behaviors create the core of the diagram. The Individual affects and is influenced by other elements in her environment, like the Interpersonal, Community/Organizational, and Policy levels; and that screening behavior both shapes and is shaped by each of these outer segments. The Interpersonal segment represents the socioculturally oriented intervention approaches needed for that SEM level. The Community/ Organizational segment represents sociocultural adaptations that can influence screening uptake within vulnerable communities and organizations serving low-income women. The Policy segment represents the over-reaching macro-system that improves healthcare access to un/under-insured women through funding and policy expansion.
created by authors

According to the socioecological framework, a public health problem such as barriers to cancer screening, is the result of a convergence of factors spanning all socioecological levels of the issue, which include sociocultural elements of important relevance (See figure 4.1). The SEM proposes that individual behavior affects and is affected by the social environment and that behavior both shapes and is shaped by multiple levels of influence (Glanz & Rimer, 1997). This model has been used to explain health promotion within communities on the basis of the premise of social, cultural, and environmental factors influencing changes in an individual's behavior (Stokols, 1996). SEM facilitates the examination of the environmental or ecological niche (family, community, political, and social environments) and is essential to better understand and improve cancer screening adherence. Here, we see the value in a multilevel SEM framework to promote behavioral changes at the individual, interpersonal, and policy levels. In short, SEM posits that individuals are affected by multiple dimensions of their environment. Therefore, strategies are best understood and implemented through a socioecological framework because a theoretical interpretation of health promotion speaks to the complex relationships among individual, social, and environmental factors (Stokols, 1996).

Understanding cultural competence through the multiple SEM avenues is uncommon, as most often cultural competency is understood as a trait of healthcare providers. However, organizations without culturally attuned processes and policies limit the problem-solving capacity of culturally competent providers. In turn, organizations themselves operate in a policy environment that may or may not favor the cultural competency of the provider. In fact, some of the strategies identified for improving cultural competence in the clinical setting and, thus, cancer screening behavior among patients, may even require revisions of policy as a first step.

Based on the identified barriers in the literature and our research, we have designed a cancer screening model to help explain and guide intervention and implementation of a program to increase adherence among low-income women of color. By applying the SEM to the design, we have identified individual, interpersonal, organizational, and policy factors that are influenced by barriers and influence the health behavior of these women. These factors create multiple layers of support for the woman and ultimately influences favorable screening. At the individual level, efforts would influence the woman's beliefs, attitudes, and knowledge about screening; the risks and benefits of screening; and the affordability and convenience of screening, all of which are at the core of the model and ultimately influence screening behavior. At the next sphere of influence, the interpersonal level, the community navigator would assist the woman with screening by showing her how the test is conducted, how to make the appointment, where they go for the procedure. The navigator would remind the woman of her appointment and assist with any follow-up services if necessary. This level would also include identifying and engaging friends, family, providers, and/or stakeholders to reinforce screening behavior, if needed. At the organizational/ community level, barriers could be addressed by healthcare organizations using mobile vans to go into hard-to-reach community sites on a daily basis, with designation to churches on Sundays and to nonhealth community sites (like hair/nail salons, grocery stores, laundromats, social service agencies, libraries, etc.) where health may not be on women's minds. This level would also involve healthcare organizations partnering with these community sites to help leverage resources and participation. At the final social structure or policy level, individual behavior change should be influenced through legislation and funding at the local, state, and national levels. These include (among many others) the development of a system that enables these women to pay nominal fees for services, offers alternative appointment scheduling methods, and explores options for prevention and treatment of uninsured women. The goal of using a multilevel approach is to allow these factors to work synergistically to facilitate the screening at the individual level. Next, we will discuss an example of how patient navigation at the interpersonal level works to facilitate screening.

Case Example #2: Toward a New Conceptual Model— Socioecological Model

Although progress has been made and overall screening utilization rates have improved over the past 25 years, low-income women who are non-adherent for getting mammograms at regular intervals remain the biggest challenge to creating the healthiest nation and ensuring the right to health among women. Although we do have some knowledge about predictors and strategies of mammography screening among low-income groups and other high-risk populations, most of it has not been examined theoretically.

Social Ecological Theory can be applied as a conceptual framework for identifying mammography screening strategies. Utilizing a SEM framework in this study, we aimed to examine the multilevel barriers to mammography screening among low-income unscreened women within public sector care systems; and explored feasible strategies that can be used among patient navigators to improve mammography uptake and maintenance among this population of underserved women.

We utilized interview data from 28 unscreened women (table 4.2) and three focus groups (table 4.3) conducted with providers from the St. Louis Regional Breast Navigator Provider Workgroup. The data included a total of 28 indi-

Table 4.2. Client Demographic Characteristics. Client Demographic Characteristics (n=28)

African American	28
Marital Status	
Single	25
Married	3
Age in years (50–59)	21
Unemployed	18
Annual Income	
Less than $10,000	15
Less than $20,000	7
Insurance coverage	19
Mammogram History	
Within past 13–25 months	21
Within past 25 months–5 yrs.	6
No mammogram	1
Women without children <18	23

vidual interviews and 11 providers spanning 11 different healthcare settings in the St. Louis county area. Grounded theory was used to guide interview prompts and to analyze the results. Barriers were conceptualized as intrapersonal barriers, interpersonal barriers, environmental barriers, community barriers, and structural barriers (table 4.4). Furthermore, cultural explanatory theories (discussed above in this chapter) contribute to an understanding of unique sociocultural barriers to mammogram screening. Providers reported feasible strategies used to inform the development of appropriate interventions for unscreened low-income women to help promote mammogram screening among low-income women.

These findings enhance our understanding of mammography screening adherence and provide a theoretical foundation for the development of future multilevel resources and interventions tailored for this population. Socioculturally sensitive adaptations of existing multilevel intervention models for low-income women are needed.

Table 4.3. Patient Navigator Characteristics (n=11)

Navigator Site Type	
Medical/Clinical Hospital	4
Community Clinics/FQHC	6
Cancer Centers	1

Table 4.4. Social Ecological Theory Levels and Codes: Representative Quotes

SEM Levels	Barriers Reported/ Aligning Strategies	Socioecological Theory Levels and Codes Representative Quotes
Intrapersonal	**BARRIERS:** • Fear of mammogram • Fear of diagnosis • Fear of financial expenses • Mistrust of healthcare providers **STRATEGIES:** • Education • Rapport and Reassurance	**(BARRIER)** "And why they just don't want to do it (have mammogram), they had a <u>scare</u>: 'I am not going to go because they are going to find something and then what am I going to do?' And then you have to tell them that breast cancer has come a long way." **(STRATEGY)** "I think you have to do it on a very personal level and allow them to be interactive with their care, instead of telling them that A, B, and C, this is what you need to do. You need to sit them down and talk to them and say, okay, so for your care, what would you like to see done?"
Sociocultural	**BARRIERS:** • Mammogram "taboo" • Secrecy **STRATEGIES:** • Education	**(BARRIER)** "In the African American women's culture, there's this secrecy and so the goal is to put on your best face, be strong, keep yourself well dressed, your hair done and that's the façade and you don't talk. And African American women and in their family typically weren't discussed . . . that maybe their mama or grandma or other family members have faced. There's just this culture of secrecy that I've heard and some ladies describe to me. **(STRATEGY)** "And so working to try and penetrate that culture in helping women; it's the educational piece. Or here's why it's important to know what your family tree looks like. And here's why it's important for you to talk about breast health and the importance of mammograms."
Interpersonal	**BARRIERS:** • Provider time constraints • Patient/Provider misunderstandings about guidelines **STRATEGIES:** • Active listening • Patient/provider guideline education	**(BARRIER)** "We have a real issue in our clinics with the providers being split in half when they get the mammograms because of the taskforce guidelines. I've got some providers who believe every year is fine and then I've got some providers who are encouraging women to come back in two years and so we're kind of struggling with that as well." **(STRATEGY)** "In terms of not only the guideline changes, but also the rationale behind it because we get the questions too about HPV testing and cervical cancer. Help us make sense of this; keep us up to date on the changes in treatment for breast cancer. What's the current thinking? Why are you thinking this?"

SEM Levels	Barriers Reported/ Aligning Strategies	Socioecological Theory Levels and Codes Representative Quotes
Environmental	**BARRIERS:** • Financial constraints • Caregiving • Logistical conflicts/ Competing daily priorities • Access • Lack of motivation/ incentive **STRATEGIES:** • Caring for the caregiver • Flexibility • More collaborative efforts • Screening incentives	**(BARRIER)** "They have so many more things to manage. You can problem solve and you get one thing solved, but you've got 3 or 4 more things you've got to do too. And I think sometimes that is overwhelming. Sometimes transportation and where you've got to go and how you've got to go is overwhelming. They have grandchildren and great-grandchildren. I had a lady who had two great-grandchildren that lived with her." **(STRATEGY)** "And I say, okay, since you're taking care of that person, let me take care of you. So while you're worrying about taking care of them and providing all their transportation needs, scheduling their appointments, let me do that for you. And all I need for you to do is show up. And once I put it that way, they're like, oh okay."
Institutional	**BARRIERS:** • Inefficient healthcare system • Long wait times **STRATEGIES:** • Education about behavioral skills	**(BARRIER)** "We're always looking at how we reduce wait times. Sometimes it's just impossible with the way that our system works. But what can you do with the wait times that no longer make them 'wait times,' but turn them into something else? I think it's creative things like that, that really can improve our healthcare system." **(STRATEGY)** "If I do happen to go to the surgical consultation with them when the provider leaves out, I'll ask, 'Did you understand everything? Do you have any questions for me? Do you have any questions for him? Do you have any questions you think you're going to have before you leave or after you leave?' I say, 'Well, if so, just call me.' I say this so you fully understand everything before we leave out of here."

A social ecological framework for patient navigators and healthcare providers, highlights socioculturally competent strategies which would include:

- Intrapersonal: Tailored educational information in print, breast cancer survivor narratives in video formats (administered in community venues)
- Interpersonal: Patient navigator and provider cultural competence training, regular provider education on screening guidelines
- Environmental: Community mobile units, transportation and childcare offered
- Institutional: Walk-in appointments, appointments offered in evening and weekends, scheduling in conjunction with other appointments

SEM can serve as a theoretical guide for the adoption of future adapted models for mammography adherence screening. Future analyses should include a larger, more representative sample of unscreened women, in which actual statistical analyses could be conducted to assist in strengthening assertions and to empirically test and unpack multilevel intervention components.

Qualitative methods allow group members to voice their concerns, thoughts, and feelings in their own words and language of origin. In the second case example, focus group research demonstrates the power of cancer narratives as a way for African American and Latina breast cancer survivors to give meaning to their experiences. Little has been published about the influence of cultural values and attitudes on peer coaching during cancer diagnosis and treatment among minority women from their own perspectives.

Case Example #3: Peer Coaching

Peer coaching is an intervention involving the selection of patients with the motivation and personal skills to engage in one on one activities with other patients. In this case it was cancer. Peer coaches training includes basic patient education on the illness, principles on creating action plans and setting goals. They typically provide support for care coordination, disease management, communication and also management of issues and stressors—family stress, child care needs, etc. (based on their experience and knowledge of the community) (Steinberg, Fremont, & Khan, 2006). Focus groups explored cancer patient reactions to peer coaching during cancer diagnosis and treatment. Broad themes explored included the following: (a) the impact of the peer coaching experience, (b) personal reactions to the coaching experience, (c) reasons for study participation and intentions to participate in research in the future, and (d) willingness to participate in clinical trials and the impact of peer coaching on this intention. The institutional review board of the Washington University Medical Center, Human Studies Committee approved the research protocol. All participants received a detailed explanation of the study before providing signed consent.

Two, sex-specific, focus groups were conducted in 2006; data from four female participants are reported here. Participants were diagnosed with breast cancer and recruited from a study affiliated with the Siteman Cancer Center Program for the Elimination of Cancer Disparities (Sanders Thompson, 2015). Participants were recruited by project staff and received a reminder call the day before the scheduled focus group. Participants received a payment for their participation.

The focus groups were 90 minutes. All sessions were audio taped and each session's audiotape was professionally transcribed verbatim and reviewed by the Dr. Sanders Thompson. In addition, an assistant completed detailed field notes based on the sessions. Researchers independently read and developed general codes based on the content of the transcripts and field notes. The data analysis team, then, met and reviewed codes and discussed any discrepancies until a final code was agreed upon by consensus. Upon completion of coding, team members individually formulated core ideas and general themes for each sex. The full team, then, met to discuss the core ideas and general themes that had been generated. The discussions yielded a set of findings about peer coaching and its impact on participation in research, particularly early phase clinical trials.

One participant had completed her treatment, and two participants were continuing to receive some form of adjuvant treatment. One participant disclosed that her physician had recommended further treatment that she declined. One female participant reported that she had not screened due to fear of radiation and lack of symptoms, whereas two others had not been adherent at the time of diagnosis because of busy work schedules and the discomfort of mammograms. The participants reported that they lacked knowledge of cancer signs and symptoms, although one participant acknowledged her increased cancer risk due to family history. One participant complained that she had difficulty with her initial diagnosis and had to seek a second opinion. She stated that she believed that this might have allowed her cancer to spread.

All participants described the cancer experience as stressful, resulting in fear and a sense of loss. They noted that not knowing survivors of breast cancer intensified their reactions to their diagnosis. The participant who declined further treatment also noted that she responded to her initial diagnosis with denial, refusing treatment for a year and relying on her faith for healing. All participants reported that they had satisfactory support from their family, friends, churches, and through faith.

None of the women were aware of the term peer coaching, but all participants remembered the term when the process was described. Female participants described the peer coaching experience positively, even though they had low recognition of the term. These participants stated that they had no expectations of the experience when they agreed to participate. The women described themselves as "givers" who would not have requested assistance although they needed it. They stated that they participated primarily to obtain the monetary incentive, but the experience benefited them in ways that they had not anticipated. Participants described the peer coach as an asset who was nice, helpful, and supportive. The peer coaches reportedly "removed a burden" from participants' families, filled a void, provided needed information, "gave them hope" and helped them "see possibilities." They also discussed the experience as increasing their understanding of and trust in their treatment and treatment providers. The women reported that the peer coaches were easy to talk to. According to female participants, peer coaches could be trusted because they had been through the cancer experience; for this reason, women consulted them when they needed to process issues related to their own cancer experiences and worries. The coach provided helpful reminders of appointments, and assisted in locating resources. In addition, the peer coach was available to discuss symptoms and reactions when medical staff could not be available or did not realize that issues might be important.

Peer coaching appeared to reduce stress, improve adjustment to an identity as a cancer patient, and provide needed information, support, and assistance in managing the complexities of receipt of treatment among the group of participants. Participants suggested that in the future the timing of the end of peer coaching experiences should be examined. They suggested that coaching continue until the end of all treatment (i.e., surgeries, chemotherapy, and radiation therapy). Participants felt that any loss of support while treatment continued was problematic. Participants reported sadness and disappointment as they transitioned away from this service. To ease this transition, the female participants suggested that all participants receive monthly check-in calls for several months after program cessation.

The peer coaching experience promoted a positive attitude toward research. Participants noted an increased willingness to either consider or participate in similar types of research in the future. Participants suggested that appeals based on service to the African American community, made by African American recruiters or peer coaches, would be important determinants of future participation. Who requests their participation and what organization(s) this person or persons represent were cited as important issues. Participants reported that they liked the personal, low-key, non-pressured recruitment used in the Barriers to Early Phase Clinical Trials study. Male participants

influence of family members, emphasizing the importance of the Navigator-Client relationship, empathizing with the women regarding their stressors, acknowledging women's screening apprehensions, providing appropriate self-disclosure about the navigator's personal challenges with health, listening actively, asking about stressors and barriers, asking about general health and life events, placing follow-up calls after screening, and emphasizing the navigator as a partner and a resource for health. The following dialogue was an example of a navigator engaging and trying to build rapport with a 2-1-1 caller ("Caller") who needed a mammogram:

> Caller: I had gotten myself in a bit of financial trouble and now I am in the situation where I am facing foreclosure. All of my 'steam' has kind have gone to prevent that from happening.
>
> Navigator: You sound like you are very active, and it dovetails with some of the things I will be talking to you about . . . taking care of your health. . . . You do have a lot of things going on, so having a health setback would really derail you.
>
> Caller: This is such service! I don't want to overdo your time.
>
> Navigator: Always feel free to give me a call; you don't have to wait for me to call you. I understand how hard it is for you when you lose a job and have so many other things to take care of.
>
> Caller: There's help out there, but I've always been so independent. I think it's time I started getting some help.
>
> Navigator: No problem. That's what I'm here for—to help you. So, don't feel like you are imposing on me because I'm here for you and I'm here to help you out.

Often, given women's experience of multiple, or overwhelming, problems, there was a need for *focusing* skills, which were used to help prioritize which barriers and stressors to work on. Navigators encouraged women to choose one stressor or barrier on which to focus, to evoke change around that focus. Focusing tasks involved assisting a woman with prioritizing health referrals and assessing her interest and readiness in completing the referral(s). The following is an example of a dialogue, which reflects a simple focusing quote used by a navigator to help parse out a woman's barriers, thereby identifying the life stressor that the woman in need of mammography screening wanted to work on before using screening services:

> Navigator: You don't have to do everything all at once. We will be working together for about four months. Out of all the things we just talked about, which one of these things would you like to take care of first?
>
> Caller: So many things are difficult . . . I have co-dependency; I'm aware of it, and I'm trying to change. I am dealing with a man who was homeless, and he

has a drinking problem, and I need to find out where he can go to get help. He needs to be in a place where it would be a controlled, Christian environment, and I don't know where to take him. He was living in a warehouse, and they changed ownership so he could no longer be there, so here I am, taking him on.

Navigator: Have you tried calling 2-1-1 for services just for him, like a homeless shelter or Christian services to find help for him?

Caller: No, I haven't tried that, and I need to do that. I just think he needs to be in a nice environment where he will be watched so that he would not be able to get a hold of any liquor. Thank you for that reminder!

Once a woman decided on which barrier or stressor to focus on, navigators listened for ways to help women elaborate and to evoke more brainstorming discussion about alleviating or reducing barrier(s), stressor(s), and ambivalence around screening behavior. Navigators usually attempted to evoke this type of thinking by posing an open-ended question, which is illustrated in this dialogue focused on Pap testing:

Navigator: What would make you feel more motivated to try and get that [Pap test] taken care of?

Caller: Probably nothing really, because I guess I am in one of those slumps in where I don't want to do anything. I'm just discouraged (about the job hunt process). I'm just in a rut and just don't want to do nothing.

Navigator: Sometimes getting out of the house, getting some exercise, will make you feel better and get some positive energy going in your life . . . maybe that will translate hopefully. Think of it (taking care of health) as one less thing on your list to take care of, and you are able to get it for free.

Case Management

Patterns in case management technique were reflected by navigators in three primary ways: (a) addressing barriers to care and stressors, (b) collaboration and continuum of care tasks, and (c) planning. Specifically, with regard to addressing barriers to care and stressors, navigators referred women with social service needs back to United Way 2-1-1, checked social service assistance eligibility requirements, and provided counseling services information. With regard to collaborating and the continuum of care tasks, navigators streamlined processes, updated information and searched referral resources, searched additional services and locations, reviewed action items from previous contact, arranged and found information about transportation for screening appointments, suggested best times to contact study navigators and other resources, walked women through screening and testing processes, and informed women about information needed to bring to an appointment. This is reflected in the following dialogue between a navigator and a woman in need of a mammogram:

> Caller: I prefer [to be seen] at [de-identified hospital] because I received a bad surgery from another hospital, and I don't want to go to that hospital, even though it is close to my house. I don't want to go there.
>
> Navigator: If I can find transportation for you to go get your Pap done at [de-identified hospital] or if I can find a location that is close to you (but not at the facility you don't want to go to) would you be willing to go then?
>
> Caller: That's amazing! That is really, really is amazing! Wow! I really need to hear that.
>
> Navigator: Great! I'll be calling on you, checking on you from time to time to check on your progress. I'll be a good resource for you for those procedures.

As early as the first contact with women, navigators also helped women plan to act on the screening referrals: for example, planning for a woman to seek assistance for emotional and social service needs, confirming scheduled appointments and appointment completion, and arranging follow-up calls. This is reflected in the following dialogue between the navigator and a woman in need of a mammogram:

> Navigator: I can come up with a list of places for you to go that take Medicare and can either waive or break the co-pay up into installments. Are you looking to go somewhere in the city or county? In St. Louis? [De-identified hospital] does not turn anyone away if they can't pay a co-pay, and they have sliding scale fees.
>
> Caller: There is one in Maplewood I can go to because I walk a lot due to having no transportation. I think it's a People's Health Center.
>
> Navigator: It is, and it's a Federally Qualified Health Clinic, meaning that they won't turn you away due to an inability to provide a co-pay, and they can also give you a referral for your mammogram and for your colonoscopy. A lot of what we talk about are things to help give you peace of mind to help screen or prevent cancer. . . . You don't have to do everything all at once. . . . We will be working together for about 4 months. This sounds like this would be a good starting place for you. When you go for your appointment, just bring a photo ID and proof of income. Maybe, you and I can set up a time for me to call you again to see how you are coming with the appointment?

Delivering Information and Education

Whenever possible, navigators attempted to use plain language to deliver information and education about (a) the study, (b) community and healthcare systems, and (c) breast and cervical cancer screening. This allowed navigators to clarify misconceptions, reiterate screening guidelines and recommendation(s), and assist women in weighing the costs and benefits of referral resources and screenings. With regard to providing study-related information and education , the navigator would explain her role as "health coach," emphasize details about the length of time they would work together, share contact information, provide clarification about 2-1-1, and discuss role expectations.

Examples of information and education about community and healthcare systems included explanation of the *Show Me Healthy Women* (SMHW) program and/or *Federally Qualified Health Center* (FQHC) programs, researching information about mobile mammography schedules, and explaining that clinics may waive co-pays or divide bills into smaller payments. Specific ways in which navigators provided information and education about screenings involved discussing screening guidelines and the importance of family history of cancer. Illustrations of screening information and education are reflected in this dialogue between a navigator and a woman needing a mammogram:

> Caller: I got that from my mother. She taught us that if you let someone touch your breast it would give you cancer (laughter)
>
> Navigator: No, that's not true, breast cancer isn't caused by trauma to the breast; it is caused by an overgrowth of cells.

The next quote is an example of information and education dialogue between a navigator and woman needing a Pap test:

> Caller: You know I am going to call that [SMHW referral] today. I haven't had a Pap in many years, and I go to the doctor and he doesn't recommend one during the physical checkup, and I believe all women need those Paps.
>
> Navigator: It's something you should talk to your doctor about. Once you get over the age of 65, if you have 3 normal Pap tests and had no abnormal results in the past 10 years, you can stop getting them.

Here is another example of a simple educational opportunity between a navigator and a caller in need of a Pap test:

> Caller: I'm not too big on going to the doctor. It will probably be awhile before I get to doing that. I just don't like doctors. I just don't go to the doctor unless I absolutely have to.
>
> Navigator: Sometimes, we take care of everything but ourselves until something happens that we can't ignore or put it aside, that if we get screened a little bit earlier, it would not get more serious.

Empowerment

We discerned patterns of navigators empowering women with strength-based approaches, using affirmations. Affirmations are statements of support that point out the woman's strengths and are said in a genuine manner. Examples of this include commending a woman for following through with scheduling an appointment and praising her for healthy behavior(s). The dialogue below provides illustrations taken from calls with a woman in need of a mammogram:

> Caller: A lot of times people have problems, and people judge you for it. I have a dependence problem, and I have been struggling with it for a long time . . . . I don't know if counseling would help as opposed to some [other] kind of treatment that they can provide. Because unless you walk down those roads yourself, you don't know what it's like. Every day is a challenge. I had attempted to go through treatment before. To me, they [other people] are constantly throwing it up [judging me], and it causes that desire to peak. I don't want that in my life anymore. I need to change.

> Navigator: It seems like you have been dealing with problems from the past for many years that are affecting what is going on now. Sometimes, it helps to calm down, take a breath, and get yourself together. We're all human and things happen, but the good thing about it is that we can rebound and come back. As long as we're alive, we have another chance.

> Caller: You don't know how much of a comfort it is to talk to somebody because I have a problem, and I have to accept it, and I can't deal with it on my own. I am trying to move forward. I want to make my children proud; they live a good life, and I want to be an addition to them and not take away from what they are doing. It's really fulfilling to listen to nice, kind people on the phone.

> Navigator: I do care, and I want to make sure that you get all the services that you need and make sure that you are comfortable to get your health straight so you can take care of everything else you have to take care of.

Here, we also see another illustration of a navigator and a woman in need of a mammography screening:

> Caller: I am also seeking some kind of mental health counseling. I was a rape victim, and from that rape, I have a 17-year-old son. I need to be stable, but I'm not. It's killing me. I pretend to be okay, but it's not working. I feel a lot of shame [about being raped], and I pretend that it's okay, but it's not.

> Navigator: I think it's really great that you know you need help, and there's no shame in it.

> Caller: I've been really trying but a lot of places have appointments that are months down the road, and that's not helping me, or they are just doing assess-

ments because they don't have a therapist on site, so what am I supposed to do in the meantime?

Navigator: Have you contacted an organization called Safe Connections? They work with survivors of domestic violence and sexual abuse.

Discussion

The purpose of this study was to identify and describe what transpired in real-time interactions between navigators and low-income women in an intervention study that demonstrated significant benefits of patient navigation . In the study, we found four core navigation skills used to promote women's use of mammography and Pap testing: case management , motivational interviewing techniques, information and education , and empowerment.

Although we identified some of the same highly valued elements of navigation found in the literature (Carroll, 2010; Derose, Fox, Reigadas, & Hawes-Dawson, 2010; Sadler et al., 2007), we also found that adherence barriers could possibly be reduced using key *motivational interviewing* techniques. Motivational strategies included three important skills, which happen to also be three of the four classic motivational interviewing processes: (a) engaging, (b) focusing, and (c) evoking. Previous literature suggests that high motivation for health concerns leads to an increase in health-promoting behaviors (Sandler et al., 2007), so improving motivation should be targeted. This was also demonstrated in a study in which telephone calls with targeted motivational techniques (as opposed to simply sending a reminder card) increased mammography screening adherence (Taplin et al., 2000). Even in cases in which women have access to and are well informed about screening and testing, there is a need to emphasize motivational strategies (Hendren et al., 2010; Jean et al., 2010) to help improve mammography screening use.

It is important to note that motivational interviewing has been more traditionally used to change addiction behaviors; however, screening adherence can also be an important health behavior that can have a major effect on unfavorable cancer outcomes. Health outcomes are often highly influenced by and dependent on the patient's own behavioral choices—on doing something new or doing something differently (Rollnick, Miller, & Butler, 2008). Motivational interviewing has been more recently adapted for use by healthcare practitioners and used in challenging patient circumstances, in which a similar range of health behavior concerns arise and practitioners feel that patients' health and adherence is not necessarily something they can control. It is true that healthcare practitioners have little or no direct control; however, letting go of some control does not mean lack of influence. It is quite possible to influence that which we do not personally control (Rollnick, Miller, & Butler, 2008).

This study highlights the importance of strong *case management* skills, which complements motivational interviewing techniques used to assist women whose financial need is beyond question. Patient navigators assisted with identifying needed financial services, resources, and opportunities within the system, while also providing empowering guidance along the way. Navigators collaboratively assessed the needs of the women and arranged, coordinated, monitored, evaluated, and advocated for a package of multiple services to meet their complex needs, which were mostly financial in nature. When helping to address socioeconomic and psychosocial needs of the women, as well as the social service and healthcare systems, the patient navigators could develop and maintain rapport with women. Addressing case management needs first was extremely important in getting the women into mammography screening and Pap testing.

Consistent communication with the delivery of *information and education* is a critical factor that influences adherence (Allen et al., 2008; Eggleston et al., 2007) and is shown to be a common thread that ties together the identified core elements of navigation in this study. Although face-to-face interactions might be ideal for facilitating greater communication with women who have overwhelming stressors and little support (Derose et al., 2010), providing telephone communication still adds an additional layer of interaction with clients. However, because women will require consistent screening and testing for several decades after initiation, this initial engagement could lead to greater adherence with mammography screening and Pap testing (Eggleston et al., 2007; Stoddard et al., 2002). With sufficient resources, ideally, we should try to find a way to train navigators to intervene with women beyond the telephone contact, to have the ability to get to know and see participants regularly, which can facilitate spontaneous follow-up (Derose et al., 2010). Although we want effective public health interventions that serve large populations and are scalable, like phone navigation, we still need to determine whether a patient will truly benefit from a more personalized, face-to-face intervention or whether they would prefer a series of phone conversations. Nonetheless, the consistent communication of information and education in patient navigation interactions is one of the most important aspects of patient adherence, and navigation is a simple tool that facilitates this communication and ensures that patients move from being nonadherent to adherent in seeking mammography screening and Pap testing services (Stoddard et al., 2002).

Women in this study were found to experience layers of life events, chronic strain, life trauma, and discrimination stressors, which, when experienced, can be overwhelming and may affect mammography screening and Pap testing participation. Barriers were not isolated to personal stressors, as women also described structural barriers (co-pays or insurance issues and the inability to contact the agency) within most stressor categories. Although most women were educated (i.e., high school graduates and/or having had some college), education did not protect them from economic hardship. Nor did their education protect most of them from being unemployed, as most women were either out of work or unable to work. Most women were never married, divorced/separated, or widowed, which contributed to the lack of support for these vulnerable women. These results highlight the importance of *empowering* women and increasing women's self-efficacy by teaching them personal skills to overcome psychological and physical barriers to mammogram screening. Increased self-efficacy may enhance their motivation to get a mammogram (Tolma, Reininger, Evans, & Ureda, 2006).

Because of the "multiple confounding" (Wells, Palinkas, Shon, & Ell, 2013) layers of stressors and sensitive psychosocial issues—sometimes related to trauma, abuse, and discrimination—we also need to ensure navigators are formally trained to identify mental health or behavioral health risk issues, perhaps by clinical social workers. Ideally, navigators should be trained to look and listen for risk issues (e.g., depression and anxiety related to suicidality or homicidal, and direct links to behavioral health professionals, as opposed to just referring women back to another referral linkage source. It is also important for navigators to know when to refer to a licensed mental health professional for further assessment. The incorporation of mental health training for patient navigators is likely to help reduce disparities in acceptance and receipt of screening and testing (Ell et al., 2010).

Although the navigators' focus was supposed to be on health, clear evidence exists that they spent much of their time on reducing barriers and life stressors. Therefore, future navigation interventions should incorporate training and skill building that allows navigators to emphasize the personal and structural barriers and to discuss stressors of need first, before seeking to address health-related adherence behavior (e.g., making and coordinating appointments, translating medical terminology into plain language, and providing appointment reminders). Although it might take a little longer to address psychosocial needs and stressors, women might be more motivated to work on preventive health issues if assistance for their presenting psychosocial issues are initiated first (Farmer, Reddick, D'Agostino, & Jackson, 2007; Russell, Perkins, Zollinger, & Champion, 2006). This also helps build rapport and trust in the navigator, which are particularly important for this group of women experiencing sensitive stressors.

In addition, when considering the sustainability of future community-based navigation projects, it is important to recognize the time sensitivity involved in such work. This study reveals that navigators often made numerous telephone call attempts to reach women and followed women for several months to obtain screening. This could create a limitation for the adoption of the intervention with programs that have a limited budget. A more sustainable approach to this type of work will be to use existing community capacity and appeal to politicians to create financial incentives for existing community-based agencies and healthcare programs that conduct community-based prevention work with this target population.

Next Steps

This study provides new insight into successful telephone navigation strategies with vulnerable women in need of mammography and Pap testing. The future framing of patient navigation, within the context of hard-to-reach populations in poverty, should expand and adapt traditional "barrier reduction" patient navigation training to include systematic, evidence-based interventions such as problem-solving treatment, motivational interviewing, and tailored educational information. The next step will be to better address the significant elements of patient navigation, which will have the greatest impact on regular and preventive screening and testing, and will likely come from relatively simple interventions that can be sustained over time (Stoddard et al., 2002). The challenge is to address the life stressors so that devoting time and energy to other urgent needs, like health and prevention, becomes possible. On the navigator's part, it will take persistence and assertiveness, not only when dealing with patients' barriers, but also structural barriers, which sometimes involve a dysfunctional medical system (Jean et al., 2010).

Patient Navigation Gaps

Despite the effectiveness of navigation interventions, there are four main limitations when attempting to get nonadherent women to initiate and maintain mammography screening. First, although a feature of some navigation programs is the use of problem-solving elements (Lasser, Murrillo, Lisboa et al., 2011), systematic evidence-based problem-solving techniques, like *Problem Solving* Treatment (PST) (Nezu, Nezu, & Houts, 1994); are not used. PST is a cognitive-behavioral treatment found effective in treating psychosocial coping among minorities with comorbidities, particularly when socio-environmental stressors are a significant factor. Second, a key element of navigation is to provide knowledge and information, which has been shown effective in increasing behavioral initiation in many other intervention studies (Nezu, Nezu, & Houts, 1994); however, information is not always culturally tailored for all groups, like tailored educational information (TEI) (Kreuter, Sugg Skinner et al., 2004). Evidence exists that standardized printed recommendations are less effective than tailored recommendations that address women's specific screening and risk status and perceptions about breast cancer and mammography (Skinner, Strecher, Hospers, 1994). In addition, tailored educational information should be tailored specifically for a higher risk audience (Lopez & Castro, 2006). Third, navigation focuses on motivational components, but not on systematic evidence-based motivational interviewing techniques, shown to increase mammography screening (Taplin, Ichikawa, & Yood, 2004) and other health-promoting behaviors. Fourth, navigation interventions often focus on efforts to change general patterns of behavior, as opposed to focusing on increasing individuals' inclination and ability to practice specific risk-reduction acts, like *behavioral activation* (BA) (Lejuez, Hopko, & Hopko, 2001) which is critical to assuming more active involvement in care by asking more appropriate and relevant questions about mammography, thus improving self-efficacy (Wolf, Chang, Davis, & Makoul, 2010). There exist only a few mammogram studies that incorporate elements of BA; however, these are in different countries and settings, with populations in England (Steadman & Rutter, 2004) and in Korea (Kang, Thomas, Kwon et al., 2008).

Case Example #5: Toward a New Intervention: Navigation-Information-Motivation-Behavioral Skills

From the same sample in case example #2, we conducted semi-structured telephone interviews with 28 low-income uninsured and underinsured African-American women, 40 to 70 years, without a mammogram within the past 12 months (Wells, Shon, McGowan, & James, 2015). Women were recruited from 21 hair and nail salons and Laundromats within the five North St. Louis city zip codes with the highest breast cancer mortality rates. Transcripts were analyzed using grounded theory.

This study found the individual relevancy of information, motivation, and behavioral skills affect screening adherence (Wells, Shon, McGowan, & James, 2015). The data suggested the reordering of the traditional IMB components to the following: information, behavioral skills, and motivation. Information and behavioral skills first, work together for motivation to occur, and thus behavior adherence. In addition, the need for specificity of behavioral skills, categorized into systematic (i.e., number to call, where to go) or procedural (information or knowledge about mammogram procedure). Thus, having both accurate information and having the necessary behavioral skills, activates the motivation to get screened.

These findings enhanced our understanding of mammography screening adherence and provided a theoretical foundation for the development of a new explanatory change model based on prevention, which expected to help oncology healthcare clinical and population health providers and the community, improve screening outcomes for other hard-to-reach, unscreened populations.

Toward a New Model

The Information-Motivation-Behavioral (IMB) Model is a well-known evidence-based adherence model, which asserts that information, motivation, and behavioral skills are the fundamental determinants to screening behavior (Fisher & Fisher, 2000). In accordance with IMB, the extent to which women are well informed, are motivated to act, and possess behavioral skills required to act effectively determines how likely they will be to act favorably (e.g., initiate and maintain regular mammography). IMB serves as a theoretical guide for the adoption of an adapted model, which improves upon classic navigation. The *Navigation-Information-Motivation-Behavioral* (NIMB) Model asserts that, in combination with "barrier reduction" patient navigation techniques, problem-solving, information, motivation, and behavioral skills are the fundamental determinants of behavior (e.g., getting screened). Figure 4.2 shows the proposed adaptations to the traditional IMB model. This figure

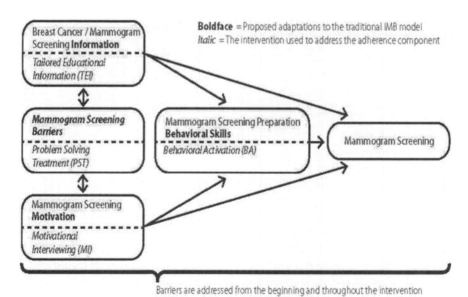

Figure 4.2.   Navigation-Information-Motivation-Behavioral Model
created by authors

illustrates the interrelationships among the relevant NIMB constructs and operations used to translate into an evidence-based mammography intervention. So, for an unscreened woman, "barrier-reduction" navigation activities, combined with problem-solving, might be needed first (and throughout) to address the daily stressors, practical issues, and circumstances faced among those living in poverty.

Studies support this model, showing that for populations of poverty, meeting basic human needs is perceived as more important than obtaining cancer prevention and screening. For this population, laundromats (Kreuter, Green, Cappella et al., 2007) hair (Sadler, Thomas, Gebrekristos, Dhanjal, & Mugo, 2000) and nail salons (Kim, Linnan, Kulik, Carlisle, Enga, & Bentley, 2007) stand out as promising public places for delivering breast cancer and mammography educational information to low-income and African American women. Thus, information (e.g., relevant research data, health promotion information, preventive or risk details about cancer or mammography behavior, and information on positive outcomes from mammography initiation and maintenance) and motivation (the conscious realization of the importance of mammography and having a positive attitude), along with social support, are potentially independent constructs. This means that well-informed individuals are not necessarily motivated to engage in cancer screening behaviors, and/or motivated individuals are not necessarily well informed about screening practices. In fact, navigators are effective in providing the needed support to dispel fears among women of color about cancer, encourage adherence to screening guidelines, and help women seek appropriate care options. Information and motivation act as tools to develop behavioral activation skill, which is an additional critical determinant of whether people who adopt information and are motivated would be capable of effectively bringing about the expected behavior change.

The translational nature of this proposed model and intervention is best accomplished with stakeholder input and partnerships, which can increase the relevance of research to practice to improve community health. We recommend the first phase of our proposed intervention would start with the use of formative research (i.e., focus groups with a patient navigator provider group and interviews with unscreened women) to "give voice" to inform research questions, practice needs, and the adaptation of the NIMB intervention. As a result, this phase would provide a sound foundation for bolstering the translation strategy. At the higher end of this stakeholder engagement continuum, we propose creating a formal partnership with organizations that would ultimately implement the NIMB intervention (e.g., hair and nail salons, churches, laundromats). In future studies, the use of peer community health navigators (CHNs) who are cancer survivors or women of color who have had a personal experience with cancer and are familiar with the St. Louis community, might have an additional benefit in that navigators will be able to identify with the issue and eliminate some of the trust issues that exist for this population.

The use of evidence-based clinical interventions within a community-engaged research (CEnR) context is a "paradigm shift" from traditional models of cancer prevention and control. Navigation services would not be embedded or constrained within an existing paradigm of a traditional clinical healthcare system, which would fill a substantial gap in our knowledge of how interventions make it into the "real-world" CEnR and practice. Additionally, the qualitative phases used in the formative phase of such a project would "give voice" to the intervention model.

Traditional navigation interventions that address personal psychosocial and systems barriers need to be coupled with other relevant evidence-based intervention techniques (i.e., PST, TEI, MI, BA) to improve breast cancer mammogram initiation and maintenance in non-adherent populations. We propose a model that expands and adapts traditional navigation to include systematic, evidence-based interventions within the context of CEnR, which are needed to help reduce cancer disparities among low-income women of color. This model can help enhance our understanding of mammography screening adherence and provide a theoretical foundation for the development of future tailored public health interventions for this population.

NOTE

1. We would like to thank and give credit to Matthew Kreuter, PhD, PI of parent study—Integrating cancer control referrals and navigators into United Way 2-1-1 (NCI Center for Excellence in Cancer Communication Research [CECCR]). This larger study provided the foundation from which sub-study research and case examples were created for this volume.

Downtown St. Louis City
photo by Nikisha Bridges

Chapter Five

Poverty and Public Health

. . . Poverty is a health issue.

—Colorado Center on Law and Policy, 2018

As cancer disparities continue to persist for low-income and women of color, the promotion and attainment of health equity becomes a matter of paramount importance. Historical inequality in socioenvironmental settings have contributed to marked health disparities. Addressing these causes and contributors to women's health disparities is a complex process that requires intervention from a socioecological framework, at micro-, meso-, and macro-levels of influence. For prevention and intervention initiatives to decrease disparities at the population level, multilevel factors must be accounted for and addressed. *Poverty and Place: Cancer Prevention among Low Income Women of Color,* examines ways in which cancer health disparities exist due to class and context inequities even in the most advanced society of the world. This volume, while articulating health disparities in the St. Louis metropolitan area, seeks to move beyond deficit models to focus on health equity. As Braveman (2014) noted "health equity means social justice in health (no one is denied the possibility to be healthy for belonging to a group that has historically been economically/socially disadvantaged). Health disparities are the metric we use to measure progress toward achieving health equity. A reduction in health disparities (in absolute and relative terms) is evidence that we are moving toward greater health equity)" (p. 3).

This concluding chapter provides a summary analysis of the preceding chapters of *Poverty and Place.* In addition, we have offered commentary on future research in the area and a discussion of broader national policy considerations.

As the volume unfolded, we began to understand that health inequities affected not only physical health, but affects and is affected by broader micro
and macro environments including public policy or the lack thereof and the
intergenerational transfer of a host of social, political and economic determinants. Such influences both conditioned and shaped psychological states
and subsequent physiological stress reactions through the social isolation
engendered. These issues caused women to retreat into their homes, limit interaction, and increase feelings of loneliness and hopelessness. Efforts to deal
with environmental threats depleted women's physical and psychological
resources over time. Recognizing that health care costs continued to increase
along with the diversity in our society, the volume discussed a multitude of
factors that facilitated or posed barriers to cancer treatment and adherence
in a population drawn from the St. Louis metropolitan area, including North
City St. Louis, Missouri and the river city of East St. Louis, Illinois. We saw,
undeniably, that one's health affects, and is affected by everything.

Chapter 1 provided insights on the ground-level through an exploration
of the history, prevalence, and the influences of the social determinants of
health, utilizing GIS and illustrations of the neighborhoods in North St.
Louis City, Missouri, and East St. Louis, Illinois. We delved deeper into
the depths of cancer disparities in these communities and among women.
In the case of the greater St. Louis community, the social determinants that
negatively affected health outcomes stemmed from poverty and degraded
socioenvironmental conditions. Policies that supported the movement of
White families from urban centers into suburban areas, coupled with housing discrimination against African Americans were instrumental in the in-
tentional racial segregation of St. Louis as the policies helped determine the
stratification of the St. Louis population by race and by income (Gordon,
2009; Phillips, 2016).

Chapter 2 provided an introduction to the St. Louis Metropolitan area,
through a rich discussion of the range of social determinants of health (poor
nutrition, deteriorated infrastructure, crime, unstable housing, low education,
unemployment, racism, etc.). In this chapter, we gained an understanding
of how social determinants were inextricably linked to health and we saw
that health was and is created by the conditions of our society and environment. We gained an understanding that most of what makes us healthy occurs outside of a hospital or a physician's office. Geospatial (GIS) mapping
and testimonials demonstrated ways in which this region exemplifies highly
segregated urban and decaying suburban communities of color with known
cancer disparities. Through original research, the volume explored the local neighborhood effects and community impact on lifestyle decisions to
illuminate the issues faced by those engaged in cancer prevention among

low income women of color. Some of the most profound concerns included homelessness, residential segregation and housing quality, disinvestment in neighborhoods and communities, access to and provision of adequate and appropriate healthcare, lack of civic engagement, underachievement of schools, unemployment, environmental hazards, curtailment of social welfare programs, and under-resourced public services.

Chapter 3 provided an overview of the social and cultural attitudes and concerns raised by residential segregation, poverty, and low income as they related to low adherence to health recommendations, particularly cancer screening. The volume also shed light on the impactful and influential role of the social determinants of health on health disparities (WHO Commission on Social Determinants of Health, & World Health Organization 2008). As stated previously, the World Health Organization defines the social determinants of health as the conditions in which people "are born, grow, live, work, and age" (WHO Commission on Social Determinants of Health, & World Health Organization, 2008). The complex ways that macro level social determinants (WHO Commission on Social Determinants of Health, & World Health Organization 2008) combine with social and cultural attitudes (Napier, Ancarno, Butler Calabrese, Chater, & Chatterjee, 2014) to affect cancer prevention behaviors in low-income communities were discussed.

We noted the recognition of and efforts to call attention to how mistrust of the healthcare system affects health behavior (LaVeist et al., 2000; Kurz & Scharff, 2003), as well as the ways culture affects what and how we discuss health issues (Thompson et al., 2015). We also highlighted the variable influence that religion can have on cancer screening, HPV vaccination and other health behaviors (Thompson Sanders et al., 2010; Thompson Sanders et al., 2012; Thompson Sanders et al., 2014). The Missouri MICA system, indicated that in 2011, 25.90% of residents of St. Louis indicated that they had engaged in no leisure time physical activity (DHSS-MOPHIMS Community Data Profiles, 2017), providing an example of a regional health disparity relevant to cancer. The negative impact of living in a poor, segregated community was addressed. Lack of access to supermarkets and grocery stores (Golan et al., 2008; Diez Roux & Mair, 2010), parks and other safe and walkable spaces for physical activity were discussed as barriers to the ability to integrate a cancer prevention lifestyle (Diez Roux & Mair, 2010). We noted differences in tobacco use among women that may be associated with experiences of discrimination and stress (Jesse et al., 2006; Webb & Carey, 2008; Nguyen et al., 2010) and advertising in low-income and racial/ ethnic communities (NCI, 2017) targeted for use of a product that is known to contribute significantly to cancer incidence and mortality. Provider and navigator quotes discussed the impact that differences in the location of healthcare services, the concentration of providers and high quality services have on efforts to promote and coordinate cancer screening among low-income, racial/ethnic minority women.

Findings confirmed that overall rates of physical activity and healthy eating are lower among individuals who are low-income and less well educated, as well as racial/ethnic minorities who are more likely to experience residential segregation, poverty and low-income (Golan, et al., 2008; Diez Roux & Mair, 2010). In addition, the rates of smoking and difficulties quitting were higher in these communities (Jamal, et al., 2016). And, barriers remained for the implementation of one of the most important strategies for addressing disparities in cancer mortality, screening. The barriers to screening highlighted issues of equity that are central to the issues raised in this volume.

Findings also indicated that the sustainable adoption of the proposed adapted NIMB model would also require information exchange between care providers and routine monitoring of patient adherence. We need to focus on developing and disseminating evidence-based strategies to meet the social and health needs of poor women in ways that do not undermine their sense of autonomy and control that is important to their overall sense of well-being. Such strategies require an understanding of evidence-based intervention dissemination and implementation, which includes a longitudinal perspective that takes into consideration the dynamic relationships between patients and providers and between providers in the safety net care systems in the community. These public sector care and community settings are increasingly the provider of preventive care, and for underserved patients, neighborhoods and community settings as the preferred venues. We found that accessibility induced less stigmatization while building more trust in tandem with systematic assessment and treatment. However, it is important to remember that specific patient and provider preferences, cultural perceptions, and socioeconomic factors often facilitated or impeded adoption and sustainability. Health care providers need to draw on the knowledge and resources of vulnerable communities to choose interventions that best match the experiences of their own community members, demonstrating respect that will lead to greater trust of medical providers and improve treatment adherence. A holistic orientation naturally makes the connection between prevention and intervention from the individual to the community populations, combining the dual aims of promoting health and conducting multilevel research interventions that address these multiple barriers and determinants.

In chapter 4 we gained an understanding of the discrete barriers and stressors that influenced screening and strategies that helped reduce these barriers, within a theoretical context. We looked at multiple models that included both clinical, local grassroots, organizational and community levels of influence to address adherence. We understand that solutions are not created within the health sector, alone, but rather in environments in which women live. We began to look at various theoretical models as a framework, which could be used to address health equity. We saw profound public health implications for determining the barriers for these groups in adhering to preventive cancer recommendations and developing effective interventions and strategies that providers can use to improve uptake and adherence.

In addition, we presented five exemplary cases used to illustrate economically poor women's perspectives on cancer screening and the stressors involved with adherence. We acknowledge that these conditions contribute to the increasing gaps in health status between rich and poor, and white and non-White in this region. However it is important to also acknowledge unique stressors in urban areas of poverty. We do not dismiss the positive assets, skills, strengths and resources in these communities. These communities proved to be knowledgeable and committed to the wellbeing of their community members. As has been illustrated, there are rich resources through hundreds of faith-based organizations in this region, strong supportive networks (e.g. Harris-Stowe University), engaged community members and organizations (e.g. Jackie Joyner-Kersee Foundation), among others. Based on our research, what is needed is a comprehensive model to strengthen existing community resources. We do not want to constantly focus on deficits and look at these communities from a deficit perspective, but rather recognize that such communities possess unique strengths to promote health and well-being.

In *Poverty and Place*, we have highlighted critical aspects of a practical multidimensional model of community engagement. We discussed important influences of the various levels of research, policy and practice. But more pointedly, we support a new model of community engagement that focuses on individuals in the broader ecological context, and includes community education, clinical care, community outreach, community service, research, policy and advocacy (Ahmed, Young, DeFino, Franco, & Nelson, 2017). We feel this model helps to advance the art and science of community engagement and collaboration. No longer can we narrowly focus on individual behavior change with less attention to the broader contextual social and structural determinants of health and well-being. By taking a broader perspective, we seek to address some of the limitations over time, while also maintaining and sustaining community engagement and partnerships. We no longer accept the 'parachute' model of research, policy and practice, that reinforces and sustains the problems associated with the status quo.

BROADER POLICY CONSIDERATIONS

Overcoming racial/ethnic and socioeconomic disparities in cancer requires an equity lens. Given differences in history and demographics, state and local health departments will need to establish data collection and analysis standards that permit monitoring of all people, including those who are members of populations with high disparities or live in regions of high disparity. More importantly, jurisdictions must monitor programs and services for equitable outcomes across demographic categories. Substandard and inconsistent data collection across states, as evidenced in East St. Louis, Illinois, poses yet another barrier to creating effective and data-driven approaches to decrease disparities and increase health equity among low income and ethnic minority women.

There is also a need to consider how policy decisions will impact equity in cancer outcomes, as well as health equity broadly. For example, access to cancer screenings (mammography, cervical, colorectal) is affected by legislative decisions on Medicaid expansion, funding for programs such as the National Breast and Cervical Cancer Early Detection Program (NBCCEDP) and provider reimbursement rates for cancer screening. Funded by the CDC and partner organizations, NBCCEDP provides free breast and cervical cancer screenings for women meeting certain age, income and insurance guidelines. Women who have employer based, federal or state market place or Medicaid insurance are generally ineligible for screening through the program. However, states vary in funding and how extensively they advertise the program and their eligibility. In Missouri, approximately 101,000 Missouri women are eligible for NBCCEDP services, but the program serves only about 8.5% of the eligible population due to funding levels. (Small Area Health Insurance Estimates (SAHIE), 2018). Medicaid expansion reduces the need for NBCCEDP, but many working women fail to qualify for Medicaid and cannot afford employer based or market place insurance making availability and knowledge of availability important. Provider reimbursement rates in state Medicaid programs might stimulate greater participation and thereby access to services for poor and minority women.

Navigator and lay health worker services are important in assisting less well educated, low literacy and low health literacy women to obtain cancer screenings, adhere to cancer screening guidelines and in managing treatment if diagnosed with cancer. Although there is evidence for the use of navigator and lay health workers to support preventive behavior and treatment adherence, these services are not uniformly performed or reimbursed.

Future Research Directions

The authors of *Poverty and Place* envision expanding this work to other important behavioral and disease-specific illness domains outside of cancer (e.g.,

HIV/AIDs anti-retroviral medications, hormonal contraceptive medications, diabetes regimen, heart disease medication), where adherence can also be a problem (Wells, Thompson, Yeakey, Ross, & Notaro, forthcoming). This future research will provide the necessary knowledge to draw on (i.e., disseminating and implementing a longer-term clinical adherence intervention for patient navigators and other healthcare providers working in community settings). Our future work will not only make a significant contribution to the field of adherence research in the cancer prevention and control arena, particularly in providing a better understanding of how to improve low-income and minority population clinical trials, cancer screening, and other preventive health activities. Our broader focus is toward the improvement of health equity.

We must begin to translate evidence-based adherence strategies and interventions into routine cancer care for providers in safety net care systems and in the community. We need future research not only in St. Louis metropolitan community-based settings, but in other neighborhood and community environments with similar social, economic and political trajectories. Strategies should address the psychosocial needs and barriers of non-adherent low-income minorities, their providers, and within organizational systems that lead to intervention adaptations in safety net care systems and in the communities that serve them.

One strategy that *Healthy People 2020* recognizes is the importance of health communication strategies and information technology to improve health outcomes and achieve health equity ("Healthy People," 2010). It emphasizes *health literacy* as a tool for decreasing disparities (Riley, Dodd, Muller, Guo, & Logan, 2012) by fostering balanced patient and provider communication (Augustus et al., 2009). Achieving health literacy in complex healthcare environments requires that patients are armed with accurate, accessible information that they can understand, a criterion least often met for those who are poor and uneducated (Bowen et al., 2006). People with limited health literacy generally have lower medication adherence rates, higher hospitalization rates, and poorer health outcomes (Karten, 2007). Although online websites have become important sources of healthcare information, low health literacy may impede their full utilization (Donelle & Hoffman-Goetz, 2006). Narrative forms of communication—including entertainment education, literature, testimonials, and storytelling—are also emerging as important tools for communicating information about cancer. Communication-based interventions are essential for improving cancer patients' ability to understand information during medical visits, resulting in improved treatment adherence (Parker et al., 2005).

Given the social ecology of health and health care, interdisciplinary and transdisciplinary providers are needed, who are particularly sensitive to broader social contexts not only in the assessment of problems, but in the complex diagnosis of solutions. Taking a multi-level approach to understanding health inequity allows us to draw from a menu of interventions that range from the individual to the community levels. These interventions can be used separately or in combination to tailor treatment approaches to the needs of individuals.

For many years, oncology and other health care providers focused on the individual-level utilizing intrapersonal treatment modalities focused on treatment of and coping with disease. Far too often, group, neighborhood, or community-level interventions were excluded. More recently, we have begun to shape agendas by participating in intervention research and advocacy for policy change, including policies to shift public funding from cancer treatment to cancer prevention. We are beginning to see the value in expanding interventions into communities.

Moreover, research is needed in the development, implementation and sustainability of successful interventions. Most psychotherapeutic interventions were primarily developed for and evaluated with middle-class White populations (Alvidrez et al., 1996). Culturally-sensitive adaptations of existing treatment models for low-income and ethnic minority groups are needed (Castro-Blanco, 2005). Effectiveness may vary by persons and setting, based on differences in social context (Nezu, Nezu, Friedman, Fadis, & Houts, 1998). Interventions can be tailored by skillfully blending strategies according to specific settings and situations (Maliski et al., 2004).

While not all providers are in positions to develop and test new treatment modalities, they can work together to pool resources to enhance research findings. Even if providers are unable to participate in these efforts, all involved must have accessible, relevant information on current evidence-based prevention and treatment approaches for use with racial/ethnic minority and lower socioeconomic populations. There is dire need to draw upon knowledge and resources of vulnerable communities to choose interventions, for which evidence is available, that provides the best match with the experiences and needs of their own community members. The key is to establish long-lasting relationships between academics and community stakeholders, which should become a natural enterprise, a natural partnership. The payoff is prevention and treatment approaches that have markedly greater chances of improving the lives of low income women with cancer, their social networks, and communities, no matter where they may live.

The Erosion of the Social Safety Net: Toward Broader National Policy Considerations

We the authors of *Poverty and Place* would be remiss if we did not mention the national context in which health policy and practice take place. As the title of this chapter indicates, we argue that poverty is a health issue.

We define poverty as economic insecurity, that is, the scarcity of material resources, the complete lack of means necessary to meet basic human needs such as food, clothing, shelter and protection. A recent report from the Office of the High Commission for Human Rights at the United Nations (2018), authored by Philip Alston, the Special Rapporteur, found that U.S. President Donald Trump and his policies have mounted a systematic attack on welfare programs leaving millions deprived of food, shelter and health care. The UN Report endeavored to explain the intransigence of poverty, class and racial disparities and their institutionalization across American society. In sum, the U.S. economy is delivering better living standards for only the few. Household incomes are stagnating, job opportunities are deteriorating, prospects for upward mobility are waning and economic gains are increasingly accruing to those that are already wealthy. Researchers (Yeakey et al., 2012) have called the erosion of the American Dream, 'the downward slope of upward mobility, ' as low wage workers, 'run in place,' (Yeakey et al., 2014), with little hope for social mobility and economic advance. While inequality has always been a part of American society, today, that inequality not only persists but is growing. A few signs of America's glaring inequalities, as articulated in the UN Report, bear repeating: the U.S. has the highest rate of income inequality in the industrialized West; American's live shorter and sicker lives than citizens of other rich democracies; tropical diseases which flourish in conditions of poverty are now on the rise; the US incarceration rate remains the highest in the world; voter registration levels are among the lowest in industrialized nations; and, among the thirty five member countries of the Organization for Economic Co-operation and Development (OECD) countries, the United States has the highest youth poverty rates. Given the powerful influence of the intergenerational transfer of poverty, having such large youth poverty rates in the U.S. will have devastating impacts on our country, socially, politically and economically in the years ahead. The Federal Reserve's recent annual economic survey (2017) provides further evidence of growing inequality and economic insecurity in American society. The Federal Reserve found that four out of 10 Americans are so poor that they could not cover an emergency expense of $400 without borrowing money or selling possessions. What is so disturbing is that President Trump, rather than taking measures to address the problem of inequality, seeks to define poverty out of existence, and in so doing, aggravates the problem of poverty through regressive policies.

Among the measures pursued by the Trump administration which seek to aggravate the problem of poverty are the following:

- Passage of the $1.5 trillion tax bill which slashes tax rates for corporations and the wealthy, while simultaneously instituting across the board reductions for Medicaid, the Supplemental Nutrition Assistant Program (SNAP) and housing assistance programs. As President Trump seeks to obliterate the Affordable Care Act and its Medicaid expansion, the Trump administration has rolled out a growing list of restrictions that will only serve to remove the poor from public assistance, creating an even poorer subclass of the poor.

- In addition to the tax breaks, there are new work requirements for welfare recipients, cuts up to a third in the food stamp program, recent proposals to triple the base rent for federally subsidized housing, and other government regulations that offered protections to middle class and poor families.
- Understanding our broader theoretical focus on the social ecology of public health, the Trump administration's deregulation of more than seventy six environmental rules and policies will impact the poorest Americans, first (Popovich, 2017). Harvard University scientists, using an extremely conservative estimate, project that such deregulation will cause respiratory problems for more than a million people, per decade, many of them poor children (Chen, 2018).
- The Trump administration's policies support and sustain structural racism that keep large percentages of non-Whites in poverty or near poverty as a result of enduring discrimination in housing, health care, education, civil rights, judicial processes, criminal justice, employment, and the persistently consequential racial disparities in wages. Nowhere is this strategy more clear than in the Department of Education and the Department of Housing and Urban Development and their steady march toward narrowing their approach to racial discrimination and civil rights enforcement.

No one will be left out of the intended and unintended consequences of the foregoing policies. Middle Americans and even wealthy Americans will not escape or be immune to the byproducts of such regressive policies, since the loss of social protections and their social costs will bode ill for them and society as a whole.

It bears repeating that poverty is a health issue because it erodes the social, political and economic support systems that enhance well-being and healthy life styles necessary for human development and human betterment. While the authors of *Poverty and Place* prescribe no magic potion for the elimination of poverty and health inequities, we can agree that such a recipe must begin with the acknowledgement that poverty and economic insecurity are problems for over 40 million Americans. The next step comes with the political will and commitment, among our elected representatives, to treat our fellow citizens as though we are all humans, deserving of respect and dignity to pursue our dreams. The culmination of the foregoing is the political courage to fight for the passage of a broad set of policies designed to eliminate economic insecurity and the poverty related manifestations that encompass that insecurity. The prescient words of former U.S. President Barack Hussein Obama in his Nobel lecture (2009), captures summarily the intent of our text, *Poverty and Place*:

> . . . *a just peace includes not only civil and political rights—it must encompass economic security and opportunity. For true peace is not just freedom from fear, but freedom from want. It is undoubtedly true that development rarely takes root without security; it is also true that security does not exist where human beings do not have access to enough food, or clean water, or the medicine and shelter they need to survive. It does not exist where children can't aspire to a decent education or a job that supports a family. The absence of hope can rot a society from within.*

References

Adler, N. T., Boyce, M. A., Chesney, M., Cohen, S., Folkman, S., Kahn R. L., & Syme, S. L. (1994). Socioeconomic status and health: the challenge of the gradient. *American Psychologist, 49*, 15–24.

Aggarwal, A., Pandurangi, A., & Smith, W. (2013). Disparities in breast and cervical cancer screening in women with mental illness: A systematic literature review. *American Journal of Preventive Medicine, 44*(4), 392–398.

Augustus, J., Kwan, L., Fink, A., Connor, S., Maliski, S., & Litwin, M. (2009). Education as a predictor of quality of life outcomes among disadvantaged men. *Prostate Cancer and Prostatic Diseases, 12* (3): 253–8.

Ahmed, S. M., Young, S. N., DeFino, M. C., Franco, Z. & Nelson, D. A. (2017). Towards a practical model for community engagement: Advancing the art and science in academic health centers. *Journal of Clinical and Translational Science.* I, pp. 310–315. doi: 10:1017/cts.2017.304

Ainsworth, B. E., Wilcox, S., Thompson, W. W., Richter, D. L., & Henderson, K. A. (2003). Personal, social, and physical environmental correlates of physical activity in African-American women in South Carolina. *American Journal of Preventive Medicine, 25*(3), 23–29.

Allen, J. D., Othus, M. K. D., Shelton, R. C., Li, Y., Norman, N., Tom, L., & del Carmen, M. G. (2010). Parental decision making about the HPV vaccine. *Cancer Epidemiology, Biomarkers & Prevention, 19*(9), 2187–2198.

Allen, J. D., Shelton R. C., Harden, E., & Goldman R. E. (2008). Follow-up of abnormal screening mammograms among low-income ethnically diverse women: Findings from a qualitative study. *Patient Education and Counseling, 72*(2), 283–292. https://doi.org/10.1016/j.pec.2008.03.024

Alston, Philip, Special Rapporteur. (2018). *Report of the Special Rapporteur on Extreme Poverty and Human Rights on His Mission to the United States of America.* Geneva, Switzerland: Offices of High Commission for Human Rights (OHCHR), United Nations.

Alvidrez, J., & Arean, P. (2002). Psychosocial treatment research with ethnic minority populations: Ethical considerations in conducting clinical trials. *Ethics & Behavior, 12*(1), 103–116.

Alvidrez, J., Azocar, F., & Miranda, J. (1996). Demystifying the concept of ethnicity for psychotherapy researchers. *Journal of Consulting and Clinical Psychology, 64*(5), 903–908.

American Cancer Society (ACS). (2013). *Cancer Facts & Figures for African Americans 2013–2014.* Retrieved from http://www.cancer.org/acs/groups/content/@ epidemiologysurveilance/documents/document/acspc-036921.pdf

American Cancer Society. (2014). *Cancer facts & figures for African Americans, 2013–014.* Retrieved from https://www.cancer.org/research/cancer-facts-statistics/ all-cancer-facts-figures.html

American Cancer Society. (2015). *Cancer facts & figures for African Americans, 2012–2014.* Retrieved from https://www.cancer.org/research/cancer-facts-statis tics/all-cancer-facts-figures.html

American Cancer Society. (2015). Cancer facts and figures for African Americans 2012–2014. *American Cancer Society: Cancer Facts and Figures.* Retrieved from http://www.cancer.org/acs/groups/content/@epidemiologysurveilance/documents/ document/acspc-036921.pdf

American Cancer Society. (2016). *Cancer facts & figures for African Americans, 2015.* Retrieved from https://www.cancer.org/research/cancer-facts-statistics/all -cancer-facts-figures.html

American Cancer Society. (2017). *Cancer facts & figures for African Americans, 2016.* Retrieved from https://www.cancer.org/research/cancer-facts-statistics/all -cancer-facts-figures.html

Amico, R. (2011). A situated-Information Motivation Behavioral Skills Model of Care Initiation and Maintenance (sIMB-CIM): An IMB model-based approach to understanding and intervening in engagement in care for chronic medical conditions. *Journal of Health Psychology, 16*(7), 1071–1081. https://doi .org/10.1177/1359105311398727.

Andersen, R. M., & Newman, J. F. (2005). Societal and individual determinants of medical care utilization in the United States. *Milbank Quarterly, 83*(4), 1–28.

Anderson, E., Wagstaff, D. A., Heckman, T. G., Winett, R. A., Roffman, R. A., Solomon, L. J., . . . Sikkema, K. J. (2006). Information-Motivation-Behavioral Skills (IMB) Model: Testing direct and mediated treatment effects on condom use among women in low-income housing. *Annals of Behavioral Medicine, 31*(1), 70–79. https://doi.org/10.1207/s15324796abm3101_11

Bailey, R. K., Geyen, D.J., Scott-Gurnell, K., Hipolito, M.M.S., Bailey, T.A., & Beal, J.M. (2005). Understanding and treating depression among cancer patients. *International Journal of Gynecological Cancer, 15*, 203–208.

Baker, E., Kelly, C., Barnidge, E., Strayhorn, J., Schootman, M., Struthers, J., & Griffith, D., (2006). The garden of Eden: Acknowledging the impact of race and class in efforts to decrease obesity rates. *Community Matters in Healthy Aging, 97*(7), 1170–1174.

Bandura, A. (1977). Self-efficacy: Toward a unifying theory of behavioral change. *Psychological Review, 84*(2), 191–215.

Bandura, A. (1986). *Social foundations of thought and action.* Englewood Cliffs, NJ: Prentice Hall.

Banks, K. H., & Sanders Thompson, V. L. (2016). Psychic pain: Residents, protesters, police and community. In Kimberly J. Norwood (Ed.) *Ferguson's fault lines: The race quake that rocked a nation.* Chicago, IL: American Bar Association.

Beavis, A. L., Gravitt, P. E., & Rositch, A. F. (2017). Hysterectomy-corrected cervical cancer mortality rates reveal a larger racial disparity in the United States. *Cancer, 123*(6), 1044–1050.

Bendik, M. K., Mayo, R. M., & Parker, V. G. (2011). Knowledge, perceptions, and motivations related to HPV vaccination among college women. *Journal of Cancer Education, 26*(3), 459–464.

Berkman, N. D., Sheridan, S. L., Donahue, K. E., Halpern, D. J., Crotty, K. (2011). Low health literacy and health outcomes: An updated systematic review. *Annals of Internal Medicine, 155*(2), 97–107.

Bernal, M. W., & Castro, F. G. (1994). Are clinical psychologists prepared for service and research with ethnic minorities? Report of a decade of progress. *American Psychologist, 49*, 797–805.

Block, G., Wakimoto, P., Metz, D., Fujii, M., Feldman, N., Mandel, R., & Sutherland, B. (2004). A randomized trial of the *Little by Little* CD-ROM: Demonstrated effectiveness in increasing fruits and vegetable intake in a low-income population. *Preventing Chronic Disease, 1*(3), 1–12.

Blumer, H. (1954). What is wrong with social theory? *American Sociological Review, 19*(1), 1–10.

Board of Governors of the Federal Reserve System. (2017). Changes in U.S. Family Finances from 2013 to 2016: Evidence from the Survey of Consumer Finances. https://www.federalreserve.gov/publications/files/scf17.pdf. Last accessed September 28, 2017.

Boehner, C. W., Howe, S. R., Bernstein, D. I., & Rosenthal, S. L. (2003). Viral sexually transmitted disease vaccine acceptability among college students. *Sexually Transmitted Diseases, 30*(10), 774–778.

Bosch, F. X., Lorincz, A., Munoz, N., Meijer, C. J., & Shah, K. V. (2002). The causal relation between human papillomavirus and cervical cancer. *Journal of Clinical Pathology, 55*, 244–265.

Bosch, F. X., & de Sanjosé, S. (2003). Human papillomavirus and cervical cancer—burden and assessment of causality. *JNCI Monographs, 2003*(31), 3–13.

Boscoe, F. P., Johnson, C. J., Sherman, R. L., Stinchcomb, D. G., Lin, G., & Henry, K. A. (2014). The relationship between area poverty rate and site-specific cancer incidence in the United States. *Cancer, 120*(14), 2191–2198.

Braveman, P. (2014). What Are Health Disparities and Equity? We Need to Be Clear. *Public Health Reports, 129* (Suppl 2), 5–8.

Brawley, L. R., & Culos-Reed, S. N. (2000). Studying adherence to therapeutic regimens overview, theories, recommendations. *Controlled Clinical Trials, 21*(5), S156-S163.

Bronfenbrenner, U. (1995). Developmental ecology through space and time: A future perspective. In P. Moen & G. H. Elder, Jr., (Eds.), *Examining lives in context: Perspectives on the ecology of human development* (pp. 619–647). Washington, DC: American Psychological Association.

Brown, D. R., & Topcu, M. (2003). Willingness to participate in clinical treatment research among older African Americans and Whites. *The Gerontologist 43*(1), 62–72.

Bruno, D. M., Wilson, T. E., Gany, F., & Aragones, A. (2014). Identifying human papillomavirus vaccination practices among primary care providers of minority, low-income and immigrant patient populations. *Vaccine, 32*(33), 4149–4154.

Budrys, G. (2010). *Unequal health: How inequality contributes to health or illness.* Lanham, MD: Rowman & Littlefield Publishers.

The California Endowment. *Building Healthy Communities.* Retrieved from: www .calendow.org/building-healthy-communities/

Camp Yeakey, C., Sanders Thompson, V. L., & Wells, A. (2014). The epilogue: Confronting the dilemmas twenty-first-century urban living in global contexts. In C. Camp -Yeakey, V.L. Thompson-Sanders Thompson & A. Wells (Eds.), *Urban ills: Twenty-first-century complexities of urban living in global contexts* (Vol. 1.; pp. 331–340; Vol 2). Lanham, MD: Lexington Books.

Carroll, J. K., Humiston, S. G., Meldrum, S. C., Salamone, C. M., Jean-Pierre, P., & Epstein, R. M. (2010). Patients' experiences with navigation for cancer care. *Patient Education and Counseling, 80*(2), 241–247. https://doi.org/10.1016/j .pec.2009.10.024

Carter-Pokras, O., & Baquet, C. (2002). What is a "health disparity." *Public Health Reports, 117*(5), 426–433.

Cassall, C. (2008). Template analysis. *The SAGE dictionary of qualitative management.* https://doi.org/10.4135/9780857020109

Castro-Blanco, D. R. (2005). Cultural Sensitivity in Conventional Psychotherapy: A comment On Martínez-Taboas. *Psychotherapy Theory, Research, Practice, Training, 42*(1), 14–16.

Census Bureau. (2018). Small Area Health Insurance Estimates: 2016. https://www .census.gov/content/dam/Census/library/publication/2018/.../p30-03.pdf. Accessed August 21, 2018.

Centers for Disease Control and Prevention (CDC). (2010). FDA licensure of bivalent human papillomavirus vaccine (HPV2, Cervix) for use in females and updated HPV vaccination recommendations from the Advisory Committee on Immunization Practices (ACIP). *Morbidity and Mortality Weekly Report, 59*(20), 626.

Centers for Disease Control and Prevention (CDC). (2011). Recommendations on the use of quadrivalent human papillomavirus vaccine in males—Advisory Committee on Immunization Practices (ACIP), 2011. *Morbidity and Mortality Weekly Report, 60*(50), 1705–1708.

Centers for Disease Control and Prevention (CDC) (2014). Human papillomavirus (HPV)-associated cancers. *Cancer Prevention and Control: Cancer Data and Statistics.* Retrieved from http://www.cdc.gov/cancer/hpv/statistics/cases.html

Centers for Disease Control and Prevention (CDC) (2014). HPV-associated cancers rates by race and ethnicity. Retrieved from https://www.cdc.gov/cancer/hpv/statis tics/race.htm

Centers for Disease Control and Prevention (CDC), Division of Behavioral Risk Factor Surveillance System (BRFSS). (2015). 2014 Missouri Behavioral Risk Factor Surveillance System key findings. Missouri Department of Health and Senior Services. Office of Epidemiology http://health.mo.gov/data/brfss/2014_BRFSS_Key_Findings_Report.pdf

Center for Disease Control and Prevention. (2015). Global Cancer Statistics. *Cancer Prevention and Control*: *Cancer Data and Statistics*. Retrieved from http://www.cdc.gov/cancer/international/statistics.html

Centers for Disease Control and Prevention (CDC), National Center for Health Statistics. (2015). National Health Interview Survey, 1987–2015. Colorectal screening. Retrieve from https://progressreport.cancer.gov/detection/colorectal_cancer#field_healthy_people_202_0_target

Centers for Disease Control and Prevention (CDC). (2015). United States Cancer Statistics: Data Visualizations. Retrieved from: https://gis.cdc.gov/cancer/USCS/DataViz.html. Accessed August 26, 2018.

Centers for Disease Control and Prevention. (2016). Health Disparities in Cancer. *Cancer Prevention and Control*: *Resources to Share*. Retrieved from http://www.cdc.gov/cancer/dcpc/resources/features/cancerhealthdisparities/

Centers for Disease Control and Prevention. (2017). Health disparities in cancer. *Cancer Prevention and Control*: *Resources to Share*. Retrieved from https://www.cdc.gov/cancer/dcpc/resources/features/cancerhealthdisparities/index.htm

Centers for Disease Control and Prevention. (2017). Rates of cervical cancer by state, 2014. Retrieved from https://www.cdc.gov/cancer/cervical/statistics/state.htm

Centers for Disease Control (CDC). (2017). Quick facts colorectal cancer (CRC) screening in Missouri. Retrieved from https://www.cdc.gov/cancer/ncccp/screening-rates/pdf/colorectal-cancer-screening-missouri-508.pdf. Accessed December 3, 2018.

Chen, A. (June 14, 2018). Trump's environmental policies could lead to an extra 80,000 deaths per decade. https:/www.theverge.com/2018/6/14/17463430/trump-environmental-policies-public-health-epa. Accessed August 21, 2018.

Chyun, D. A., Amend, A. M., Newlin, K., Langerman, S., & Melkus, G. D. (2003). Coronary heart disease prevention and lifestyle interventions. *The Journal of Cardiovascular Nursing, 18*(4), 302–318.

City-Data. (2016). St. Louis, Missouri. Retrieved from http://www.city-data.com/city/St.-Louis-Missouri.html#b

City-Data. (2017a). St. Louis, Missouri. Retrieved from https://www.citydata.com

City-Data. (2017b). East St. Louis, Illinois. Retrieved from https://www.citydata.com

Cogbill, S. A., Sanders Thompson, V. L., & Deshpande, A. D. (2011). Selected sociocultural correlates of physical activity among African American adults. *Ethnicity & Health, 16*(6), 625–641. https://doi.org/10.1080/13557858.2011.603040

Colorado Center on Law & Policy. (2018).*Colorado Health Equity Report.* Retrieved from: cclpvitalsigns.org/race-place-and-income-in-colorado/

Comparing breast cancer screening rates among different groups. (October 22, 2018). Retrieved from: https://ww5.komen.org/BreastCancer/DisparitiesInBreastCancerScreening.html

Cooper, L. A., Hill, M. N., & Powe, N. R. (2002). Designing and evaluating interventions to eliminate racial and ethnic disparities in health care. *Journal of General Internal Medicine, 17,* 477–486.

Coy, P. (2014). Injustice in Ferguson, long before Michael Brown. *Bloomberg Business Week.* Retrieved from https://www.bloomberg.com/news/articles/2014-08-21/ferguson-economic-political-conditions-fuel-protest-fury

Creswell, J. W., & Maietta, R. C. (2002). Qualitative Research. In D. C. Miller & N. J. Salkind (Eds.), *Handbook of research design and social measurement* (6th ed.). Thousand Oaks: CA: Sage.

CSDH (2008). Closing the gap in a generation: health equity through action on the social determinants of health. Final Report of the Commission on Social Determinants of Health. Geneva, World Health Organization. Retrieved from: http://apps.who.int/iris/bitstream/handle/10665/43943/9789241563703_eng.pdf;jsessionid=BFFF27059691DC8F8BE72908D1ADAA74?sequence=1

Cunningham, P. J., & Tu, H. T. (1997). A changing picture of uncompensated care. *Health Affairs, 16*(4), 167

Daley, E. M., Vamos, C. A., Buhi, E. R., Kolar, S. K., McDermott, R. J., Hernandez, N., & Fuhrmann, H. J. (2010). Influences on human papillomavirus vaccination status among female college students. *Journal of Women's Health, 19*(10), 1885–1891.

Dana, R. H. (2005). *Multicultural assessment: Principles, applications, and examples.* Mahwah, NJ: Lawrence Erlbaum Associates.

Data USA. (2017). St. Louis Missouri. *DataUSA St. Louis Missouri.* Retrieved from: https://datausa.io/profile/geo/st.-louis-mo/?compare=missouri

Delmerico, J., Hyland, A., Celestino, P., Reid, M., & Cummings, K. M. (2014). Patient willingness and barriers to receiving a CT scan for lung cancer screening. *Lung Cancer, 84*(3), 307–309.

DeNavas-Walt, C., & Proctor, B. D. (2014, September). *Income and poverty in the United States: 2013.* (Current Population Reports, P60-252). Retrieved from https://www.census.gov/content/dam/Census/library/publications/2015/demo/p60-252.pdf

Denzin, N. K. (1978). *The research act: A theoretical introduction to sociological methods.* (2nd ed.). New York, NY: McGraw Hill.

Department of Health & Human Services (DHHS), Missouri Public Health Information Management System (MOPHIMS). (2017). Community data profiles: Health and preventive practices Retrieved from https://webapp01.dhss.mo.gov/MOPHIMS/ProfileHome

Derose, K. P., Fox, S. A., Reigadas, E., & Hawes-Dawson, J. (2010). Church-based telephone mammography counseling with peer counselors. *Journal of Health communication, 5*(2), 175–188.

DeSantis, C., Naishadham, D., & Jemal, A. (2013). Cancer statistics for African Americans. 2013. *CA: A Cancer Journal for Clinicians, 63*(3), 151–166. Retrieved from http://onlinelibrary.wiley.com/doi/10.3322/caac.21173/full

DeSantis, C. E., Siegel, R. L., Sauer, A. G., Miller, K. D., Fedewa, S. A., Alcaraz, K. I., & Jemal, A. (2016). Cancer statistics for African Americans, 2016: Progress and opportunities in reducing racial disparities. *CA: A Cancer Journal for Clinicians, 66*(4), 290–308. https://doi.org/10.3322/caac.21340

Diez Roux, A. V., & Mair, C. (2010). Neighborhoods and health. *Annals of the New York Academy of Sciences, 1186*, 125–145.

Donelle, L., Hoffman-Goetz, L., Gatobu, S., & Arocha, J. F. (2009). Comprehension of Internet-based numeric cancer information by older adults. *Informatics for Health and Social Care, 34*(4), 209–224.

Drake, B. F., Abadin, S. S., Lyons, S., Chang, S. H., Steward, L. T., Kraenzle, S., & Goodman, M. S. (2015). Mammograms on-the-go—predictors of repeat visits to mobile mammography vans in St Louis, Missouri, USA: a case–control study. *BMJ open, 5*(3), e006960.

Dunne, E. F., Unger, E. R., Sternberg, M., McQuillan, G., Swan, D. C., Patel, S. S., & Markowitz, L. E. (2007). Prevalence of HPV infection among females in the United States. *Journal of the American Medical Association, 297*(8), 813–819.

Dutta, M. J. (2007). Communicating about culture and health: Theorizing culture-centered and cultural sensitivity approaches. *Communication Theory, 17*(3), 304–328.

Egede, L. E. (2003). Lifestyle modification to improve blood pressure control in individuals with diabetes. *Diabetes Care, 26*(3), 602–607.

Eggleston, K. S., Coker, A. L., Das, I. P., Cordray S. T., & Luchok, K. J. (2007). Understanding barriers for adherence to follow-up care for abnormal pap tests. *Journal of Women's Health, 16*(3), 311–30. https://doi.org/10.1089/jwh.2006.0161.

Elam-Evans, LD, Yankey, D, Jeyarajah, J, Singleton, JA, Curtis, RC, MacNeil, J., . . . Centers for Disease Control and Prevention. (2014). National, regional, state, and selected local area vaccination coverage among adolescents aged 13–17 years—United States, 2013. *Morbidity and Mortality Weekly Report, 63*(29), 625–33.

Ell, K., Katon, W., Xie, B., Lee, P., Kapetanovic, S., Guterman, J., & Chou, C. (2010). Collaborative care management of major depression among low-income, predominantly subjects with diabetes. *American Diabetes Association Diabetes Care, 33*(4), 706–713. https://doi.org/10.2337/dc09-1711

Ell, K., Xie, B., Kapetanovic, S., Quinn, D. I., Lee, P. J., Wells, A., & Chou, C. P. (2011). One-year follow-up of collaborative depression care for low-income, predominantly Hispanic patients with cancer. *Psychiatric Services, 62*(2), 162–170.

Farmer, D., Reddick, B., D'Agostino, R., & Jackson, S. A. (2007). Psychosocial correlates of mammography screening in older African American Women. *Oncology Nursing Forum, 34*(1), 117–123. https://doi.org/10.1188/07.ONF.117–123

Fayanju, O. M., Kraenzle, S., Drake, B. F., Oka, M., & Goodman, M. S. (2014). Perceived barriers to mammography among underserved women in a Breast Health Center Outreach Program. *The American Journal of Surgery, 208*(3), 425–434.

Faulkner, S. L., Baldwin, J. R., Lindsley, S. L., & Hecht, M. L. (2006). Layers of meaning: An analysis of definitions of culture. *Redefining culture: Perspectives across the disciplines*, 27–51.

Felitti, V. J., Anda, R. F., Nordenberg, D., Williamson, D. F., Spitz, A. M., Edwards, V., . . . Koss, M. P. (1998). The relationship of adult health status to childhood abuse and household dysfunction. *American Journal of Preventive Medicine,14*, 245–258.

Ferlay, J., Soerjomataram, I., Ervik, M., Dikshit, R., Eser, S., Mathers, C., . . . Bray, F. (2014). *GLOBOCAN 2012: Cancer incidence and mortality worldwide: IARC CancerBase* (No. 11). Lyon, France: International Agency for Research on Cancer. Retrieved from http://globocan.iarc.fr

Fishbein, M. (Ed.). (1967). *Readings in attitude theory and measurement.* New York, NY: Wiley.

Fishbein, M., & Ajzen, I. (1975). *Belief, attitude, intention, and behavior: An introduction to theory and research.* Reading, MA: Addison-Wesley.

Fisher, J. D., Fisher, W. A., Bryan, A. D., & Misovich, S. J. (2002). Information-motivation-behavioral skills model-based HIV risk behavior change intervention for inner-city high school youth. *Health Psychology, 21*(2), 177–186.

Fisher, J. D., & Fisher, W. (2000). Theoretical approaches to individual-level change in HIV risk behavior. In J. Peterson & R. DiClemente (Eds.), *Handbook of HIV prevention* (pp. 3–55). New York, NY: Plenum.

Fisher, J. D., & Fisher, W. A. (2000). Theoretical approaches to individual level change in HIV risk behavior. Centre for Health, Information and Prevention Documents. Paper 4. Retrieved from http://digitalcommons.uconn.edu/chip_docs/4

Fontaine, K. R., Bartlett, S. J., & Heo, M. (2005). Are health care professionals advising adults with arthritis to become more physically active? *Arthritis and Rheumatism, 53*(2), 279–283.

Franks, P., Winters, P., Tancredi, D., & Fiscella, K. (2011). Do changes in traditional coronary heart disease risk factors over time explain the association between socioeconomic status and coronary heart disease? *BMC Cardiovascular Disorders, 11*(28). Retrieved from https://www.ncbi.nlm.nih.gov/pmc/articles/PMC3130693/

Freeman, H. (1991). Race, poverty, and cancer. *Journal of the National Cancer Institute, 83*(8), 526–527. Retrieved from http://jnci.oxfordjournals.org

Freeman, H., & Chu, K. C. (2005). Determinants of cancer disparities: Barriers to cancer screening, diagnosis, and treatment. *Surgical Oncology Clinics, 14*(4), 655–669.

Gabram, S. G., Lund, M. J. B., Gardner, J., Hatchett, N., Bumpers, H. L., Okoli, J., . . . Brawley, O.W. (2008). Effects of an outreach and internal navigation program on breast cancer diagnosis in an urban cancer center with a large African-American population. *American Cancer Society, 111*(3), 602–7. https://doi.org/10.1002/cncr.23568

Galea, S., Tracy, M., Hoggatt, K. J., DiMaggio, C., & Karpati, A. (2011). Estimated deaths attributable to social factors in the United States. *American Journal of Public Health, 101*(8), 1456–1465.

Gazmararian J., Curran J.W., Parker R., Bernhardt J. M., DeBuono, B. A. (2005). Public Health Literacy in America: An Ethical Imperative. *American Journal of Preventive Medicine, 28*(3): 317–32.

Gerend, M. A., & Barley, J. (2009). Human papillomavirus vaccine acceptability among young adult men. *Sexually Transmitted Diseases, 36*(1), 58–62.

Givens, J. L., Datto, C. J., Ruckdeschel, K., Knott, K., Zubrittsky, C., Oslin, D. W., . . . Barg, F. K. (2006). Older patient's aversion to antidepressants: A qualitative study. *Journal of General Internal Medicine, 21*(2), 146–151.

Glantz, K., Rimer, B. K., & Lewis, F. M. (Eds.). (2002). *Health behavior and health education* (3rd ed). San Francisco, CA: Jossey-Bass.

Glanz, K., & Rimer, B. K. (1997). *Theory at a glance: A guide for health promotion practice* (No. 97). US Dept. of Health and Human Services, Public Health Service, National Institutes of Health, National Cancer Institute.

Glaser, B., & Strauss, A. (1967). *The discovery of grounded theory: Strategies for qualitative research.* New York: Aldine de Gruyter.

Golan, E., Stewart, H., Kuchler, F. & Dong, D. (2008). Can low-income Americans afford a healthy diet? *Amber Waves, 6*(5), 26–33. Retrieved from https://www.ers.usda.gov/amber-waves/2008/november/can-low-income-americans-afford-a-healthy-diet/

Gordon, C. (2009). *Mapping decline: St. Louis and the fate of the American city.* Philadelphia, PA: University of Pennsylvania Press.

Green, L. W., Richard, L., & Potvin, L. (1996). Ecological foundations of health promotion. *American Journal of Health Promotion, 10*(4), 270–281.

Guessous, I., Dash, C., Lapin, P., Doroshenk, M., Smith, R. A., Klabunde, C. N., & National Colorectal Cancer Roundtable Screening Among the 65 Plus Task Group. (2010). Colorectal cancer screening barriers and facilitators in older persons. *Preventive Medicine, 50*(1–2), 3–10.

Haan, M. N., Kaplan, G. A., & Syme, S. L. (1989). Socioeconomic status and health: Old observations and new thoughts. In J. D. Bunker, D. S. Gomby, & B. H. Kehrer (Eds.), *Pathways to Health: The Role of Social Factors* (pp. 76–135). Menlo Park, CA: Henry H. Kaiser Family Foundation.

Haas, J. S., Earle, C. C., Orav, J. E., Brawarsky, P., Keohane, M., Neville, B. A., & Williams, D. R. (2008). Racial segregation and disparities in breast cancer care and mortality. *Cancer, 113*(8), 2166–2172.

Hall, M. (2011). Population change during trying times: Illinois' new demographic reality. *Institute of Government and Public Affairs.* Retrieved from https://igpa.uillinois.edu/sites/igpa.uillinois.edu/files/reports/Illinois_Population_Change_IGPA_0.pdf

Hall, M. B., Carter-Francique, A. R., Lloyd, S. M., Eden, T. M., Zuniga, A. V., Guidry, J. J., & Jones, L. A. (2015). Bias within: Examining the role of cultural competence perceptions in mammography adherence. *SAGE Open, 5*(1), https://doi.org/10.1177/2158244015576547

Hammond, D., Fong, G. T., McDonald, P. W., Cameron, R., & Brown, K. S. (2003). Impact of the graphic Canadian warning labels on adult smoking behavior. *Tobacco Control, 12*, 391–395.

Health Policy Brief. (2011, October 6). Achieving equity in health. *Health Affairs.* Retrieved from http://www.healthaffairs.org/do/10.1377/hpb20111006.957918/full/

Helman, C. G. (2000). *Culture, health and illness* (4th ed.). Oxford, England: Butterworth-Heinemann.

Hendren, S., Griggs, J., Epstein, R., Humiston, S., Rousseau, S., Jean-Pierre, P., & Fiscella, K. (2010). Study protocol: A randomized controlled trial of patient navigation-activation to reduce cancer health disparities. *BioMed Central.* https://doi.org/10.1186/1471-2407-10-551

Henschke, U. K., Leffall Jr, L. D., Mason, C. H., Reinhold, A. W., Schneider, R. L., & White, J. E. (1973). Alarming increase of the cancer mortality in the US black population (1950–1967). *Cancer, 31*(4), 763.

Hochbaum, G. M. (1958). *Public participation in medical screening programs: A sociopsychological study.* Washington, DC: Government Printing Office.

Hoge, V. M. (1958). Hospital bed needs: A review of developments in the United States. *Canadian Journal of Public Health/Revue Canadienne de Sante'e Publique, 49*(1), 1–8.

Holm, C., Frank, D., & Curtin, J. (1999). Health beliefs, health locus of control, and women's mammography behavior. *Cancer Nursing, 22*(2), 149–156.

Houston, T. K., Scarinci, I. C., Person, S. D., & Greene, P. G. (2005). Patient smoking cessation advice by health care providers: The role of ethnicity, socioeconomic status, and health. *American Journal of Public Health, 95*(6), 1056–1061.

Illinois Department of Public Health (IDPH). (2013). Illinois Project for Local Assessment of Needs. Retrieved from http://app.idph.state.il.us/

Illinois Department of Public Health (IDPH).) (2015). Illinois State Cancer mortality review and update, 1986–2012. *Epidemiologic Report Series 15*(7). Springfield, IL: Illinois Department of Public Health.

Illinois Department of Public Health (IDPH). (2016a). Illinois State Cancer mortality review and update, 1986 2013. *Epidemiologic Report Series 16*(4). Springfield, IL: Illinois Department of Public Health.

Illinois Department of Public Health (IDPH). (2016b). Cancer in Illinois—2013. Illinois Department of Public Health. Retrieved from http://www.idph.state.il.us/cancer/pdf/Cancer-n-Illinois_2013.pdf

Illinois Department of Public Health (IDPH). (2016c). Illinois socio-demographic characteristics. 2014 Illinois HIV/AIDS Epidemiology Profile. Retrieved from http://www.dph.illinois.gov/sites/default/files/publications/1-28-16-OHP-HIV-factsheet-Socio-Demographic-Characteristics.pdf. Accessed December 3, 2018.

Index Mundi. (2017). Missouri Black population percentage, 2013 by county. Retrieved from https://www.indexmundi.com/facts/united-states/quick-facts/missouri/black-population-percentage#chart

Iwelunmor, J., Newsome, V., & Airhihenbuwa, C. O. (2014). Framing the impact of culture on health: a systematic review of the PEN-3 cultural model and its application in public health research and interventions. *Ethnicity & Health, 19*(1), 20–46.

Jamal, A., King, B. A., Neff, L. J., Whitmill, J., Babb, S. D., & Graffunder, C. M. (2016) Current cigarette smoking among adults—United States, 2005–2015. *Morbidity and Mortality Weekly Report, 65,* 1205–11. https//doi.org/10.15585/mmwr.mm6544a2

Jargowsky, P. A. (2015). *Architecture of segregation: Civil unrest, the concentration of poverty, and public policy.* Camden, NJ: Center for Urban Research and Education.

Jean, P., Hendren S., Fiscella, K., Loader, S., Rousseau, S., Schwartzbauer, B., Epstein, R. (2010). Understanding the process of patient navigation to reduce disparities in cancer care: Perspectives of trained navigators from the field. *Journal of Cancer Education, 26* (1), 111–120. https://doi.org/10.1007/s13187-010-0122-x

Jemal, A., Bray, F., Center, M. M., Ferlay, J., Ward, E., & Forman, D. (2011). Global cancer statistics. *CA: A Cancer Journal for Clinicians, 61*(2), 69–90.

Jesse, D. E., Graham, M., & Swanson, M. (2006). Psychosocial and spiritual factors associated with smoking and substance use during pregnancy in African American and white low-income women. *Journal of Obstetric, Gynecologic, & Neonatal Nursing, 35*(1), 68–77.

Jibaja-Weiss, M. L., Volk, R. J., Kingery, P., Smith, Q. W., & Holcomb, D. (2003). Tailored messages for breast and cervical cancer screening of low-income and minority women using medical records data. *Patient Education and Counseling, 2*(50), 123–132. https://doi.org/10.1016/S0738-3991(02)00119-2

Jones, R. M., Woolf, S. H., Cunningham, T. D., Johnson, R. E., Krist, A. H., Rothemich, S. F., & Vernon, S. W. (2010). The relative importance of patient-reported barriers to colorectal cancer screening. *American Journal of Preventive Medicine, 38*(5), 499–507.

Jones, L. (2014, February 17). Why new discoveries won't lead to a reduction in health disparities. *Like the Dew: A Journal of Southern Culture and Politics.* Retrieved from: http://likethedew.com/2014/02/17/new-discoveries-wont-lead-reduction-health-disparities/#.WfoKhreWy70

Joseph, D. A., King, J. B., Miller, J. W., Richardson, L. C., & Centers for Disease Control and Prevention. (2012). Prevalence of colorectal cancer screening among adults—Behavioral risk factor surveillance system, United States, 2010 [Supplemental material]. *Morbidity and Mortality Weekly Report, 61*(2), 51–56.

Kahng, S. K. (2010). Can racial disparity in health between black and white Americans be attributed to racial disparities in body weight and socioeconomic status? *Health & Social Work, 35*(4), 257–266.

Kallgren, C. A., Reno, R. R., & Cialdini, R. B. (2000). A focus theory of normative conduct: When norms do and do not affect behavior. *Personality and social psychology bulletin, 26*(8), 1002–1012.

Kang, H. S., Thomas, E., Kwon, B. E., Myung-Sun, H., & Jun, E. M. (2008) Stages of change: Korean women's attitudes and barriers toward mammography screening. *Health Care for Women International, 29*(2), 151–164.

Kang, H., Thomas, E., Kwon, B. E., Hyun, M., & Jun, E. M. 2008. Stages of change: Korean women's attitudes and barriers toward mammography screening. *Health Care for Women International, 29*(2), 151–164. https://doi.org/10.1080/07399330701738176

Karten, C. (2007). .Easy to Write? Creating Easy-to-Read Patient Education Materials. Clinical Journal of Oncology Nursing: 11(4): 506–10.

Kasprzyk, D., Montaño, D., & Fishbein, M. (1998). Application of an integrated behavioral model to predict condom use: A prospective study among high HIV risk groups. *Journal of Applied Social Psychology, 28*(17), 1557–1583.

Keku, T., Millikan, R., Martin, C., Rahkra-Burris, T., & Sandler, R., (2003). Family history of colon cancer: What does it mean and how is it useful? *American Journal of Public Medicine, 24*, 170–176.

Kim, K., Linnan, L., Kulik, N., Carlisle, V., Enga, Z., & Bentley, M. (2007). Linking beauty and health among African-American women: Using focus group data to build culturally and contextually appropriate interventions. *Journal of Social, Behavioral, and Health Sciences, 1*(1), 41–59. https://doi.org/10.5590/JSBHS.2007.01.1.03

King, Jr. M.L. (1963). *Dr. Martin Luther King Jr. 1963 WMU Speech Found.* Western Michigan University Archives and Regional History Collections and University Libraries. Retrieved from: https://wmich.edu/sites/default/files/at tachments/MLK.pdf. Accessed August 25, 2018.

King, N., & Ross, A. (2003). Professional identities and interprofessional relations: Evaluation of collaborative community schemes. *Social Work in Health Care, 38*(2), 51–72.

Klabunde, C. N., Vernon, S. W., Nadel, M. R., Breen, N., Seeff, L. C., & Brown, M. L. (2005). Barriers to colorectal cancer screening: A comparison of reports from primary care physicians and average-risk adults. *Medical Care, 43*(9), 939–944.

Kleinmann, A., Eisenberg, L., & Good, B. (1978). Culture, illness and care: Clinical lessons from anthropologic and cross-cultural research. *Annals of Internal Medicine, 88*, 251–258.

Kohler, B. A., Sherman, R. L., Howlader, N., Jemal, A., Ryerson, A. B., Henry, K. A., . . . & Henley, S. J. (2015). Annual report to the nation on the status of cancer, 1975–2011, featuring incidence of breast cancer subtypes by race/ethnicity, poverty, and state. *Journal of the National Cancer Institute, 107*(6), djv048.

Korber, S. F., Padula, C., Gray, J., & Powell, M. (2011). A breast navigator program: barriers, enhancers, and nursing interventions. *Oncology Nursing Forum, 38*(1), 44–50. https://doi.org/10.1188/11/ONF

Kreuter, M. W., Eddens, K. S., & Alcaraz, K. I. (2012, August). If you refer them, will they call? Use of cancer control referrals by 2-1-1 callers. In *National Cancer Conference.*

Kreuter, M. W., Eddens, K. S., Alcaraz, K. I., Rath, S., Lai, C., Caito, N., . . . Fu, Q. (2012). Use of cancer control referrals by 2-1-1 callers: A randomized trial. *American Journal of Medicine, 43*(6), S425–S434.

Kreuter, M. W., Skinner, C. S., Steger-May, K., Holt, C. L., Bucholtz, D. C., Clark, E. M., & Haire-Joshu, D. (2004). Responses to behaviorally vs culturally tailored cancer communication among African American women. *American Journal of Health Behavior, 28*(3), 195–207.

Kreuter, M., Green, M., Cappella, J., Slater, M. D., Wise, M. E., Storey, D., . . . Woolley, S. (2007). Narrative communication in cancer prevention and control: A framework to guide research and application. *Annals of Behavioral Medicine, 33*(3), 221–235.

Kurz, R. S., & Scharff, D. P. (2003, March). *A crisis of care: The community's perspective on health care in St. Louis.* St. Louis, MO: Episcopal-Presbyterian Health and Medical Charitable Trust.

Lasser, K. E., Murrillo, J., Lisboa, S., Casimir, A. N., Valley-Shah, L., Emmons, K. M., . . . Ayanian, J. Z. (2011). Colorectal cancer screening among ethnically diverse, low-Income patients: A randomized controlled trial. *Archives of Internal Medicine, 171*(10), 906–912.

LaVeist, T. A. (2005). *Minority populations and health: An introduction to health disparities in the United States.* San Francisco, CA: Jossey-Bass.

LaVeist, T., Nickerson, K., & Bowie, J. (2000). Attitudes about racism, medical mistrust, and satisfaction with care among African American and white cardiac patients. *Med Care Res Rev*: 57 Suppl 1:146–61.

Lee, B. & Jo, H. 2011. Evaluation of a navigator program for cancer screening of women in Korean communities. *Asian Pacific Journal of Cancer Prevention, 12,* 271–275.

Lejuez, CW, Hopko, DR, & Hopko, SD. A brief behavioral activation treatment for depression. *Behavioral Modification, 25*(2), 255–286.

Leventhal, H., Diefenbach, M., & Leventhal, E. A. (1992). Illness cognition: using common sense to understand treatment adherence and affect cognition interactions. *Cognitive Therapy and Research, 16*(2), 143–164.

Levin, B., Lieberman, D. A., McFarland, B., Smith, R. A., Brooks, D., Andrews, K. S., . . . & Pickhardt, P. (2008). Screening and surveillance for the early detection of colorectal cancer and adenomatous polyps, 2008: a joint guideline from the American Cancer Society, the US Multi-Society Task Force on Colorectal Cancer, and the American College of Radiology. *CA: a cancer journal for clinicians, 58*(3), 130–160.

Lin, E. H. B., Von Korff, M., Katon, W., Bush, T., Simon, G. E., Walker, E., & Robinson, P. (1995). The role of the primary care physician in patients' adherence to antidepressant therapy. *Medical Care, 33*(1), 67–74.

Lobb, R., & Colditz, G, A. (2013). Implementation science and its application to population health. *Annual Review of Public Health, 34,* 235–251. https://doi.org/10.1146/annurev-publhealth-031912-114444

Lopez, V., & Castro, F. G. (2006). Participation and program outcomes in a church-based cancer prevention program for Hispanic women. *Journal of Community Health, 31*(4), 343–362.

Lubotsky, D., & Hall, M. (2011). The demography of the immigrant population in Illinois. *Institute of Government & Public Affairs: Public Forum, 23*(3), 1–8.

Lurie, N., Somers, S. A., Fremont, A., Angeles, J., Murphy, E. K., & Hamblin, A. (2008, March/April). Challenges to using a business case for addressing health disparities. *Health Affairs, 27*(2), 334–338.

Mackun, P., Wilson, S., Fischetti, T., & Goworowska, J. (March 2011). Population and distribution change: 2000 to 2010. *United States Census Bureau.* Retrieved from https://www.census.gov/prod/cen2010/briefs/c2010br-01.pdf. Accessed December 3, 2018.

Maliski, S., Clerkin, B., & Litwin, M. (2004). Describing a Nurse Case Manager Intervention to Empower Low-Income Men with Prostate Cancer. *Oncology Nursing Forum,* 31(1), 57–64.

Markowitz, L. E., Dunne, E., Saraiya, M., Lawson, H. W., Chesson, H., & Unger, E. R. (2007). Quadrivalent human papillomavirus vaccine: Recommendations of the Advisory Committee on Immunization Practices (ACIP). *Morbidity and Mortality Weekly Report, 56*(RR02), 1–24.

Marlatt, G. A., & Gordon, J. R. (1985). *Relapse prevention: Maintenance strategies in the treatment of addictive behaviors.* New York: NY: Guilford Press.

Marlow, L. A., Waller, J., & Wardle, J. (2015). Barriers to cervical cancer screening among ethnic minority women: A qualitative study. *Journal of Family Planning and Reproductive Health Care, 41*(4), 248–254. https://doi.org/10.1136/jfprhc-2014–101082

Marmot, M.G., Kogevinas, M., & Elston, M. A. (1987). Social/economic status and disease. *Annual Review of Public Health, 8,*111–135.

Marmot, M. (2005). Social determinants of health inequalities. *The Lancet, 365*(9464), 1099–1104.

Marmot, M., Friel, S., Bell, R., Houweling, T., & Taylor, S. (2008). Closing the gap in a generation: Health equity through action on the social determinants of health. *Lancet, 372*(9650), 1661–1669. https://doi.org/10.1016/S0140-6736 (08)61690-6

Mass Law Reform Institute (MLRI). (January 17, 2018). Federal poverty guidelines–2018. Retrieved from: https://www.masslegalservices.org/content/federal-poverty-guidelines-201

Matthews Burwell, S. (April 13, 2015). *Minority Health Month: Making progress on health disparities.* Retrieved from: https://www.huffingtonpost.com/sylvia-mathews-burwell/minority-health-month-making-progress-on-health-disparities_b_7054646.html

Mayne, S. T. (2003). Antioxidant nutrients and chronic disease: Use of biomarkers of exposure and oxidative stress status in epidemiologic research. *Journal of Nutrition, 133*(Supplement 3), 9S–40S.

McKinnon, J. (August, 2001). The black population: 2000. *United States Census Bureau.* Retrieved from https://www.census.gov/prod/2001pubs/c2kbr01-5.pdf. Accessed December 3, 2018.

McLaughlin, M. (2002). Reconsidering the East St Louis Race Riot of 1917. *International Review of Social History, 47*(2), 187–212.

McQueen, A., Kreuter, M. W., Boyum, S., Thompson, V. S., Caburnay, C. A., Waters, E. A., . . . & Fu, Q. (2015). Reactions to FDA-proposed graphic warning labels affixed to US smokers' cigarette packs. *Nicotine & Tobacco Research, 17*(7), 784–795.

Meichenbaum, D., & Turk, D. C. (1987). *Facilitating treatment adherence: A practitioner's guidebook.* New York, NY: Plenum Press.

Mendez, J. E., Evans, M., & Stone, M. D. (2009). Promoters and barriers to mammography screening in multiethnic inner city patients. *The American Journal of Surgery, 198*(4), 526–528. https://doi.org/10.1016/j.amjsurg.2009.07.002

Miles, M. B., & Huberman, A. M. (1994). *Qualitative data analysis.* (2nd ed). Thousand Oaks: CA: Sage Publishing.

Miller, R. & Rollnick, S. (2013). *Motivational interviewing: Helping people change* (3rd ed). New York, NY: the Gilford Press.

Missouri Department of Health and Senior Services (MDHSS). (2011). *The burden of cancer in Missouri: A comprehensive analysis and plan, 2010–2015.* Missouri Department of Health and Senior Services. Retrieved from http://health.mo.gov/living/healthcondiseases/chronic/chronicdisease/cancerburdenreport.pdf

Missouri Department of Health and Senior Services (MDHSS). (2014). *Behavioral Risk Factor Surveillance Data for Missouri.* Retrieved from http://health.mo.gov/data/brfss/data.php

Missouri Department of Health and Senior Services (MDHSS). (2016). *Cancer inquiry.* Retrieved from http://health.mo.gov/living/healthcondiseases/chronic/cancerinquiry/index.php

Missouri Department of Health and Senior Services (MDHSS). (2016b). *Cancer inquiry.* Retrieved from http://health.mo.gov/living/healthcondiseases/chronic/cancerinquiry/index.php

Missouri Department of Health and Senior Services (MDHSS). (2016a). *Tobacco Control.* Retrieved from http://health.mo.gov/living/wellness/tobacco/smokingandtobacco/tobaccocontrol.php

Missouri Foundation for Health (MFH). (April, 2013). Coleman, A. Ed. *Health Equity Series: African American Health Disparities in Missouri.* Retrieved from https://mffh.org/wordpress/wp-content/uploads/2016/04/13AfrAmDisparities.pdf. Accessed December 3, 2018.

Montano, D. E., & Kasprzyk, D. (2002). The theory of reasoned action and the theory of planned behavior. In R. Glanz, B.K. Rimer, & F.M. Lewis, (Ed.), *Health behavior and health education* (pp. 67–98). San Francisco: Jossey-Bass.

Moreno-John, G., Gachie, A., Fleming, C. M., Nápoles-Springer, A., Mutran, E., & Manson, S. M. (2004). Ethnic minority older adults participating in clinical research: Developing trust. *Journal of Aging and Health, 16*(5), s93–s123.

Moy, B., Park, E. R., Feibelmann S., Chiang S., & Weissman J. S. (2006). Barriers to repeat mammography: Cultural perspectives of African-American, Asian, and Hispanic women. *Psycho-Oncology, 15*(7), 623–34. https://doi.org/10.1002/pon.994

Mulatu, M. S., & Berry, J. W. (2001). Health care practice in a multicultural context: Western and non-Western assumptions. In S. S. Kazarian & D. R. Evans (Eds.), *Handbook of cultural health psychology.* San Diego, CA: Academic Press.

National Cancer Institute (NCI), Division of Extramural Activities (DEA), President's Cancer Panel. (2014). Retrieved from http://deainfo.nci.nih.gov/advisory/pcp/annualReports/HPV/PDF/PCP_Annual_Report_2012-2013.pdf

National Cancer Institute (NCI). (2015a). *What is Cancer?* Retrieved from http://www.cancer.gov/about-cancer/what-is-cancer

National Cancer Institute (NCI). (2015b). Fact sheet, Human papillomaviruses and cancer: Questions and answers. Retrieved from http://www.cancer.gov/cancertopics/factsheet/Risk/HPV

National Cancer Institute (NCI). (2016a, April). *Cancer health disparities.* Retrieved from http://www.cancer.gov/about-nci/organization/crchd/cancer-health-disparities-fact-sheet#q1

National Cancer Institute (NCI). (2016b). *Cancer trends progress report: Breast cancer screening.* Retrieved from http://progressreport.cancer.gov/detection/breast_cancer

National Cancer Institute (NCI). (2016c). *SEER stat fact sheets: Female breast cancer.* Retrieved from http://seer.cancer.gov/statfacts/html/breast.html

National Cancer Institute (NCI). (2016d). *SEER stat fact sheets: Colon and rectum cancer.* Retrieved from http://seer.cancer.gov/statfacts/html/colorect.html

National Cancer Institute (NCI). (2016e). *State cancer profiles: Missouri.* Retrieved from https://statecancerprofiles.cancer.gov/quick-profiles/index.php?state name=missouri#t=4

National Cancer Institute (NCI). (2017a). *Cancer disparities research.* Retrieved from https://www.cancer.gov/research/areas/disparities

National Cancer Institute (NCI). (2017b). *Incidence rate report for Missouri by county: All cancer sites, 2010–2014.* Retrieved from https://statecancerprofiles. cancer.gov/incidencerates

National Cancer Institute (NCI). (2017c). *A socioecological approach to addressing tobacco-related health disparities.* National Cancer Institute Tobacco Control Monograph 22. (NIH Publication No. 17-CA-8035A). Bethesda, MD: U.S. Department of Health and Human Services, National Institutes of Health, National Cancer Institute.

National Cancer Institute (NCI). (2018a). Incidence Rates Table [Data file and documentation]. Retrieved from https://statecancerprofiles.cancer.gov/incidencerates/index.php?stateFIPS=00&cancer=001&race=02&sex=0&age=001&year=1&type=incd&sortVariableName=rate&sortOrder=default#results. Accessed December 3, 2018.

National Cancer Institute. (2018b). SEER Cancer Statistics Review (CSR) 1975–2014. Retrieved from: https://seer.cancer.gov/archive/csr/1975_2014/. Accessed August 26, 2018.

National Cancer Institute (NCI). (2018c). Quick profiles: Missouri: Mortality [Date file and documentation]. Retrieved from https://statecancerprofiles.cancer.gov/quick-profiles/index.php?statename=missouri#t=4. Accessed December 3, 2018.

National Cancer Institute (NCI). (2018d). Quick profiles: Missouri: Incidence [Date file and documentation]. Retrieved from https://statecancerprofiles.cancer.gov/quick-profiles/index.php?statename=missouri#t=2

Nezu, A. M., Nezu, C. M., Friedman, S. H., Faddis, S., & Houts, P. S. (1998). Problem-solving therapy for cancer patients: Overview, process, and related clinical issues. In A. M. Nezu, C. M. Nezu, S. H. Friedman, S. Faddis, & P. S. Houts, *Helping cancer patients cope: A problem-solving approach* (pp. 71–99). Washington, DC, US: American Psychological Association. http://dx.doi.org/10.1037/10283-003

Nezu, A. M., Nezu, C. M., & Houts, P. S. (1994, July). *Coping with cancer: A problem solving approach.* Paper presented at the International Congress of Behavioral Medicine, Amsterdam, The Netherlands.

Nguyen, K. H., Subramanian, S. V., Sorensen, G., Tsang, K., & Wright, R. J. (2010). Influence of experiences of racial discrimination and ethnic identity on prenatal smoking among urban black and Hispanic women. *Journal of Epidemiology & Community Health, 66*(4), 315–321. https://doi.org/10.1136/jech.2009.107516.

Obama, Barack H. (10 December 2009). A Just and Lasting Peace. https://www.nobelprize.org/nobel_prizes/peace/laureate/2009/obama-lecture_en.html. Accessed August 12, 2018.

Office of Disease Prevention and Health Promotion. (2017). *Cancer.* Retrieved from https://www.healthypeople.gov/2020/topics-objectives/topic/cancer

Office of Minority Health (OMH). (2015). *Heart disease and African Americans.* Retrieved from http://minorityhealth.hhs.gov/omh/browse.aspx?lvl=4&lvlID=19

O'Keefe, E. B., Meltzer, J. P., & Bethea, T. N. (2015). Health disparities and cancer: Racial disparities in cancer mortality in the United States, 2000–2010. *Frontiers in Public Health, 3*, 51. https://doi.org/10.3389/fpubh.2015.00051

Osborn, C. Y., & Egede, L. E. (2010). Validation of an Information-Motivation-Behavioral Skills model of diabetes self-care (IMB-DSC). *Patient Education and Counseling, 79*(1), 49–54.

Padgett, D. (1998). *Qualitative methods in social work research: Challenges and rewards.* Thousand Oaks; CA: Sage Publications.

Patient Protection and Affordable Care Act of 2010, 42 U.S.C. § 18001 et seq. (2010).

Patton, M. Q. (2002). *Qualitative research and evaluation methods* (3rd ed.). Thousand Oaks: CA: Sage Publications.

Peek, M. E. & Han, J. H. (2004). Disparities in screening mammography current status, interventions, and implications. *Journal of General Internal Medicine, 19*(2), 184–194. https://doi.org/10.1111/j.1525-1497.2004.30254.x

Peek, M. E., Sayad, J. V., & Markwardt, R. (2008). Fear, fatalism and breast cancer screening in low-income African-American women: The role of clinicians and the health care system. *Journal of General Internal Medicine, 23*(11), 1847–1853.

Peipins, L.A., Graham, S., Young R., Lewis B., Foster S., Flanagan B., & Dent A. (2011). Time and distance barriers to mammography facilities in the Atlanta metropolitan area. *Journal of Community Health, 36*(4), 675–683. https://doi.org/10.1007/s10900-011-9359-5.

Percac-Lima, S., Aldrich L. S., Gamba, G. B., Bearse, A. M., & Atlas S. J. (2010). Barriers to follow-up of an abnormal pap smear in Latina women referred for colposcopy. *Society of General Internal Medicine, 25*(11), 1198–204. https://doi.org/10.1007/sll606-010-1450-6.

Phillips, C. (2016). Researcher: St. Louis is segregation is a legacy of deliberate federal policy. St. Louis Public Radio New. news.stlpublicradio.org/post/researcher-st-louis-segregation-legacy-deliberate-federal-policy#stream/0. Retrieved July 5. 2018.

Pickett, K. E., & Pearl, M. (2001). Multilevel analyses of neighborhood socioeconomic context and health outcomes: A critical review. *Journal of Epidemiology and Community Health, 55*(2), 111–122.

Pierce, R., Chadiha, L. A., Vargas, A., & Mosley, M. (2003). Prostate cancer and psychosocial concerns in African American men: Literature synthesis and recommendations. *Health & Social Work, 28*(4), 302–312.

Pinto, B. M., & Floyd, A. (2008). Theories underlying health promotion interventions among cancer survivors. *Seminars in Oncology Nursing, 24*(3), 153–163.

Popovich, N., Albeck-Ripka, & Pierre-Louis, K. 76 Environmental Rules on the Way out Under Trump. https://www.nytimes.com/interactive/2017/10/...trump-environmental-rules-reversed-html. Accessed August 21, 2018.

Prochaska, J. O. (1979). *Systems of psychotherapy: A transtheoretical analysis.* Homewood: IL: Dorsey Press.

Purnell, T. S., Calhoun, E. A., Golden, S. H., Halladay, J. R., Krok-Schoen, J. L., Appelhans, B. M., & Cooper, L. A. (2016). Achieving health equity: Closing the gaps in health care disparities, interventions, and research. *Health Affairs, 35*(8), 1410–1415.

Rambout, L., Tashkandi, M., Hopkins, L., & Tricco, A. C. (2013). Self-reported barriers and facilitators to preventive human papillomavirus vaccination among adolescent girls and young women: A systematic review. *Preventive Medicine, 58*, 22–32.

Reagan-Steiner, S., Yankey, D., Jeyarajah, J., Elam-Evans, L. D., Singleton, J. A., Curtis, C. R., . . . & Stokley, S. (2015). National, regional, state, and selected local area vaccination coverage among adolescents aged 13–17 years—United States, 2014. *MMWR Morbidity & Mortality Weekly Report, 64*(29), 784–792.

Reece, M. (2003). HIV-related mental health care: Factors influencing dropout among low-income, HIV positive individuals. *AIDS Care, 15*(5), 707–716.

Reiter, P. L. & Linnan, L. A. (2011). Cancer screening behaviors of African American women enrolled in a community-based cancer prevention trial. *Journal of Women's Health, 20*(3). https://doi.org/10.1089/jwh.2010.2245

Rex, D. K., Boland, C. R., Dominitz, J. A., Giardiello, F. M., Johnson, D. A., Kaltenbach, T., . . . & Robertson, D. J. (2017). Colorectal cancer screening: Recommendations for physicians and patients from the US Multi-Society Task Force on Colorectal Cancer. *Gastroenterology, 153*(1), 307–323.

Riley, J. R., Dodd, V. J., Muller, K. E., Guo, Y., Logan, H. L. (2012). Psychosocial Factors Associated with Mouth and Throat Cancer Examinations in Rural Florida. *American Journal of Public Health* 102 (2): pp. e7-e14. DOI: 10.2105/AJPH.2011.300504

Rimal, R. N., & Real, K. (2005). How behaviors are influenced by perceived norms: A test of the theory of normative social behavior. *Communication research, 32*(3), 389–414.

Robinson, C. L., Advisory Committee on Immunization Practices (ACIP), & ACIP Child/Adolescent Immunization Work Group. (2016). Recommended immunization schedules for persons aged 0 through 18 years—United States, 2016. *Morbidity and Mortality Weekly Report, 65*(4), 86–87.

Rogers, R. W. (1975). A protection motivation theory of fear appeals and attitude change. *Journal of Psychology, 91*, 93–114.

Rollnick, S., Miller, W. R. & Butler, C. C. 2008. *Motivational interviewing in health care*. New York: Guilford Press.

Rolnick, S., Calvi, J., Heimendinger, J., McClure, J., Kelley, M., Johnson, C., & Alexander, G. (2009). Focus groups inform a web-based program to increase fruit and vegetable intake. *Patient Education and Counseling, 77*(2009), 314–318. https://doi.org/10.1016/j.pec.2009.03.032

Ross, W. (2014). *Better together: Public health*. Retrieved from http://www.bettertogetherstl.com/wp-content/uploads/2014/09/Better-Together-Public-Health-Report-FULL-REPORT.pdf

Rothstein, R. (2014). The making of Ferguson. *American Prospect*. Retrieved from http://prospect.org/article/making-ferguson-how-decades-hostile-policy-created-powder-keg

Rudwick, E. (1964). *Race riots in East St. Louis*. Carbondale, IL: Southern Illinois University Press.

Russell, K. M., Monahan, P., Wagle, A., & Champion, V. (2007). Differences in health and cultural beliefs by stage of mammography screening adoption in African American women. *Cancer, 109*(2 Suppl), 386–395.

Russell, K. M., Perkins, S. M., Zollinger, T. W., & Champion, V. L. (2006). Socio-cultural context of mammography screening use. *Oncology Nursing Forum, 33* (1), 105–112. https://doi.org/10.1188/06.ONF.105-112

Ryan, C. L., Bauman, K. (March 2016). Educational attainment in the United States: 2015. *United States Census Bureau*. Retrieved from https://www.census.gov/content/dam/Census/library/publications/2016/demo/p20-578.pdf. Accessed December 3, 2018.

Sadler, G. R., Ko, C. M., Cohn J. A., White, M., Weldon, R., & Wu, P. (2007) Breast cancer knowledge, attitudes, and screening behaviors among African American women: The Black cosmetologists promoting health program. *BMC Public Health, 7*(57). https://doi.org/10.1186/1471-2458-7-57

Sadler, G. R., Ko, C. M., Cohn, J. A., White, M., Weldon, R., & Wu, P. (2007). Breast cancer knowledge, attitudes, and screening behaviors among African American women: The black cosmetologists promoting health program. *BMC Public Health, 7*(57). https://doi.org/10.1186/1471-2458-7-57

Sadler, G. R., Thomas, A. G., Gebrekristos, B., Dhanjal, S. K., & Mugo, J. (2000). Black cosmetologists promoting health program: Pilot study outcomes. *Journal of Cancer Education, 15*(1):33–37.

Saint Louis Regional Health Commission (RHC). (2003). *Building a healthier Saint Louis: Recommendations for improving safety net primary and specialty care services in St. Louis City and County*. Retrieved from http://www.stlrhc.org/wp-content/uploads/2013/07/Recommendations-of-Improving-Safety-Net-Primary-and-Specialty-Care-Services-in-St.-Louis-City-and-County-Strategic-Plan-Detailed-Discussion-of-Recommendations-10-2003.doc.pdf

Saint Louis Regional Health Commission. (2012). Decade review of health status for St. Louis City and County 2000–2010: An update to *Building a Healthier St. Louis*. Retrieved from http://qocri3zgw3918amdk1xadmx1.wpengine.netdna-cdn.com/wp-content/uploads/2013/07/Decade-Review-of-Health-Status.pdf

Sanders Thompson, V. L. (2006). Coping responses and the experience of discrimination. *Journal of Applied Social Psychology, 36*(5), 1198–1214.

Sanders Thompson, V. L., Arnold, L. D., & Notaro, S. R. (2011). African American parents' attitudes toward HPV vaccination. *Ethnicity & Disease, 21*(3), 335.

Sanders Thompson, V. L., Arnold, L. D., & Notaro, S. R. (2012). African American parents' HPV vaccination intent and concerns. *Journal of Health Care for the Poor and Underserved, 23*(1), 290–301.

Sanders Thompson, V L., Lewis, T., Williams, S.L. (2013) Refining the use of cancer-related cultural constructs with African Americans. *Health Promotion and Practice, 14* (1), 38–43. https://doi.org/10.1177/1524839911399431. PMID: 21460257

Sanders Thompson, V. L., Harris, J., Clark, E.M., Purnell, J., & Deshpande, A.D. (2014). Broadening the examination of socio-cultural constructs relevant to African American colorectal cancer screening. *Psychology, Health & Medicine, 20*(1), 47–58.

Sanders Thompson, V., Lander, S., Xu, S., & Shyu, C. (2014). Identifying key variables in African American adherence to colorectal cancer screening: The application of data mining. *BMC: Public Health, 14*, 1173. https://doi.org/10.1186/1471-2458-14-1173

Sanders Thompson, V. L., & Wells, A. (2014). The intersection of poverty and health: Are race and class far behind? A case study. In C. Camp -Yeakey, V.L. Thompson-Sanders Thompson & A. Wells (Eds.), *Urban ills: Twenty-first-century complexities of urban living in global contexts* (Vol. 1.; pp. 109–132; Vol 2). Lanham, MD: Lexington Books.

Sanders Thompson, V., Drake, B., James, A., Norfolk, M., Goodman, M., Ashford, l., Jackson, S., Witherspoon, M., Brewster, M. & Colditz, G. (2015). A community coalition to address cancer disparities: Transitions, successes and challenges. *Journal of Cancer Education, 30* (4) 616–622. DOI 10.1007/s13187-014-0746-3

Sarma, E. A. (2015). Barriers to screening mammography. *Health Psychology Review, 9*(1), 42–62.

Scarboro, M. (May 10, 2017). How high are cigarette taxes in your state? Retrieved from:https://taxfoundation.org/state-cigarette-taxes/

Schmidt, S., & Parsons, H. M. (2014). Vaccination interest and trends in human papillomavirus vaccine uptake in young adult women aged 18 to 26 years in the United States: An analysis using the 2008–2012 National Health Interview Survey. *American Journal of Public Health, 104*(5), 946–953.

Schootman, M., Jeffe, D. B., Lian, M., Gillanders, W. E., & Aft, R. (2008). The role of poverty rate and racial distribution in the geographic clustering of breast cancer survival among older women: a geographic and multilevel analysis. *American Journal of Epidemiology, 169*(5), 554–561.

Schraufnagel, T. J., Wagner, A. W., Miranda, J., & Roy-Byrne, P. P. (2006). Treating minority patients with depression and anxiety: What does the evidence tell us? *General Hospital Psychiatry, 28*, 27–36.

Scott, E. K. (2005). Beyond tokenism: The making of racially diverse feminist organizations. *Social Problems, 52*(2), 232–254.

Scott, J. (2005, May 16). Life at the top in America isn't just better, it's longer. *New York Times*. Retrieved from https://www.nytimes.com/2005/05/16/us/class/life-at-the-top-in-america-isnt-just-better-its-longer.html

Seefeldt, V., Malina, R.M., & Clark, M.A., 2002. Factors affecting levels of physical activity in adults. *Sports Medicine, 32*(3), 143–168.

Sharma, M. (2012). Information-Motivation-Behavioral Skills (IMB) model: Need for utilization in alcohol and drug education. *Journal of Alcohol and Drug Education, 56*(1), 3S-7S.

Shelton, R. C., Thompson, H. S., Jandorf, L., Varela, A., Oliveri, B., Redd, W. H. (2011). Training experiences of lay and professional patient navigators for colorectal screening. *Journal of Cancer Education, 26*(2), 277–284. https://doi.org/10.1007/s13187-010-0185-8

Sher, I., McGinn, L., Sirey, J. A., & Meyers, B. (2005). Effects of caregivers perceived stigma and causal beliefs on patients' adherence to antidepressant treatment. *Psychiatric Services, 56*, 564–569.

Siegel, R., Ma, J., Zou, Z., & Jemal, A. (2014). Cancer statistics, 2014. *CA: A Cancer Journal for Clinicians*, *64*(1), 9–29.

Singh, G. K., Siahpush, M., & Kogan, M. D. (2010). Neighborhood socioeconomic conditions, built environments, and childhood obesity. *Health affairs*, *29*(3), 503–512.

Singh, G. K., Williams, S. D., Siahpush, M., & Mulhollen, A. (2012). Socioeconomic, rural urban, and racial inequalities in US cancer mortality: Part I—All cancers and lung cancer and Part II—Colorectal, prostate, breast, and cervical cancers. *Journal of Cancer Epidemiology*, *2011*, 1–27. https://doi.org/10.1155/2011/107497

Skinner, C. S., Strecher, V. J., Hospers, H. (1994). Physicians' recommendations for mammography: Do tailored messages make a difference? *American Journal of Public Health*, *84*(1), 43–49.

Smedley, B. D., Stith, A. Y., & Nelson, A. R. (Eds). (2003). Unequal treatment: Confronting racial and ethnic disparities in healthcare. Washington, DC: The National Academies Press.

Smith, R. A., Manassaram-Baptiste, D., Brooks, D., Doroshenk, M., Fedewa, S., Saslow, D., . . . & Wender, R. (2015). Cancer screening in the United States, 2015: A review of current American Cancer Society guidelines and current issues in cancer screening. *CA: A Cancer Journal for Clinicians*, *65*(1), 30–54.

Sorensen, G., Emmons, K., Hunt, M. K., Barbeau, E., Goldman, R., Peterson, K., . . . Berkman, L. (2003). Model for incorporating social context in health behavior interventions: Applications for cancer prevention for working-class, multiethnic populations. *Preventive Medicine, 37*(3), 188–197.

Spinetta, J. J. (1984). Methodology in behavioral and psychosocial cancer research. Development of psychometric assessment methods by life cycle stages. *Cancer, 15*(53), 2222–2227.

Steadman, L. & Rutter, D. R. (2004). Belief importance and the theory of planned behavior: Comparing modal and ranked modal beliefs in predicting attendance at breast screening. *British Journal of Health Psychology, 9*(4), 447–463.

Steadman, L., & Rutter, D. R. (2004) Belief importance and the theory of planned behaviour: Comparing modal and ranked modal beliefs in predicting attendance at breast screening. *British Journal of Health Psychology, 9*, 447–463.

Steele, C. B., Rim, S. H., Joseph, D. A., King, J. B., Seeff, L. C., & Centers for Disease Control and Prevention. (2013). Colorectal cancer incidence and screening -United States, 2008 and 2010. *Morbidity and Mortality Weekly Report Surveillance Summary*, *62*(3), 53–60.

Steinberg, M. L., Fremont, A., Khan, D. C. (2006). Lay patient navigator program implementation for equal access to clinical care and clinical trials. *Cancer, 107*, 2669–77.

Stewart, B. W. K. P., & Wild, C. P. (2014). *World cancer report, 2014*. Lyon, France: World Health Organization.

Stoll, C. R., Roberts, S., Cheng, M. R., Crayton, E. V., Jackson, S., & Politi, M. C. (2015). Barriers to mammography among inadequately screened women. *Health Education & Behavior*, *42*(1), 8–15.

Stone, K. M., Karem, K. L., Sternberg, M. R., McQuillan, G. M., Poon, A. D., Unger, E. R., & Reeves, W. C. (2002). Seroprevalence of human papillomavirus type 16 infection in the United States. *Journal of Infectious Diseases*, *186*(10), 1396–1402.

Strecher, V. J., McEvoy DeVellis, B., Becker, M. H., & Rosenstock, I. M. (1986). The role of self-efficacy in achieving health behavior change. *Health Education & Behavior, 13*(1), 73–92.

Szaboova, V., Svihrova, V., & Hudeckova, V. (2014). Selected risk factors for cervical cancer and barriers to cervical cancer screening. *Acta Medica Martiana, 14*(2), 25–32.

Taplin, S. H., Barlow, W. E., Ludman, E., Maclehos, R., Meyer, D. M., Seger, D., Curry, S. (2000). Testing reminder and motivational telephone calls to increase screening mammography: A randomized study. *Journal of the National Cancer Institute, 92*(3), 233–242. https://doi.org/10.1093/jnci/92.3.233

Taplin, S. H., Ichikawa, L., & Yood, M. U. (2004). Reason for late-stage breast cancer: Absence of screening or detection, or breakdown in follow-up? *Journal off the National Cancer Institute, 96*(20), 1518–1527.

Theising, A. J. (2003). *Made in USA: East S. Louis—The rise and fall of an industrial river town.* St. Louis, MO: Virginia Publishing.

Thompson, V. L. S., Kalesan, B., Wells, A., Williams, S. L., & Caito, N. M. (2010). Comparing the use of evidence and culture in targeted colorectal cancer communication for African Americans. *Patient Education and Counseling, 81*, S22–S33.

Tolma, E. L, Reininger, B. M., Evans, A., & Ureda, J. (2006) Examining the theory of planned behavior and the construct of self-efficacy to predict mammography intention. *Health Education & Behavior, 33*(2), 233–251. https://doi.org/10.1177/1090198105277393

Torre, L. A., Bray, F., Siegel, R. L., Ferlay, J., Lortet-Tieulent, J., & Jemal, A. (2015). Global cancer statistics, 2012. *CA: A Cancer Journal for Clinicians, 65*(2), 87–108.

Truth Initiative. (May 1, 2017). Tobacco use in Missouri 2017. Retrieved from https://truthinitiative.org/tobacco-use-missouri-2017. Accessed December 3, 2018.

Turner, R. J., & Avison, W. R. (2003). Status variations in stress exposure: Implications for the interpretation of research on race, socioeconomic status, and gender. *Journal of Health and Social Behavior, 44*(4), 488–505.

United States Census Bureau. (2000). *Profile of general demographic characteristics.* Retrieved from https://www.census.gov/

United States Census Bureau (2014). *Poverty in the United States.* Retrieved from http://www.census.gov/hhes/www/poverty/

United States Census Bureau. (2016). Quick facts: Missouri. Retrieved from https://www.census.gov/quickfacts/MO

United States Census Bureau. (2017). QuickFacts: St. Louis city, Missouri [Data file and documentation]. Retrieved from https://www.census.gov/quickfacts/fact/table/stlouiscitymissouricounty/HSG860216#HSG860216 U.S. Department of Health and Human Services (USDHHS). (2008). *2008 Physical Activity Guidelines for Americans* (ODPHP Publication No. U0036). Washington, DC: U.S. Department of Health and Human Services. Retrieved from http://www.health.gov/paguidelines

U.S. Department of Health and Human Services (USDHHS). (2009). *Health, United States, 2008.* Hyattsville, MD: Centers for Disease Control and Prevention, National Center for Health Statistics. Retrieved from https://www.cdc.gov/nchs/data/hus/hus08.pdf

U.S. Department of Health and Human Services (USDHHS). (2014). *The health consequences of smoking: 50 years of progress. A report of the surgeon general.* Atlanta, GA: U.S. Department of Health and Human Services, Centers for Disease Control and Prevention, National Center for Chronic Disease Prevention & Health Promotion, Office on Smoking and Health. Retrieved from https://www.surgeon general.gov/library/reports/50-years-of-progress/index.html

U.S. Department of Health and Human Services (USDHHS), & U.S. Department of Agriculture (USDA). (2015). *Dietary guidelines for Americans, 2015–2020* (8th ed.). Retrieved from http://health.gov/dietaryguidelines/2015/guidelines/

U.S. Department of Health and Human Services, Office of Minority Health (2010). *National Partnership for Action to End Health Disparities. The National Plan for Action Draft as of February 17, 2010.* Retrieved from http://www.minorityhealth. hhs.gov/npa/templates/browse.aspx?&lvl=2&lvlid=34

U.S. Preventive Services Task Force (USPSTF). (2013). *Lung cancer screening.* Retrieved from http://www.uspreventiveservicestaskforce.org/Page/Document/ UpdateSummaryFinal/lungcancerscreening

U.S. Preventive Services Task Force (USPSTF). (2015). *Final update summary: Lung cancer: Screening.* Retrieved from http://www.uspreventiveservicestask force.org/Page/Document/UpdateSummaryFinal/lung-cancer-screening

U.S. Preventive Services Task Force (USPSTF). (2016). Screening for colorectal Cancer: US Preventive Services Task Force Recommendation Statement. *Journal of the American Medical Association, 315*(23):2564–2575. https://doi.org/10.1001/ jama.2016.5989

U.S. Preventive Services Task Force (USPSTF). (2017). Published recommenda-tions. Retrieved from https://www.uspreventiveservicestaskforce.org/BrowseRec/ Search?s=cancer

Van Heeringen, K., & Zivkov, M. (1996). Pharmacological treatment of depression in cancer patients: A placebo-controlled study of Mianserin. *British Journal of Psychiatry, 169*, 440–443.

Vega, W. A., Karno, M., Alegria, M., Alvidrez, J., Bernal, G., Escamilla, M., . . . Loue, S. (2007). Research issues for improving treatment of U.S. Hispanics with persistent mental disorders. *Psychiatric Services, 58*(3), 385–394.

Voices for Illinois Children. (2009). *Illinois Kids Count, 2009.* Retrieved from http:// www.voices4kids.org/publications-multimedia/kids-count-reports/illinois-kids -count-2009/

Washington University in St. Louis and Saint Louis University. (2014). *For the Sake of All: A report on the health and well-being of African American in St. Louis and why it matters for everyone.* Retrieved from https://forthesakeofall.files.wordpress. com/2014/05/for-the-sake-of-all-report.pdf. Accessed August 25, 2018.

Webb, M. S., & Carey, M. P. (2008). Tobacco smoking among low-income black women: Demographic and psychosocial correlates in a community sample. *Nicotine & Tobacco Research, 10*(1), 219–229. https://doi.org/10.1080/14622200701767845

Wee, C. C., McCarthy, E. P., & Phillips, R. S. (2005). Factors associated with colon cancer screening: The role of patient factors and physician counseling. *Preventive Medicine, 41*, 23–29.

Weinstein, N. D. (1988). The precaution adoption process. *Health Psychology, 7*(4), 355–386.

Weinstein, N. D., & Sandman, P. M. (2002). The precaution adoption process model and its application. In R. J. DiClemente, R. A. Crosby, M. C. Kegler (Eds.), *Emerging theories in health promotion practice and research* (pp. 16–39). San Francisco, CA: Jossey-Bass.

Wender, R., Fontham, E. T., Barrera, E., Colditz, G. A., Church, T. R., Ettinger, D. S. & LaMonte, S. J. (2013). American Cancer Society lung cancer screening guidelines. *CA: A Cancer Journal for Clinicians 63*, 106–117.

Wells, A., Gulbas, L., Sanders-Thompson, V., Shon, E. J., & Kreuter, M. (2013). African American breast cancer survivors participating in a support group: Translating research into oncology practice. *Journal of Cancer Education,* 29(4), 619–625. https://doi.org/10.1007/s13187-013-0592-8

Wells, A., Palinkas, L., & Ell, K. (2014). Understanding barriers to retention after a clinical treatment trial drop out: Translating qualitative research and theory to practice. *Journal of Clinical Trials, 4*(168). https://doi.org/10.4172/2167-0870.1000168

Wells, A., Palinkas, L., Shon, E., & Ell, K. (2013). Cancer patients in depression treatment: Dropouts and completers. *Journal of Behavioral Health Services and Research*, 1–14. https://doi.org/10.1007/s11414-013-9354-y

Wells, A. A., Shon, E. J., McGowan, K., James, A. (2017). Perspectives of low-income African-American women non-adherent to mammography screening: The important of information, behavioral skills, and motivation. *Journal of Cancer Education, 32*(2), 328–334. https://doi.org/10.1007/s13187-015-0947-4

Wells, A., Thompson, V., Yeakey, C., Ross, W., & Notaro, S. (forthcoming). *Cancer Navigation for Low-income and Women of Color: Tools and Strategies*, Oxford, UK: Oxford U. Press.

White, M. C., Espey, D. K., Swan, J., Wiggins, C. L., Eheman, C., and Kaur, J. S. (2014). Disparities in cancer mortality and incidence among American Indians and Alaska Natives in the United States. *American Journal of Public Health, 104*(3), 377–387.

Wilkerson, I. (2010). *The warmth of other suns: The epic story of America's Great Migration.* New York, NY: Random House.

Wilbur, J., Chandler, P. J., Dancy, B., & Lee, H. (2003). Correlates of physical activity in urban Midwestern African-American women. *American Journal of Preventive Medicine, 25*(3Suppl 1), 45–52.

Willems, S., De Maesschalck, S., Deveugele, M., Derese, A., & De Maeseneer, J. (2005). Socioeconomic status of the patient and doctor-patient communication: Does it make a difference? *Patient Education and Counseling, 56*, 139–46.

Williams, D. R., Neighbors, H. and Jackson, J. S. (2003). Racial/ethnic discrimination and health: Findings from community studies. *American journal of public health, 93*, 200–208.

Wisk, L. E., Allchin, A., Witt, W. P. (2014). Disparities in human papillomavirus vaccine awareness among U.S. parents of preadolescents and adolescents. *Sexually Transmitted Diseases, 41*,117–122.

Wolf, M. S., Chang, C. H., Davis, T., Makoul, G. (2010). Development and validation of the Communication and Attitudinal Self-Efficacy Scale for cancer (CASEcancer). *Patient Education and Counseling, 57*(3):333–341.

Wolf, M. S., Chang, C., Davis, T., & Makoul, G. (2005). Development and validation of the Communication and Attitudinal Self-Efficacy scale for cancer (CASEcancer). *Patient Education and Counseling, 57*(3), 333–341.

World Health Organization Commission on Social Determinants of Health & World Health Organization. (2008). *Closing the gap in a generation: health equity through action on the social determinants of health: Commission on Social Determinants of Health final report.* World Health Organization.

Yeakey, C. C. & Shepherd, D. L. (2012). The Downward Slope of Upward Mobility in A Global Economy. In Yeakey, C. C. (Ed.). *Living on the Boundaries: Urban Marginality in National and International Contexts.* Bingley, UK: Emerald Publishers, Inc., pp. 3–22.

Yeakey, C. C. & Shepherd, D. L. (2014). 'Running in Place:' Low Wage Work in a High Tech Economy. In Yeakey, C. C., Thompson, V. L., & Wells, A. J. (Eds.). *Urban Ills: Twenty First Century Complexities of Urban Living in Global Contexts, Volume One.* Lanham, MD: New York: Lexington Books.

Young, R. F., Schwartz, K., & Booza, J. (2011). Medical barriers to mammography screening of African American women in a high cancer mortality area: Implications for cancer educators and health providers. *Journal of Cancer Education, 26*(2), 262–269.

Zenk, S. N., Schulz, A. J., Hollis-Neely, T., Campbell, R. T., Holmes, N., Watkins, G., . . . Odoms-Young, A. (2005). Fruit and vegetable intake in African Americans: Income and store characteristics. *American Journal of Preventive Medicine, 29*(1), 1–9.

Index

Page references for figures and table are italicized.

About the Authors

Anjanette Wells, PhD, is assistant professor in the School of Social Work, College of Allied Health Sciences, at the University of Cincinnati. She is a researcher in the Precision Cancer Cluster, with her focus being community-based cancer prevention and adherence. Her research interests developed with her clinical experiences in the homes and communities of patients as a home health social worker in Los Angeles, California, where she has substantial direct practice experience in outpatient community clinics, in-patient hospitals, psychiatric units, and private practice. Dr. Wells teaching focuses on advanced clinical social work practice, research methods, diversity, and theory courses.

Vetta L. Sanders Thompson, PhD, is E. Desmond Lee Professor of Racial and Ethnic Studies, focuses on the health and well-being of ethnic and racial minority communities, particularly the African-American community. Sanders Thompson serves as a Co-Director of the Institute for Public Health Center for Community Health, Partnership and Research. An associate member of the Siteman Cancer Center, she works closely with the Program for the Elimination of Cancer Disparities. Dr. Sanders Thompson's other work has focused on racial identity, psychosocial implications of race and ethnicity in health behavior and use of health services.

Will Ross, MD, MPH, is principal officer for community partnerships, associate dean for diversity and inclusion at Washington University School of Medicine, and professor of medicine in the Division of Nephrology. In addition to recruiting and developing a diverse group of medical students, residents and faculty, he helped create a network of free medical clinics in St. Louis. He is a charter and founding member of the St. Louis Regional Health

Commission, Chairman of the St. Louis City Board of Health, and a former member of the Centers for Disease Control Health Disparities Committee. Dr. Ross is a founding associate editor of *Frontiers in Public Health Education and Promotion.* Dr. Ross formerly served as the chief medical of St. Louis Regional Medical Center, the last public hospital in St. Louis.

Carol Camp Yeakey, PhD, is the Marshall S. Snow Professor of Arts & Sciences and the Founding Director of the Interdisciplinary Program in Urban Studies and the Center on Urban Research and Public Policy, at Washington University in St. Louis. Her primary area of research is social welfare policy as said policy pertains to marginalized children, young adults and families and the neighborhood contexts in which they live. Having published an extensive list of books and research articles in national and international venues, she has held media interviews on pressing urban issues with the *New York Times, The Washington Post,* Al Jazeera, Russian (Sputnik) News, *Agence France Presse*, Canadian Broadcasting Company, and ABC World News Australia, among many others. Her next authored volume *"Where are the poor to live? Gentrification in Global Contexts"* will be published by Palgrave/Macmillan in Spring 2019.

Sheri Notaro, PhD, MPH, brings over 19 years of experience in higher education administration to her role as Associate Dean for Graduate Student Affairs in the Graduate School at Washington University in St. Louis. Notaro directs both the Chancellor's Graduate Fellowship and the Liberman Graduate Center. She serves as a liaison to the Research Graduate Affairs Committee of the Board of Trustees, overseeing the annual selection of graduate and professional student representatives to the Board. She serves as an affiliated faculty of the Center for Urban Research and Public Policy and the Interdisciplinary Program in Urban Studies. Dr. Notaro's research focuses on health disparities across the lifespan.

Foreword by Holden Thorp: Holden Thorp is the Provost an Executive Vice Chancellor for Academic Affairs at Washington University in St. Louis. He is also the Rita Levi-Montalcini Distinguished University Professor and holds appointments in both chemistry and medicine. A co-author of two books about higher education, in his research career, Thorp developed technology for electronic DNA chips and co-founded Viamet Pharmaceuticals and Innocrin Pharmaceuticals, which are commercializing new drugs for fungal disease and cancer, respectively.